UNEMPLOYMENT AND RESISTANCE
IN TUNISIA

Disruptions: Political Protests, Social Movements and Revolutions in the Middle East
Series Editor: Adham Saouli

Published and forthcoming titles

The Egyptian Muslim Sisterhood in the Aftermath of the Arab Uprisings: Activism, Gender and Politics
Erika Biagini

Unemployment and Resistance in Tunisia: The Democracy–Security Nexus
Saerom Han

edinburghuniversitypress.com/series-disruptions

UNEMPLOYMENT AND RESISTANCE IN TUNISIA

THE DEMOCRACY–SECURITY NEXUS

⸕

Saerom Han

EDINBURGH
University Press

Edinburgh University Press is one of the leading university presses in the UK. We publish academic books and journals in our selected subject areas across the humanities and social sciences, combining cutting-edge scholarship with high editorial and production values to produce academic works of lasting importance. For more information visit our website: edinburghuniversitypress.com

Edinburgh University Press Ltd
13 Infirmary Street,
Edinburgh, EH1 1LT

First published in hardback by Edinburgh University Press 2024

Typeset in Jaghbuni by
Cheshire Typesetting Ltd, Cuddington, Cheshire

A CIP record for this book is available from the British Library

ISBN 978 1 3995 0708 0 (hardback)
ISBN 978 1 3995 0709 7 (paperback)
ISBN 978 1 3995 0710 3 (webready PDF)
ISBN 978 1 3995 0711 0 (epub)

Contents

Acknowledgements

I could not have completed this book without the support, encouragement and advice of many people and institutions to whom I am deeply grateful. First, I owe a debt of gratitude to the Tunisian unemployed protesters, civil society and human rights activists, unionists, journalists and researchers who took their time to share their stories and knowledge with me. The numerous interviews and conversations that I had with them in their houses, on streets and in cafés helped me learn and grow. This book would not have come to fruition without them.

I deeply thank Andrea Teti, my supervisor and now colleague and caring friend, for his never-ending support, encouragement and insights which he has been giving me ever since I began this project in 2015. I am grateful to Cristina Flesher Fominaya and Ilia Xypolia for providing invaluable help, intellectual inspiration and suggestions on my drafts whenever I knocked on their doors. I thank Emma Murphy who not only offered me her constructive comments on my PhD thesis at my viva, but also tirelessly encouraged me to finish this book. I would also like to thank Natasha Danilova, Trevor Stack and Pamela Abbott for their generous support during and after my time in Aberdeen.

I wish to thank the Centre for Citizenship, Civil Society and Rule of Law (CISRUL) for providing me with the funding for my PhD research on this project and my fieldwork in Tunisia. I am also grateful to the Economic and Social Research Council (ESRC) for funding my postdoctoral research fellowship in the School of Government and International Affairs at Durham University. I was able to develop my doctoral thesis into this book thanks to the ESRC fellowship and my colleagues there, particularly Emma Murphy, Rory McCarthy and Anoush Ehteshami, who warmly welcomed me in Durham.

Acknowledgements

This book would not have been possible without Edinburgh University Press. I would like to thank Adham Saouli for providing invaluable comments and suggestions on my drafts. I am also grateful to Emma House, Louise Hutton and Isobel Birks for their assistance in the process of completing this book. All errors and shortcomings are mine alone.

Parts of this book have appeared in journal articles, and I would like to acknowledge these publications: a shorter and earlier version of the analysis in Chapters 4, 5 and 6 on the (counter)securitising practices was published as 'Securitization of the unemployed and counter-conductive resistance in Tunisia', *Security Dialogue*, 52(2), 2021, pp. 156–73, and part of the discussion on the relationship between mobilisations in neoliberal times in Chapter 7 has appeared in 'Transitional justice for whom? Contention over human rights and justice in Tunisia', *Social Movement Studies*, 21(6), 2021, pp. 861–32.

Finally, I want to thank my family for always believing in me and encouraging me to pursue what I value.

Abbreviations

ADB	African Development Bank
AQIM	Al-Qaeda in the Islamic Maghrib
AST	Ansar al-Sharia in Tunisia
ATFD	L'Association Tunisienne des Femmes Democrates
BTS	Banque tunisienne de solidarité
CNPR	Committee for Political Reform and the National Council for the Protection of the Revolution
CVE	Countering Violent Extremism
FNS	Fonds National de Solidarité
FTDES	Tunisian Forum for Economic and Social Rights
IFIs	International Financial Institutions
IS	Islamic State
ISIE	Superior Independent Instance for the Elections
KUNJK	Katibah Uqbah bn Nafa'a and Jund al-Khalifah
LPR	League for the Protection of the Revolution
LTDH	Tunisian League for the Defense of Human Rights
NCA	National Constituent Assembly
NDQ	Tunisian National Dialogue Quartet
NSF	National Salvation Front
OIC	Organisation of the Islamic Conference
RCD	Democratic Constitutional Rally
SNJT	National Union of Tunisian Journalists
UDC	Union of University Graduates
UGET	General Union of Students of Tunisia
UGTT	Tunisian General Labour Union
UNHRC	United Nations Human Rights Council
UTICA	Tunisian Confederation of Industry and Trade and Handicrafts
WFP	World Food Programme

Series Editor's Foreword

Disruptions is a book series that examines the origins and impact of socio-political events, ideas and actors on the contemporary Middle East. It is particularly interested in scholarly work that explores the role of innovative norms, activism and resistance in generating new social and political possibilities for the peoples of the region. The Arab uprisings of 2011, which disrupted several socio-political orders in the region, constituted the end of the post-colonial phase in the region which started in the 1950s and 1960s. After almost five decades of state-building attempts, several regimes – including Syria, Egypt, Tunisia, Libya, Morocco, Jordan, Iraq, Yemen and Bahrain – faced unprecedented challenges to their rule. Whilst the 1950s and 1960s witnessed popular revolts that targeted the colonial powers and their local allies, the 2011 uprisings aimed at the regimes' unrelenting repression, corruption and dependence on external powers. In the uprisings, people demanded and imagined a society where their freedoms and dignity can be respected. The uprisings failed to realise their goals. Regimes fought back. Syria, Yemen, Libya and Iraq succumbed into prolonged civil wars. The monarchical regimes of Saudi Arabia, Kuwait, the UAE, Qatar, Morocco, Jordan and Bahrain managed to diffuse the uprisings through a combination of political and economic means and outright violent repression. In Egypt and Tunisia, the revolutions that toppled long-serving autocrats, Mubarak and Ben Ali, respectively, failed to consolidate their nascent democracies.

But despite this failure, the uprisings constituted a formative moment in the history of the region. They generated disruptive norms and discourse on political freedoms and human dignity; they exposed regimes' violence and repression and other political techniques of survival; they disrupted regimes' monopoly over the political and ideological spheres; and, ultimately, they offered a much-needed repertoire of collective action for regime contenders to draw on for future battles. On this last point, the uprisings did not only disrupt regimes' political power, but they also challenged the ideological frameworks of regime opponents and tested their political capabilities and skills. Contentious politics in the region, however, is far from being over.

The *Disruptions* series aims to explore and trace challenges to domination, whether in the form of protests, revolutions, social movements, emerging norms and other forms of resistance that will shape the Middle East region in what one day may be perceived as *the people's century*. The series will explore these topics by drawing on primary and secondary data gathered from the region and through innovative theoretical and methodological frameworks.

This book, the first of the *Disruptions* series, is Saerom Han's *Unemployment and Resistance in Tunisia: The Democracy–Security Nexus*. Han's work presents a timely exploration of the politics of change in Tunisia, a country that promised a steady albeit not necessarily smooth transition to democracy in the post-revolutionary period. Contrary to many expectations Tunisia has, sadly, failed to consolidate its democratic experiment. Capitalising on the endemic political divisions, institutional paralysis, absence of economic growth and a poor response to the COVID pandemic, President Kais Saied was elected president in 2019. To the surprise of many, he gradually re-centralised power in the presidency and suspended the parliament the 2021. His continuous attempts to re-configure the power structure and to repress his main rivals in Tunisia reveals a dangerous return to autocratic rule, or what some have called 'democratic backsliding'. In contrast to the mainstream literature that focuses on the constraints to democratic transition and consolidation, Han's work invites us to discover some of the *continuities* of Bin Ali's autocratic rule during the consolidation phase. Her study shows how the narrative of Tunisia's 'new democratic model', which the new elite employed, came to play a key role in the securitisation and consequent repression of marginalised social movements and protests in the country.

The high levels of unemployment, which increased from 13.5 per cent in 2010 to 15.3 per cent in 2019 (and was as high as 24 per cent among the youth), in the post-revolutionary period generated numerous and regular protests. Han's work examines these protests by focusing on how the elite weaponised the so-called 'war on terror', which constitutes a residue of the Bin Ali regime, to control and regulate the behaviour of marginalised and unemployed groups. The book explores whether elite counter-terrorism narratives and practices changed in the post-revolutionary period; whether there are links between counter-terrorism efforts, new democratic orders and socio-economic protests; and how each actor articulates their narratives in various contentious episodes.

Drawing on a Foucauldian framework and primary data, including extensive fieldwork in Tunisia, Han focuses on the Union for Unemployed Graduates (UDC) and the Maknassy unemployed movement to examine forms of mobilisation and narrative articulation at both national and local levels. The examination of these case-studies sheds theoretical and empirical light on the relationship between democracy and security as well as on the symbolic and material resistance that these groups undertake. Securitisation, so Han emphasises, does not only consist of coercive means. It also forms a main component in the discourse of liberal-democracy (or 'governmentality', in Foucauldian parlance) that portrays certain actors as a 'threat' to or 'deviant' from democratic society and rule and that justifies regulation or repression. But, crucially, Han's study also shows that the unemployed resisted the discourse of the governing elites and, thus, disrupted their attempts to regulate the movement 'by re-appropriating, distorting, and deconstructing the dominant narrative […] producing new subjectivities'. Moreover, by rectifying the governing elite's narrative, the protesters problematised the fundamental reason, 'terrorism', which the elites are promoting to account for instability. Thus, the protesters contributed to shifting the attention to the main source of socio-political grievance: unemployment and marginalisation.

The election of President Saied, a law professor with no party affiliation, by a majority of frustrated Tunisians is telling, as Han reminds the reader. 'What we need to pay attention to', she reveals, 'is the wide gap and tension between the political and economic system aspired to and demanded by the people, on the one hand, and the actual democratisation process over the last decade, on the other'. *Unemployment and Resistance in Tunisia* paves the way for understanding some of the flaws of the actual democratisation process in Tunisia. It also reminds us how rugged the road to democracy can be.

Adham Saouli
Professor of International Relations
University of St Andrews

1

Introduction: Is Terrorism a Threat to Democratisation?

Sabri Milyan, a twenty-year-old unemployed man, was among several youths who took to the streets on 6 February 2015. Protesting the prolonged socio-economic marginalisation of their town Dehiba, adjacent to the border of Tunisia and Libya, the youths initiated a street march and called for the right to work and for regional development. On the night of the same day, the local residents witnessed more than eighteen police buses arriving in their town; their purpose was only known the day after, when the armed security forces randomly raided their houses. A violent confrontation between the security apparatuses and the protesters took place the next day, when Milyan was shot in the back and immediately died. The Interior Ministry expressed regret about his death and their determination to respect the right to peaceful protests. Simultaneously, they justified the use of live bullets as an appropriate and legitimate measure, arguing that the potential for terrorist infiltration from Libya to Tunisia due to the instability caused by the unemployed protests was too great. While Milyan's death led to further protests at the local level and an investigation of the incident, led by civil society organisations, in the same month, it did not result in any national-level campaigns or movements against the authorities. Milyan's case was handed over to the military court of Sfax, where at the time of this writing no verdict has yet been made.

During my fieldwork in Tunisia in 2016–17, I met Habib Mahfoudh,[1] a father of three daughters and a previously unemployed but now precarious worker. In the middle of our conversation about the political and economic situation in Tunisia and his participation in street protests, he started talking about his experience of being interrogated by the Interior Ministry on suspicions of terrorism. Since 2011, Mahfoudh has been able to work in a local public institute as a casual worker, with the government promise to provide him with a tenured public-servant position after four

1

years of work. His monthly wage, however, was no more than half of the 435 dinars (approximately 145 USD), the full sum of the wage that he was supposed to receive. While working two part-time jobs in a street café and a wholesale market for fruit and vegetables in addition to his work at the public institute, he had actively participated in casual workers' protests particularly since 2015, as the authorities showed no willingness to meet their promises. It was when Mahfoudh came to Tunis to organise a protest in March 2016 that he encountered two plainclothes police officers in his motel room. He then spent two days in a place which he did not know and was interrogated about his trip to Libya in the past, as well as his alleged connection to terrorist groups. There was no serious torture other than some beating and harassment, Mahfoudh said. He shortly concluded that the police officers provided no evidence whatsoever to associate him with terrorism and that the purpose of this interrogation was to intimidate him and discourage him from participating in street protests.

It was only a month before Mahfoudh's interrogation that Habib Essid, then prime minister of Tunisia, praised the role of the army and the security forces in controlling a wave of protests organised by unemployed youths in Kasserine and elsewhere in January 2016, highlighting that the security apparatuses respected 'the right to peaceful demonstration guaranteed by the Constitution'.[2] The reason for the security intervention in the protests, so Essid said, was to prevent 'terrorist gangsters' from exploiting the protests with the aim to weaken the state. The security forces intervened to defend Tunisia's 'new democratic model' from those terrorists damaging public and private property, as well as to safe-guard Tunisia's 'republican' security.[3] He concluded that 'we had to declare a curfew, which greatly improved the situation'.[4]

Milyan and Mahfoudh's stories, as well as Essid's method of protecting democracy, illustrate two interrelated facets of Tunisia's new democratisation process, which took place after the Uprising. First, the struggle of the socio-economically disadvantaged Tunisians has continued, as their demands for employment and the reduction of regional disparities between coastal and interior regions have not been addressed. Although the successive governments that came after Zine El Abidine Ben Ali's dictatorial rule and the political and economic elites in general expressed their full support for fundamental reforms in favour of the deprived regions and socio-economic justice, the post-uprising socio-economic structure did not differ much from that in the era of Ben Ali – that is, neoliberal economic policies continued to prevail.[5] This has led to an upsurge of socio-economically-motivated protests across Tunisia, particularly in the marginalised regions. While the country has witnessed various forms of collective actions based on different demands since the Uprising, protests with socio-economic demands have recently outnumbered protests with other demands such as civil and political rights. According to the data provided by Vatthauer and Weipert-Fenner, for instance, approximately 176 socio-economic protests took place in 2015, whereas the same year witnessed 143 protests with non-socio-economic demands.[6]

Second, social movements for socio-economic justice increasingly became the target of control in the name of the so-called 'War on Terror' in the context of democratisation. This was particularly the case with protests organised by unemployed and precarious youths whose modes of action and demands were often more radical than that of unionised workers. The problem of unemployment, which was one of the key reasons behind the mass mobilisations in 2010 and 2011, has continued to remain a main source of grievance and dissatisfaction among the population. The successive governments have promised to tackle high unemployment rates, but the unemployment rate gradually increased from 13.5 per cent in 2010 to 15.13 per cent in 2019. The situation was even more dire for young Tunisians. More than a third of Tunisian youths aged between fifteen and twenty-four were unemployed in 2019. The continued market-driven employment policies were accompanied by the increasing association of (mobilised) unemployed individuals and groups with threats of terrorism, which finds its reference in the visibility of political and radical Islamists as well as several violent attacks that took place after the Uprising.

Like the neoliberal economic agenda, the manipulation of the War on Terror is not a new story in Tunisia. As several scholars have pointed out, counter-terrorism was abused by the Ben Ali regime to justify its 'police state' and human rights violations.[7] What changed after 2011, however, is that the ruling elites' attempt to control unemployed movements and their counter-terrorism agenda now operated in a decreasingly authoritarian context. Despite divergent views on the initial post-uprising trajectory of Tunisia, most observers pointed out the increasing level of political freedom as one of the key achievements. In addition to regularly held free and fair elections, the public now was able to enjoy the unprecedented – albeit still limited – level of freedom of speech and assembly as compared to the era of Ben Ali, as indicated by the increasing number of social mobilisations since 2011.[8] The post-uprising governments' endeavour to develop institutional democracy was widely acknowledged by domestic and international actors alike, albeit with the warning that, in order to protect and consolidate its democracy, Tunisia must find solutions for the threat of terrorism and for the social instabilities caused by rampant unemployment and inequalities.

Do counter-terrorism narratives and practices after the Uprising differ from that under the Ben Ali regime? If so, in what ways? Are there any links between the War on Terror, the new democratic orders and socio-economic protests? In what ways are the protests discursively associated with terrorism, and what are the impacts of such an articulation on the post-uprising democratisation and *vice versa*? What does contentious politics around democracy imply about the reconfiguration of political, economic and social orders over the past ten years? Do they, for instance, tell us something about the recent radical political transformations led by President Kais Saied, which, according to some, are a clear sign of creeping authoritarianism? After his decision to freeze the parliament, fire the prime minister and lift the immunity for parliament members in July 2021, Tunisia was described to face 'its worst crisis in a decade of democracy'.[9] Saied' suspension of the parliament was regarded as 'an assault on democracy'[10] and an act that 'puts the democracy at great risk of unraveling'.[11] Some even took the event as an indicator showing how the desire for democracy is a baseless hope in the Muslim world at large.[12] Which democracy was challenged and in danger, and why?

There is growing scholarly interest in terrorism,[13] mobilisations for socio-economic justice[14] and democracy[15] in Tunisia. However, scant attention has been paid to how and by whom the mobilisations and terrorism (and counter-terrorism) have become intertwined in the context of democratisation, and to what effects. In this book, I aim at addressing these questions by drawing on a Foucauldian understanding of liberal democracy, security and resistance. Specifically, I focus my analysis on unemployed movements and examine how they became associated with counter-terrorism narratives and practices within a liberal democratic framework, as well as how the protesters experienced and reacted to the securitisation of the unemployed. Based on the analysis, I argue that the governing elites' securitisation of the unemployed contributed to the management of unemployed populations, especially unemployed protesters, so as to be able to think and act in conformity with a neoliberal modality of democracy. Yet, governing the unemployed subject through securitising practices has not been without challenges. I highlight that the securitisation of the unemployed in the name of the War on Terror went hand in hand with the unemployed protesters' active involvement in such securitisation. Having become part of the broader struggle over the right to work, the protesters' 'counter-securitising' practices operated mainly to alter, distort and redirect the ways in which they were securitised, rather than to reject the status of being securitised as such.

Based on the case-study of the securitisation of the unemployed, this book seeks to make three contributions to our understanding of the democracy–security nexus as well as socio-economic mobilisations in Tunisia and beyond. First, it offers an alternative way of thinking about the democratisation of Tunisia, by unpacking its intersection with securitisation in the context of the (global) neoliberal regime. Several studies have shown that the pre-2011 neoliberal agenda still remains in place.[16] However, the continuation of the old *economic policies* is only a partial story. Close observation reveals that various governing mechanisms 'for democracy' in Tunisia were drawn to serve the *status quo*, while disregarding the possibilities for radical changes in political, economic and social orders.[17] The continued marketisation of the Tunisian economy in this sense is not necessarily an unfortunate obstacle to the otherwise successful democratisation. Rather, it is closely linked to the instrumentalisation of liberal democracy for a 'neoliberal governing'. Neoliberal governing, in this book, is understood not as a top–down process or a set of economic policies, but as a regime of power entailing a multiplicity of technologies through which heterogeneous and often competing actors participate in the conduct of the self and others through the principle of freedom in conformity with market imperatives. It is a mode of governance whose logic of the market economy goes beyond the narrowly defined economic domain and encompasses political, social and cultural realms. This way of approaching neoliberalism shifts our attention from economic policies to various governing as well as resisting practices within neoliberal power relations. The current 'crisis' of democracy in Tunisia cannot be understood properly without taking into account the intimate connection between liberal democratisation and neoliberal governing.

Second, the book reassesses the notion that the counter-terrorism agenda is a set of state-driven authoritarian measures against democratic norms and values.[18] I call into question this presumed truth by approaching it as a dominant discourse that is historically shaped and reshaped through complex power relations. In Tunisia, counter-terrorism, which was extensively pursued by the pre-2011 authoritarian regime, re-emerged in the context of the increasing fear of the rise of Islamists after 2011 and served the securitisation of the unemployed subject, not exclusively but significantly, through liberal democratic norms, institutions and actors, including civil society. Governing unemployed populations in the name of the War on Terror provides an important exemplary case of how the pre-2011 political and economic orders came to reconfigure their relationship to new norms, as well as their strategies of domination within the newly democratising context.

Lastly, this book offers a novel way of thinking about agency vis-à-vis the securitisation of unemployed mobilisations, which has been a salient but largely under-investigated phenomenon in post-2011 Tunisia. It does so by exploring how unemployed protesters experienced and resisted ways of being securitised and what forms of (alternative) subjectivities they produced. By taking a bottom–up perspective, this book emphasises the importance of agencies in understanding the politics of mobilisations.[19] That being said, my analysis takes structure (neoliberal power relations) equally seriously and places unemployed protests within the context of the reconfiguration of a new democratic regime in a neoliberal way. In other words, the main interest of this book lies in identifying and understanding the dynamics of the securitisation of unemployed protests and resistance to it *in relation to* neoliberal attempts to govern and manage the problem of unemployment.

The remainder of this chapter reviews the existing literature on terrorism and democracy in Tunisia, provides a brief preview of why and how I use Foucault's work and explains the methods and outline of the book.

Is Terrorism a Threat to Democratisation?

With its popularity in political and public debates in post-uprising Tunisia, the issue of terrorism and its effects on the country's nascent democracy have attracted scholarly attention, particularly after two violent attacks on foreign tourists occurred in 2015. Several studies have presented terrorism as a direct threat to democratisation, due to its negative impact on the newly emerging democratic system. For instance, scholars have pointed to free and fair elections and the new constitution as some of the positive indicators for democratisation, while describing 'terrorist attacks' by global jihadi groups such as the Islamic State (IS) and local Salafi groups as the main threat to Tunisian democracy, given their negative impact on the already vulnerable economy.[20] Studies have also articulated the rise of radical Salafi movements as closely linked to terrorism in Tunisia, suggesting a balanced de-radicalisation policy based on the cooperation between state and civil society in order to effectively fight extremism and protect the process of democratisation.[21]

Yet, another body of literature has seen Tunisian authorities' illiberal and violent counter-terrorism policies as a potential sign of resilient authoritarianism that threatens Tunisia's young democracy. While acknowledging the authorities' 'proactive' response to global jihadi groups, Aaron Y. Zelin has raised concerns about the counter-terrorism laws that restrict travel and freedom of speech.[22] He has further called for US guidance and assistance in sectors such as rule of law and security reform. According to Anouar Boukhars, while Tunisia achieved a consensual elite settlement, its democracy was still fragile as the authoritarian discourse and police brutality were 'back in full swing'.[23] This illiberal tendency, so he has argued, contributed to the radicalisation of many socio-economically marginalised youth, particularly those in the border areas.[24] Importantly, Maryam Ben Salem and Fadil Aliriza have pointed to the ways in which authorities have linked terrorism to social movements, criticising that the state prioritised repressive counter-terrorism policies over human rights.[25]

While varying in their foci, many studies on terrorism tend to explicitly or implicitly postulate Tunisia as being in transition towards democracy, with terrorism and/or counter-terrorism as a key obstacle to this process. This appraisal of Tunisia as moving towards democracy is indeed found in the broader literature on the country's post-authoritarian transformations. Given its relatively peaceful process of negotiations between key political actors and the following establishment of democratic institutions, Tunisia has been evaluated as a successful democracy, albeit experiencing bumps in the road. Scholarly attention has been devoted to the factors that contributed to the transition to democracy. For instance, several studies have engaged with the notion of a 'strong civil society' to emphasise the important role that Tunisian society played during and after the Uprising.[26] Similarly, some have focused on how social media successfully mobilised the public against authoritarianism and in the consolidation of democracy.[27] A significant number of studies has also identified the moderation of political Islamists (especially the Ennahda movement)[28] and their peaceful negotiations and consensus with secular elites,[29] as a key element that made possible Tunisia's democracy.

Despite various contributions that they make to the study of Tunisian politics, existing studies on democracy often remain unclear about their conception of democracy, making one wonder what they exactly mean by the term 'democracy'. The reason for this lack of conceptualisation within the literature appears in part due to the assumption that there exists a form of democracy which is so hegemonic and monolithic that it cannot be subject to dispute – that is, liberal democracy. Based on this assumption, the dominant Western model of democracy, or the so-called 'Weber-Schumpeter-Dahl model'[30] – according to which democracy is predominantly associated with elements such as rule of law, free and fair elections, and independent civil society, with particular emphasis on the conditions of political stability and market economy – has prevailed in both academic and public narratives of democracy in Tunisia. As we will see throughout this book, this model of democracy was arguably what former Prime Minister Essid was determined to protect by declaring a curfew in 2015.

This book suggests that analysing the securitisation of the unemployed subject in the context of democratisation requires a re-assessment of three tendencies in the current debate on the relationship between terrorism and democracy. The first is the tendency to uncritically use the term 'terrorism' and negatively associate it with democracy, without taking into account that it is a politically (and morally) loaded label, especially in countries such as Tunisia. It risks reiterating the idea of 'democracy under the threat of terrorism' that had been discursively used by the Ben Ali regime and its international partners in the process of controlling and transforming Tunisian society. It is now well documented that Ben Ali's authoritarian rule was constituted and meticulously managed through exclusion and repression,[31] and his rhetoric of the threat of Islamist terrorism was tactically utilised to justify such rule domestically and internationally. The aggressive promotion of democracy by the US and the EU under the Ben Ali regime was also closely tethered to their efforts to integrate Tunisia into the global market and the global War on Terror.[32]

Second, there is a growing concern about the authorities' policing measures over social movements in the name of counter-terrorism, often articulating them as the return of Ben Ali's police and 'authoritarian' regime and as being in opposition to what is considered 'democratic'. Several studies have contributed to our understanding of the ways in which the post-2011 regime utilised the War on Terror agenda to control marginalised youth by, for instance, investigating how the coalition government discursively linked its counter-terrorism policies to workers' strikes and unemployed protests,[33] as well as how the youth in the southern border areas were radicalised as a result of police violence.[34] Repressive means such as arbitrary arrests targeting religious-looking youths, political activists and social movement actors are still in place. However, drawing a sharp line between what is democratic and what is authoritarian and associating the state apparatuses' control over social mobilisations through counter-terrorism with the latter is somewhat simplistic, not least because the state's use of violence after the Uprising was in a way 'democratically sanctioned and supervised by duly elected representatives of the people'.[35] This view also neglects the fact that even 'advanced' liberal democracies significantly rely on coercive means in order to protect and promote their democratic values. While the above-mentioned case of Milyan and several reports on state repression should not be ignored, describing the post-2011 regime's counter-terrorism agenda as merely authoritarian is misleading and precludes a more nuanced understanding of how the counter-terrorism agenda can operate through democratic norms such as rule of law, political freedom and the notion of citizen. This is to say that governing mechanisms in the name of the War on Terror may be much more subtle in practice and the binary of democratic and authoritarian often becomes blurred.

Finally, the debate on the relationship between democracy and terrorism tends to predominantly focus on state institutions, such as the military and the police, and does not pay sufficient attention to the voice and role of civil society and social movement actors. This state-centric approach raises the question of agency, particularly non-state actors who are considered to be affected by the association of terrorism with bottom–up mobilisations in Tunisia. The lack of attention given to non-state actors arguably lies in the implicit assumption which conceives counter-terrorism as promoted and implemented solely by the state, while construing civil society as being separated from the state. Consequently, civil society and social movement actors are portrayed as either passively responding to or opposing state-driven security policies. Yet, close observation of their attitudes towards and practices in relation to counter-terrorism since 2011 suggests that they are neither submissively governed by nor actively resisting the state. While many human rights activists and protesters have been critical of the state's security policies, such as the new anti-terrorism laws,[36] they have also been active advocates for counter-terrorism, as reflected in grassroots anti-terrorism street marches, as well as in campaigns to push the authorities to implement anti-terrorism laws and control radical Islamists and Tunisians returning from Syria. Guendalina Simoncini's work on Ben Guerdane's local inhabitants' response to jihadism in 2016 provides an illustrative example of how bottom–up resistance is implicated in the War on Terror.[37] How are we then to understand the ambivalent position of civil society and social movement actors in which they criticise the authorities' counter-terrorism agenda, while simultaneously demanding and collaborating with them to fight against terrorism? And what does these non-state actors' involvement in counter-terrorism tell us about the relationship between domination and resistance in Tunisia?

This book seeks to offer an alternative reading of the interlocking relationship between terrorism, democracy and social movements. It does so, firstly, by approaching democracy not as a 'neutral analytical category', but as a 'category of action',[38] practised by multiple actors for their competing political and economic goals. Instead of focusing on the question of what challenges Tunisia's democratisation is facing, it is primarily concerned with the question of what type of political-economic system the post-uprising regime envisages and relates democracy to, and how. Secondly, terrorism is seen as a discourse entailed in such politics of democracy rather than an objective threat to democracy. This way of approaching terrorism shifts our attention towards what is being practised in the name of the War on Terror and how such practices are linked to democracy. Finally, it sees civil society and social movement actors as players who are as important as state institutions and domestic elites in the construction of the terrorism–democracy nexus. In doing so, instead of conceptualising them as standing in sharp opposition to top–down security policies, it explores how they become the object of and at the same time agent of such a nexus while interacting with political and economic elites.

Why Foucault?

In developing a framework to make sense of the democracy–terrorism nexus and its relationship to unemployed movements, this study draws on a Foucauldian approach to democracy, security and resistance. I explain in great detail why and how I use Foucault in Chapter 2, but I would like to briefly mention here that this choice is driven by three main considerations.

Firstly, while democracy as such is not among the subjects that Foucault rigorously investigated, his understanding of liberalism as a set of practices that obeys 'the internal rule of maximum economy'[39] can offer insights about which political-economic orders the liberal model of democracy related itself to and promoted in democratising Tunisia. A growing body of literature has pointed to the limitations and rigidity of the democratisation/transitology approach to post-uprising transformations, emphasising the need to shift from the old and much-criticised democratisation versus authoritarianism debate to more attention to contentious politics and non-traditional actors.[40] What is relatively under-studied, however, is the question of what sort of politics the dominant democratisation paradigm performs and how it interacts with bottom–up politics on the ground. There is a small but significant literature that assesses the close ties between liberal democratisation and the neoliberalisation of Arab societies,[41] the politics of democracy knowledge production[42] and its role in 'concrete political struggles'.[43] The Foucauldian approach deployed here is in line with this critical turn in the study of democracy. It offers a framework that revisits democratisation both as a theory and as a set of political practices and explores what subjectivities it shapes and governs.

Secondly, and related to the above point, the Foucauldian critique of neoliberalism developed in this book helps us understand the War on Terror in Tunisia as not merely an authoritarian logic external to democracy, but as a 'technology of government'[44] within a neoliberal regime of power. As Mitchell Dean has highlighted in his application of Foucault to explicate the authoritarian dimension of liberal government, coercive measures need to be understood as a 'necessary component of the liberal attempt to govern free individuals', since making free societies always entails the categorisation of those who cannot (yet) exercise their freedom properly and thus must be coerced to be able to do so.[45] According to Dean, what distinguishes liberal governments from other coercive systems in Foucault's analysis is that the former justifies and operates interventions and regulations mainly through a 'knowledge of civil society' and the mobilisation of empowered civil society agencies.[46] Understanding authoritarianism as being implicated in liberal government opens up possibilities for unpacking the interlocking relationship between the dominant modality of democracy and counter-terrorism agenda promoted and implemented in Tunisia. Approached in this way, securitisation (as understood as the construction of a subject/object as a threat) can be studied as a governing technology – or, in Foucault's terms, a dispositif – that consists of not only coercive but also liberal components by which a knowledge of security is constituted at a particular historical moment and which serves a neoliberal governing.

Lastly, Foucault's notion of power as inherently relational helps us approach the dominant terrorism–democracy nexus not as a fixed and well-established order imposed on Tunisian society, but as being subject to constant processes of construction and reconstruction. As elaborated extensively in Chapter 2, power in Foucault is not a synonym of domination which indicates a more or less stable system of order. In the most fundamental sense, power is instead understood at the level of human interactions, which are in constant flux but nonetheless condition the 'possible field of actions of others' through the formation of discourses.[47] The notion that power is exercised not only by those governing but also by those governed makes processes of discursive formation inherently contested. Foucault therefore sees the role of those governed as well as those resisting as an integral part of the construction and reconstruction of hegemonic discourses (the terrorism–democracy nexus, in this particular case).

Putting together these three elements offers a unique and innovative approach to contentious politics taking place between those participating in the management and governance of Tunisian society, on the one hand, and those governed and resisting, on the other, in post-revolutionary contexts. This book is not the first to use Foucault for understanding power dynamics in Tunisia and the Arab region more broadly.[48] However, except for a few studies,[49] Foucauldian ideas have been predominantly used to explain forms of domination and not contesting actors and practices *per se*. The study of anti-system or anti-policy mobilisations in the MENA region has instead been done mainly in two ways. Scholars have focused on macro-level factors shaping or constraining bottom–up resistance. Marxist and Post-Marxist approaches to the uprisings are some of the examples that privilege structuralist understandings and focus on the question of *why* things had (and will have) to happen or not happen.[50] Yet, many studies have challenged structure-oriented explanations of grassroots protests in the region, calling for more research on micro-level dynamics, strategic actions and repertoires of contention observed within the mobilisations themselves. Mostly through their engagement with tools of social movement studies, they contribute to our understanding of *how* things happened or did not happen.[51]

These two perspectives are not in contradiction and can be mutually beneficial to each other. An emerging body of studies on collective actions in Tunisia suggests that the relationship between structure and agency is not pre-determined and that a greater focus on their *interactions* is required in order to better understand the politics of mobilisations.[52] In line with these studies, I propose that a Foucauldian understanding of contentious politics can provide a unique way of thinking about the relationship between structure and agency. It can do so by shedding light on the contentious and at the same time mutually constitutive relationship of domination and resistance. This book empirically shows this through the analysis of why and how unemployed populations were securitised. In doing so, it does not suggest and employ the Foucauldian approach as a 'better' framework that exhaustively explains all aspects of domination and resistance. Rather, I use it as complementary to scholarly efforts to critically examine the convoluted relationship between the two, as well as the political economy of democratisation in Tunisia; this can offer broader implications for the study of the Arab uprisings and their effects.

In developing this Foucauldian framework, I particularly draw on his notions of 'governmentality' and 'counter-conducts', which I consider to be crucial for understanding his ideas of power and resistance theoretically and for analysing the relationship between democracy, security and the unemployed resistance in Tunisia empirically. Defined as 'the conduct of conduct', governmentality refers to the exercise of power – the main concern of which is to shape, manage and guide the conduct of its populations at a distance – and the governing technologies which operate through discursive practices constitutive of particular forms of autonomous subjectivities. It is a synthetic notion in which Foucault's idea of power/knowledge and his critique of neoliberal government are elaborated. For the purposes of this book, I use governmentality as an analytic of 'the institutions, procedures, analyses and reflections, the calculations, and tactics'[53] that, while being performed by heterogeneous actors, together constitute the securitisation of the unemployed subject.

Whereas governmentality is mainly concerned with ways of governing, counter-conduct directs our attention to points of resistance and ways of resisting within relations of power. Foucault's notion of counter-conduct can be understood as a form of resistance the objective of which is to be conducted differently and to conduct the self, the strategies of which are shared by conducting practices. What makes this notion unique in analysing resistance is that it captures a particular aspect of resistance that operates not external to but within governmentality, interacting with and constituting the very relations of power. Counter-conductive resistance is immanent in governmentality, in the sense that it is located within the fields of discourse shared by conducting forces. It is also a productive and constitutive force within governmentality in that, instead of rejecting the status of being conducted, it continuously intervenes in, challenges and attempts to modify the relations of power to which it is subject or, more precisely, *the ways* in which it is conducted by utilising their freedom. In this book, counter-conduct serves as part of the governmentality analytic with which to investigate not only the exercise of power and domination through the securitisation of the unemployed, but also its very limitations.

Investigating Unemployed Mobilisations and the War on Terror

I believe that it is important to give an account of why I chose unemployed mobilisations as an instance of studying the democracy–security nexus in Tunisia and to outline briefly the data and methods used in this book. I began my field research in Tunisia in 2016. For a period of seven months, from October 2016 until April 2017, I conducted fifty in-depth and semi-structured interviews, as well as several dozen informal conversations with security experts, former military officials, leftist intellectuals, human rights and civil society activists and researchers, journalists, workers and unemployed protesters in Tunis, Gafsa, Sidi Bouzid, Kasserine, Gabes, El-Kef and Tataouine. The main goal of my interviews was to explore how different actors perceived and evaluated the process of democratisation, terrorism, socio-economic mobilisations and, specifically, the state's counter-terrorism approach. When necessary, follow-up interviews and conversations were also conducted through both online and in-person meetings.

While I decided to focus on 'socio-economic mobilisations' as a space of resistance, which actors or groups needed particular attention remained open prior to the fieldwork. My initial plan was to study workers' unions, as they played a visible role throughout and after the Uprising. Yet, in the process of interviewing people and reading media sources for the first half of my fieldwork, it became clear that it was unemployed populations who came to be the key target of the association of social mobilisations with terrorism. The reason behind why workers who belonged to trade unions were less associated with terrorists appears partly because of the powerful influence and legitimacy of the Tunisian General Labour Union (UGTT) within Tunisian society. Also, while several austerity measures were planned and announced by the authorities, workers were in a relatively more privileged position than the unemployed populations, in terms of both symbolic and material resources, thereby making them prefer 'peaceful' bargaining with the authorities over the highly disruptive and radical modes of action on which many unemployed protesters occasionally relied. Based on this observation, I chose unemployed protesters as the case subject and devoted the second half of my fieldwork to studying their interactions with the authorities as well as with the political and economic elites.

It should be made clear that defining the unemployed in any emerging economy is fuzzy, as the boundary between unemployment and employment has become increasingly blurred with the growing number of informal/casual workers. Tunisia is no exception in this regard. Several interviewees who introduced themselves as 'unemployed' in my interviews either were working or had experience of working as temporary or part-time workers in street cafes, restaurants and so on. The self-identification as unemployed while working as precarious workers mainly rested on the perception that they had been forced into precarious jobs that did not correspond to their educational level. Instead of including (and excluding) certain individuals according to a ready-made category of 'unemployed', I categorised my interviewees as unemployed if they self-identified as unemployed.

In analysing unemployed movements, this book specifically focuses on two groups: the Union for Unemployed Graduates (Union des diplômés chômeurs, UDC) and the Maknassy unemployed movement. These two cases were chosen in order to examine the unemployed movements at both the national and the local level. Organised by a small number of leftist university graduates in 2006, the UDC officially established a national union for the unemployed in 2011. Whereas the UDC presents itself as the representative organisation for unemployed youth across the country, the Maknassy movement locally emerged in Sidi Bouzid to demand the right to work and regional development. Despite lacking resources, the Maknassy movement in 2016 attracted public attention thanks to its creative modes of resistance. The analysis of the two case-studies has allowed me to compare how unemployed protests with different organisational structures, symbolic and material resources, as well as a range of resistance strategies, similarly or differently responded to the process of securitisation. In addition to field interviews, Facebook pages run by the two groups were used as an important data source. Observing their Facebook pages was useful, not only because they offered a more holistic picture of the methods of the two movements, but also because they enabled a triangulation of the findings from different data sources. The UDC and Maknassy movements used their Facebook pages as the main channel to publicise their activities, plans and demands. Given their robust online activism, I was able to collect various types of content, including written statements, pictures, videos and web links relevant to this study.

For the purposes of this study, I use the term 'ruling elites' and 'governing elites' to broadly refer to those exercising significant influence over the process of planning, calculation, implementation and dissemination of the arts of government. As such, my analysis of dominant securitising acts has included not only state figures, institutions and politicians, but also actors that are conventionally categorised as 'non-state', such as businessmen, experts and previously regime-friendly news media outlets. Based on my reading of the Tunisian media sources and conversations in the field, I limited the time-period for critical discourse analysis from the beginning of 2014 to the end of 2016, as the elites' association of socio-economic protests with terrorism significantly increased with the technocrat governments since January 2014.

The local digitalised news archives were used as a main source of data, as most public speeches, announcements and interviews made by government institutions, political parties, security experts and influential non-state figures and groups were accessible through digital news outlets. In order to gather the data in a systematic way, I first collected all news archives (476 in total) that included the two Arabic terms '-*Irhab*-' (terror) and '-*Ihtijaji*-' (protest) in their titles or content; to do so, I used Turess, a news database that contains news archives published from forty-seven local media outlets in Tunisia. The 476 news archives were then reviewed to exclude 258 archives that were either repetitive in their content or 'irrelevant'[54] to the research topic. The remaining news archives were coded based on speech actors, themes, referent objects and their 'securitising' effects. A narrative was considered as having securitising effects when socio-economic protests were framed as a worrisome or dangerous issue in reference to terrorism and/or counter-terrorism. Through this final stage of data selection, 109 speech acts were selected for critical discourse analysis.

Outline of the Book

Chapter 2 commences with a critical review of the liberal notion of democracy and the way in which it is used as an analytical framework, the so-called 'transitology', in the analysis of post-authoritarian transformations in developing countries, including Tunisia. Then I introduce Foucault's notion of governmentality and discuss how liberal democracy can work as an effective tool for neoliberal governing. To better investigate the exercise of neoliberal governing and its limitations, I also bring Foucault's notion of counter-conduct into the discussion. As defined as an analytic of a struggle 'to be led differently, by other men and towards other objectives', counter-conduct helps explore contentious and at the same time mutually constitutive interactions between domination and resistance. The chapter then explains how governmentality and counter-conduct together provide a useful analytic for the securitisation of the Tunisian unemployed in the context where the division between 'democratic' mobilisations and 'authoritarian' ruling has become increasingly obscured since 2011. The remainder of the chapter discusses how I translate the Foucauldian analytical framework into a discourse analysis of the (counter)securitisation of the unemployed subject.

Before providing an in-depth analysis of the empirical data, Chapter 3 provides a genealogy of the neoliberal governing in Tunisia in order to situate the analysis in its context. Rather than search for a continuity or discontinuity between the pre- and post-uprising regimes, the chapter revisits the contemporary history of Tunisia since the end of the Bourguiba era and offers a narrative of how a neoliberal governing emerged in Tunisia through a set of contingent changes witnessed after the Uprising. These changes were significantly driven by the fear of political Islam and the notion of Islamist terrorism, and the systematic securitisation of unemployed youth since 2014 was an important instance of how the nexus of the post-2011 War on Terror and neoliberal governing operated. This narrative also challenges the view that assumes the hegemonic political, economic and security order as constituted and maintained by a handful of political and economic elites. It does so by showing how the notion of civil society and actors within it played a key role in the reconfiguration of illiberal and liberal mechanisms of government, constituting the current neoliberal regime in Tunisia.

Chapter 4 analyses how the ruling elites' securitising practices linked the unemployed subject to terrorist. It shows that the elites constructed and substantiated a chain of equivalence between the unemployed and terrorism with a meta-narrative of 'the self- governable and self-responsible

unemployed' which was built through three hierarchically connected signifiers: Islamist terrorism, democracy and economic development. Building
on the investigation of the three signifying narratives, this chapter also
elaborates on how these narratives operated to regulate the conduct of the
unemployed in general and the protesters in particular. Thus, it examines
the ways in which the elites in their reactions to the unemployed mobilisations drew on commonly perceived liberal democratic values – such
as rule of law, human rights and free, fair elections – and economic
development and how these served to shape and govern the unemployed
as self-governable and entrepreneurial democratic citizens.

Chapters 5 and 6 turn to how unemployed protesters responded to
the ways in which they were associated with terrorism, by examining
the discursive practices performed by two unemployed movements, the
UDC and the Maknassy Unemployed Movement. After briefly introducing each movement, the two chapters explicate their counter-narratives,
counter-meta-narratives and counter-subjectivities. Chapter 5 shows how
the UDC, as self-proclaimed national union representing all unemployed
voices, actively intervened in and challenged the elites' securitising practices, producing three hierarchically linked counter-narratives: the state's
involvement in the rise of Islamist extremism, the state's violation of constitutional rights and, lastly, the elimination of unemployment to fight terrorism. It also illustrates how these narratives were utilised in the process
of counter-subjectifying the unemployed as a victim of and revolutionary
against (state) terrorism. Taken together, my analysis of the UDC's narratives and subjectivities shows that its counter-securitising practices both
reproduced and challenged the elites' techniques of neoliberal governing
from within.

In Chapter 6, I analyse the Maknassy unemployed movement in comparison to the UDC's case. The first section outlines the development of
the Maknassy unemployed struggle in the context of the post-2011 War
on Terror and discusses how the elites' securitisation of the protesters
partly but significantly affected the protesters' way of engaging with street
mobilisations, leading them to intervene in the production of the counter-
terrorism discourse. The second section then demonstrates that, while
presenting some significant variations from the UDC's case, the Maknassy
protesters' responses to the elites' securitising practices and the struggle
for the right to work in general entailed the ambiguities discovered in the
UDC's counter-securitising practices. Similar to the UDC, the protesters resisted not by rejecting but by re-appropriating the elites' security
rationales and techniques; in doing so, they sought to govern the self as a
not so governable subject, while at the same time sustaining the neoliberal

governing by taking up a liberal mode of protest in the name of civil disobedience and disciplining themselves at the site of protest.

The final chapter provides a brief summary of the key findings and arguments made in the preceding chapters and discusses their importance for the understanding of Tunisia's transformation. In particular, I highlight what several unemployed protesters called 'the dilemma of democracy'. The dominant (liberal) democracy was a dilemma for them because they now had the freedom to speak out for their rights; however, not only was this freedom forced to be exercised in 'liberal ways', but also their resistance within the liberal boundary was easily ignored by the elites. The UDC and Maknassy protesters' counter-securitising practices show how the protesters both lived within and attempted to challenge this dilemma. The chapter also discusses what the Tunisian case tells us about unemployed mobilisations in neoliberal times in general and indicates future research directions in the field of democracy, security and contentious politics.

Notes

1. Interview with Habib Mahfoudh, aged thirty-six, casual worker and activist, Medinine, 22 February 2017. Throughout this book, I use pseudonyms to ensure the anonymity of interview participants.
2. Attounissia, 'Rai's al-Hukumah lil Nawab'.
3. Ibid.
4. Ibid.
5. Bayat, 'Social movements, activism and social development in the Middle East', p. 47; Cavatorta, 'No democratic change ... and yet no authoritarian continuity'; Merone, 'Enduring class struggle in Tunisia'.
6. Vatthauer and Weipert-Fenner, 'The quest for social justice in Tunisia', p. 10.
7. See, for instance, Perkins, 'Playing the Islamic card'; Ben Rejeb, 'United States policy towards Tunisia'.
8. While there is variation in the number of protests in Tunisia counted by academic and NGO researchers, their data nevertheless point out a dramatic increase in public mobilisation, particularly since 2015. Jan-Philipp Vatthauer and Irene Weipert-Fenner, for instance, show that, whereas the annual average number of the socio-economic protests from 2011 to 2014 was forty-seven, the number increased to 176 in the year of 2015 (Vatthauer and Weipert-Fenner, 'The quest for social justice in Tunisia').
9. Amara and Mcdowall, 'Tunisian democracy in turmoil after president sacks government', 27 July 2021.
10. Ibid.
11. Yee, 'Tunisia's democracy verges on collapse as president moves to take control'.

12. Brake, 'Muslim and democratic? From Tunisia to Afghanistan, there's no such thing'.

13. See, for instance, Fahmi and Meddeb, 'Market for jihad'; Ben Salem, 'The national dialogue collusive transactions and government legitimacy in Tunisia'; Ajala, 'Tunisian terrorist fighters a grassroots perspective'.

14. See, for example, Beinin and Vairel, *Social movements, mobilization, and contestation in the Middle East and North Africa*; Beinin, *Workers and thieves*; Hill, *Democratisation in the Maghreb*; Bayat, *Revolution without revolutionaries*; Weipert-Fenner, 'Unemployed mobilisation in times of democratisation'.

15. See Stepan, 'Tunisia's transition and the twin tolerations'; Brody-Barre, 'The impact of political parties and coalition building on Tunisia's democratic future'; Young, 'Exploring "Non-Western Democracy"'.

16. Also see Paciello, 'Delivering the revolution?'; Cimini, 'The economic agendas of Islamic parties in Tunisia and Morocco', p. 63.

17. Han, 'Transitional justice for whom?' p. 2.

18. Aliriza, 'Tunisia at risk'; Boukhars, 'The geographic trajectory of conflict and militancy in Tunisia'.

19. There is a growing body of studies that focus their analysis on the capacity and strategies of grassroot movements in the region. See, for example, Beinin and Vairel, *Social movements, mobilization, and contestation in the Middle East and North Africa*; Pilati, Acconcia, Suber and Chennaoui, 'Between organization and spontaneity of protests'; Bishara, 'Legacy trade unions as brokers of democratization? Lessons from Tunisia'.

20. Quamar, 'Tunisia'.

21. See, for example, Fahmi and Meddeb, 'Market for jihad'; Ajala, 'Tunisian terrorist fighters, a grassroots perspective'. On the call for state-civil society cooperation for de-radicalisation, see also Watanabe and Merz, 'Tunisia's jihadi problem and how to deal with it'.

22. Zelin, 'Tunisia's fragile democratic transition'.

23. Boukhars, 'The fragility of elite settlements in Tunisia'.

24. Boukhars, 'The geographic trajectory of conflict and militancy in Tunisia'.

25. Ben Salem, 'The national dialogue collusive transactions and government legitimacy in Tunisia'; Aliriza, 'Tunisia at risk'.

26. Netterstrøm, 'The Tunisian general labor union and the advent of democracy'; Rapanos, 'The role of human development in the transition to democracy after the Arab Spring'.

27. See, for instance, Breuer and Groshek, 'Online media and offline empowerment in post-rebellion Tunisia'.

28. Stepan, 'Tunisia's transition and the twin tolerations'; Filali-Ansary, 'Tunisia'.

29. Brody-Barre, 'The impact of political parties and coalition building on Tunisia's democratic future'; Stepan and Linz, 'Democratization theory and the "Arab Spring"'; Young, 'Exploring "Non-Western Democracy"'.

30. Ayers and Saad-Filho, 'Democracy against neoliberalism'.

31. See Sadiki, 'Bin Ali's Tunisia'.
32. Durac and Cavatorta, 'Strengthening authoritarian rule through democracy promotion?'; Powel, 'The stability syndrome US and EU democracy promotion in Tunisia'.
33. Aliriza, 'Tunisia at risk'.
34. Boukhars, 'The geographic trajectory of conflict and militancy in Tunisia', p. 10.
35. Cavatorta, 'No democratic change ... and yet no authoritarian continuity', p. 781.
36. Aliriza, 'Tunisia at risk'.
37. Simoncini, 'Beyond the "Epopee of Ben Guerdane"'.
38. This approach is in line with Andrea Teti's critique of the study of democratisation in MENA (Teti, 'Beyond lies the wub', p. 7).
39. Foucault, *The essential works, 1954–1984*, vol. 1, p. 74.
40. See, for example, Asseburg and Wimmen, 'Dynamics of transformation, elite change and new social mobilization in the Arab World'; Völkel, 'Complex Politics in Single Numbers?'; Valbjørn, 'Upgrading Post-democratization Studies'; Valbjørn, 'Three ways of revisiting the (post-)democratization debate after the Arab Uprisings'.
41. Powers, 'Cartelization, neoliberalism, and the foreclosure of the Jasmine Revolution'.
42. Sadiki, 'Towards a "democratic knowledge" turn?'
43. Teti, 'Beyond lies the wub', p. 5.
44. Ibid. p. 76.
45. Dean, 'Liberal government and authoritarianism', p. 40. For the appraisal of Foucault's notion of power as the interdependence between liberal and illiberal means, see also Hindess 'Politics as government'; Death, 'Governmentality at the limits of the international'.
46. Dean, 'Liberal government and authoritarianism', p. 45.
47. Foucault, 'The subject and power', p. 221.
48. Several studies have shown how governmentality helps problematise and explicate power dynamics between the international and the local, as well as between state and society in the Arab region. See, for instance, Hibou, 'Domination and control in Tunisia'; Hanafi, 'Framing Arab socio-political space'; Malmvig, 'Governing arab reform'; Tagma, Kalaycioglu and Akcali, '"Taming" Arab social movements'; İşleyen, 'The European Union and neoliberal governmentality'; Akçalı, *Neoliberal Governmentality and the Future of the State in the Middle East and North Africa*.
49. See Malmvig, 'Governing Arab reform: Governmentality and counterconduct in European democracy promotion in the Arab world' and 'Eyes wide shut'; Diskaya, 'Don't ask, don't tell'; Abdalla, 'Neoliberal policies and the Egyptian trade union movement'.
50. See, for instance, De Smet, *Gramsci on Tahrir*; Munif, 'The Arab Revolts'; Achcar, 'Hegemony, domination, corruption and fraud in the Arab region'.

51. Pilati, Acconcia, Suber and Chennaoui, 'Between organization and spontaneity of protests'.
52. Asseburg and Wimmen, 'Dynamics of transformation, elite change and new social mobilization in the Arab World'; Jasper and Volpi, 'Introduction'; Volpi and Clark, 'Activism in the Middle East and North Africa in times of upheaval'.
53. Foucault, 'Governmentality', p. 102.
54. In the following cases, I consider the archives irrelevant to this research and consequently excluded them from the data set: when the term 'terror' was used as part of the name of a particular body (such as 'special force for counter-terrorism'); when the term 'protest' was used to describe protests organised for non-socio-economic causes (such as a protest organised by a branch of the security force to demand the enactment of a law for protecting security agencies with reference to terrorism); when the term 'protest' was used as a synonym of a 'complaint' that does not involve any physical protests; and when the term 'terror' or 'protest' was used to report or discuss non-domestic issues (such as 9/11 terror).

2

A Foucauldian Approach to Democracy, Resistance and Security

[O]ne doesn't have a power which is wholly in the hands of one person who can exercise it alone and totally over the others.[1]

[T]here is no Power, but power relationships.[2]

The 'Confused Combination' of Liberalism and Democracy

Democracy has been one of the most popular themes when discussing post-authoritarian political economy in developing countries around the world. Traditionally, the debate followed the so-called 'transitology paradigm' whose questions and approaches are anchored in the assumed identification of processes of post-authoritarian transformation with democratisation. Most transitology studies have been based on Guillermo O'Donnell and Phillippe C. Schmitter's work on transitions, in which particularly the role of elites is highlighted as a key factor of successful democratisation.[3] Having enjoyed its greatest popularity in the 1990s among comparativists who were keen to apply the model to regime changes in different regions, the transitology paradigm has also attracted much criticism. Thomas Carothers has famously criticised its 'democratic teleology' and 'belief in the determinative importance of elections' and argued that it fails to grasp what is actually happening in post-authoritarian countries.[4] Emphasising the uncertainty of regime changes and the necessity to go beyond the narrow definition of democracy, 'post'-transitologists have sought to re-evaluate countries previously considered as moving towards democracy, by using new labels such as 'feckless pluralism',[5] 'electoral authoritarianism and pseudo democracy',[6] a 'hybrid mix of electoral forms and authoritarianism',[7] or 'semi-democratic'.[8]

When it comes to the study of Arab politics, several scholars have been quick to raise concerns over the re-appearance of the democratisation/ transitology paradigm in the aftermath of the uprisings. Pace and Cavatorta, for instance, have argued that, while having much to contribute, the democratisation approach together with the authoritarian resilience paradigm needs to be re-visited to avoid their rigidity and shortcomings in comprehending political changes in the Arab region.[9] Similarly, Asseburg and Wimmen have challenged the way in which the post-uprising devel- opments are presented as a linear process towards democracy or authori- tarianism, calling for an alternative approach that sees them as open-ended and dynamic processes of transformation.[10] Yet, as Pace and Cavatorta have pointed out, the debate on democracy and democratisation itself is not dismissible as being outdated or irrelevant to the study of the Arab transformations.[11] This is particularly the case with Tunisia, where build- ing a new and truly functioning democratic system has been a key concern of international actors, domestic policy-makers, as well as many civil society and social movement forces.

Part of the problem with the debate over democracy and democratisa- tion in the region is rather that it tends to uncritically reiterate the dominant notion of democracy, where its fundamental principles and mechanisms revolve around a liberal idea of individual liberties and duties. By liberal idea, I am specifically referring to the classical Anglo-American under- standing of liberalism.[12] It produces a particular version of democracy (hereafter liberal democracy) in which democracy is thought of as a political system exercised by elected representatives of the people, with emphasis on autonomous civil society and minimal state intervention. In this system, the role of the state is required to be limited to facilitating individual freedom, mainly through the protection of the rule of law and certain human rights.[13] It prioritises individuals over society and civil/ political rights over social/economic rights.

A large body of the literature on democracy and democratisation has deployed this classical liberalism in defining, categorising and evaluating what are (and what are not) democratic systems. Take, for example, Carothers' criticism of transitology: while being critical of the tradi- tional way of studying democracy, he has still reified the hegemony of liberal democracy by creating non-democracy categories such as 'feck- less pluralism' which, according to him, differ to a large extent from 'well-established liberal democracy'. His approach to the problem of democracy shows how the abstract dichotomy of liberal and illiberal that is deeply entrenched in the mind of many democracy scholars and advocates operates to unwittingly re-affirm liberal democracy as a true and universal good, while concretising its abstract through the construction of different regime types.

The tendency to equate democracy with liberal democracy neglects and, in doing so, (unwittingly) contributes to making invisible potential alternative models such as social democracy. Central to the conception of social democracy, according to Sheri Berman, is the 'belief in the primacy of politics and a commitment to using democratically acquired power to direct economic forces in the service of the collective good'.[14] Whereas liberal democracy revolves around an individualist understanding of society, freedom and rights, social democracy places great emphasis on collective rights and well-being. Likewise, the latter considers social and economic rights as important as the civil and political rights promoting the welfare state model, its active role in the economy and control over the market.[15] Values such as basic human rights and the rule of law are not unique to liberal democracy. Social democracy also promotes these values but, as Hobson states, 'it differs in its ordering of priorities and the means used to achieve these shared goals'.[16]

Arguably, the (mostly) unspoken belief that liberal democracy is the indisputably ideal political system has the effect of depoliticising this category of democracy by rendering it a value-neutral analytical tool. While highlighting different conditions, factors or actors in their works, scholars who have explicitly or implicitly identify liberal democracy as a universal and ideal form of democracy usually ask questions such as 'is a given country a democracy?' and 'what conditions make democracy possible?' and 'how can a country achieve a stable democracy?'[17] They do not ask how the traditional Anglo-American liberal idea and priorities shape democracy in a particular way and what implications they have about the exercise of domination in political, economic and social realms in presumably post-authoritarian contexts. They neglect the fact that liberal democracy, which has become a global project today, 'rests on the *confused* combination'[18] of the two.

Hobson has pointed out that the notion of democracy has changed over time and that, thus, there is nothing universal in the currently dominant liberal model of democracy, suggesting that it 'was born of historical contingencies'.[19] Providing a brief genealogy of liberal democracy, he has discussed how democracy, which nineteenth-century liberal thinkers such as Alexis de Tocqueville perceived as potentially dangerous given the tension between liberty and equality, began to be gradually equated with liberalism in Western Europe and the United States. He went on to argue that the emergence of liberal democracy was not what liberals wished for, but that 'it emerged in part from a *miscalculation* in the strategy used to entrench liberal rights, combined with a gradual recognition that the best way to manage democracy's seemingly unavoidable rise was to limit and control it as best they could'.[20]

Hobson's genealogy of liberal democracy indicates that it is an outcome of the contingent history of liberalism and democracy, in which the former attempted to manage and utilise the latter to ensure the survival of liberal values. His appraisal of liberal democracy also suggests that it is necessary to problematise how the problem of democracy is approached by shifting our attention away from asking whether a country is democratic or how a country can achieve democracy, and towards asking *how* liberalism operates through the democratic will of the majority of the people and with *what* political, economic and social effects. These alternative questions lead us to study liberal democracy as 'not merely a neutral analytical category, but one deployed and adapted by political actors in their concrete practices'.[21] As I will discuss in the following section, a Foucauldian approach to democracy, liberalism and neoliberalism is useful, not only for identifying liberal democracy as a *historically* conditioned set of rationalising practices that call themselves democratic, but also for elucidating the increasing intimacy between the liberal democratic system and neoliberal governing today.

Liberal Democracy and Neoliberal Governing

Foucault's approach to democracy can be subsumed by his analysis of liberalism as a technology of government that obeys the rule of 'maximum economy', as understood as maximum achievement of political and economic objectives through a minimalist governance of populations.[22] While any exercise of government requires a rationalisation for maximal benefit and minimal cost, liberal rationalisation, according to him, started from the principle of society (and not the state) 'as both a precondition and a final end', which in turn enables the development of technologies of government based on the suspect: 'one always governs too much'.[23] It is based on this principle of society that democracy operates as a way of governing. For Foucault, it is not an internal or intrinsic logic as such but the *effectiveness* of the 'democracies of the state of right' that binds democracy and liberalism together.[24] Democracy is effective for liberalism in that its formal properties such as citizens' participation in elections are not only compatible with but also crucial to the operation of liberal governments whose very existence is dependent on the 'liberties and capacities of the governed exercised within an economy'.[25]

The principle of society and emphasis on individual liberties and free market should not be taken to lead to diminishing states. On the contrary, the question of targets and objectives of state intervention has been central to the debate among early liberals and neoliberals. That being said, some significant transformations in classical economic liberalism were carried out by neo-liberals in the twentieth and twenty-first centuries.[26] According to Foucault, they argued that the traditional liberal formula of creating a space of economic freedom under state supervision (but without intervention) needed to be turned around: it was the market economy that must be the principle of the state and not the other way around. Also, what was required for the market economy to fully function was no longer *laissez-faire*, as liberals had imagined it in the eighteenth and nineteenth centuries. Neoliberals instead called for an active and intervening state on the basis that competition, which is the essence of the market, 'can only appear if it is produced, and if it is produced by an active *governmentality*'.[27]

The term 'governmentality', which first appeared in Foucault's genealogy of the modern state, evolved as a more general analytical tool in his analysis of the neoliberal regime of power in his 1979 lectures. He noted that 'what I have proposed to call governmentality, which is the way in which one conducts the conduct of men, is no more than a proposed analytical grid for these relations of power'.[28] Neoliberalism is conventionally represented as a set of national and global economic policies, from cutting subsidies and privatising public entities to easing foreign investment restrictions and the dismantling of welfare systems. Yet, the governmentality approach directs attention to neoliberal *governing*; the operation of neoliberal governing encompasses political, economic, social and cultural domains, and its central epistemic values are reduced to economic rationality, market freedom and self-interest.

How does neoliberal governing based on the expansion of market economy and the intervening state actually operate? Taking the German variant of neoliberalism in the twentieth century as an example, Foucault has noted that the neoliberal government intervened in the conditions (and not the mechanisms) of the market economy through regulatory actions that *actively* encouraged its fundamental tendencies, such as the reduction of costs.[29] In doing so, the primary objective of the regulatory actions becomes price stability, not price control or systematic job creation. Full employment, for instance, should not be an objective of government intervention. To the contrary, a certain level of unemployment is considered necessary for the economy in neoliberal government, in that it renders unemployed populations workers 'in transit between an unprofitable activity and a more profitable activity'.[30] More importantly, government intervention requires organising actions around seemingly non-economic but, according to Foucault, market conditions more fundamental and structural than price stability.[31] These include technology, legal framework, education, climate and, crucially, populations. For instance, what was considered imperative by neoliberals in the process of integrating European agriculture into a market economy in the twentieth century was first and foremost the reduction of the agricultural population, which required active government intervention to encourage migration.[32] For Foucault, the logic of subjecting populations and their ways of being, thinking and acting to government intervention was a key feature of neoliberal governing and as such required particular attention.

Neoliberal governing in Foucault relies on a 'secularised and modernised' form of pastoral power, as understood as governing by guiding the conduct of individuals and by inciting subjectivities that render them a *homo oeconomicus*.[33] This is because, while the market economy needs citizens who actively and voluntarily maximise their capacity as men of production and enterprise, they do not naturally become so. They need to be encouraged and nurtured to be autonomous, responsible and risk-taking citizens, through education, a legal framework and various social policies.[34] Therefore, as Lemke has put it, the state in the neoliberal regime of power 'not only retains its traditional functions, but also takes on new tasks and functions' which are '*indirect* techniques for leading and controlling individuals without at the same time being responsible for them'.[35]

From this standpoint, liberal democratic values such as strong and autonomous civil society, rule of law and democratic procedures that encourage the participation of the governed in the process of ruling are not merely the reflection of the 'will' of political subjects or universal and natural principles, as liberal democrats often conceptualise. Rather, they can also serve as constitutive mechanisms of neoliberal governing. This is to say that, while neoliberalism is not necessarily democratic, it seeks to define and enhance democratic institutions in a particular way so that citizens can exercise and regulate their rights and liberties in conformity with market imperatives and take responsibilities for their welfare.[36] It should be highlighted that the construction of autonomous and participatory citizen in this particular way operates only through the creation and management of exceptions, requiring regulatory and coercive practices imposed on individuals whose exercise of freedom is incompatible with market principles. Rather than existing external to liberal rationalities, the coercive dimension becomes a 'necessary component of the liberal attempt to govern free individuals'.[37] In this sense, neoliberalism is not a 'type' of power that is immune to sovereign or disciplinary techniques.

Governmentality provides an analytic of such multifaceted neoliberal governing practices that constitute autonomous citizens, so as to ensure that their freedom is exercised *properly*.

From this governmentality perspective, the post-uprising trajectory in Tunisia cannot be understood without taking into account the operation of a neoliberal governing to constitute its citizens as flexible and rational *homo oeconomicus*. While there has been no fundamental change in terms of the socio-economic structure, the process of democratisation has reconfigured the ways in which the logic of market economy functions in the country. The economic liberalisation under the Ben Ali regime was characterised by its heavy reliance on authoritarian techniques and crony capitalism. From the governmentality perspective, this form of market economy through authoritarian means was at best acceptable in that it guaranteed a small but nonetheless significant space for market capitalism; at worst it was problematic and in need of modification because it hampered the full functioning of the market logic beyond the economic realm. In order for market mechanisms to fully function, the logic of maximising productivity, competitiveness and 'self-responsibilisation' had to be expanded as the ultimate goal of human actions, redefining the meaning of the social as a whole.[38] In this sense, the overthrowing of a dictatorial regime at the hands of the Tunisian people in January 2011 and the following process of building democratic institutions provided an experimental momentum for a neoliberal regime to function properly.

That neoliberal governing operates in Tunisia does not mean that it has now become a 'neoliberal society' as such. Nor does the governmentality approach postulate that Tunisian society is being governed solely through freedom. As I have highlighted, neoliberal attempts to subjectify civil society actors as active, autonomous and responsible citizens fundamentally rely on the construction and management of deviants whose exercise of freedom does not fit the kind of freedom promoted by the logic of the global market. Therefore, sovereign and coercive measures to govern them so as to be free in a proper way become necessary. While, unlike under the Ben Ali regime, monitoring and openly criticising the authorities became not only possible but also considered a sign of democracy in the post-uprising context, there simultaneously emerged multiple techniques to govern deviant ways of thinking and behaving which are deemed threatening to the consolidation of a liberal democratic system and the integration of Tunisia into the global market. In other words, after the Uprising, neoliberal governing became *an* integral part of power relations, the aim of which was to direct and guide bottom–up democratic desires so as to be exercised in compliance with the logic of maximum economy.

Unemployed populations, among others, have increasingly become subject to such neoliberal governing in Tunisia, not least because of their often-radical forms of protest that 'disrupt' business as usual. Arguably, the very existence of unemployment as a social problem is dependent on the operation of the neoliberal regime of power in that the eradication of unemployment as such is not within the neoliberal agenda; what it attempts to do instead is to manage the unemployment *at a distance*. From the perspective of neoliberals, as Foucault has argued, the problem of unemployment must not be directly intervened regardless of its rate, but must instead be governed through other means such as price stability.[39] As I will emphasise in Chapter 4, the management of the unemployment issue in Tunisia significantly relied on techniques of the self, which operated to shape the conduct of the unemployed subject so as to be autonomous, self-responsible and entrepreneurial citizens whose political freedom can conform to the stability of liberal democracy and market imperatives.

An understanding of how neoliberal governing operated in Tunisia, however, requires further consideration of the location and role of the unemployed resistance. Tunisia has witnessed continued mobilisations of the unemployed against neoliberal economic policies even after 2011, indicating that the unemployed were not merely a passive and docile subject. This raises the question of whether the unemployed resistance existed as external to the neoliberal governing in Tunisia. If not, were the protesters themselves part of the heterogeneous ensemble constitutive of neoliberal technologies? If the unemployed resistance was implicated in neoliberal power, how are we to conceptualise such resistance without reducing it to a mere reproduction of the Tunisian neoliberal regime? These questions also raise the issue of whether governmentality, and more fundamentally Foucault's notion of power, have anything to offer for the understanding of the self-proclaimed anti-neoliberal movements, such as that organised by unemployed protesters, and if so, how. To address these questions, the next section will turn to the possibility of resistance in Foucault's conception of power. This conception, in turn, will bring us to the issue of how his understanding of resistance represented by the notion of 'counter-conduct' can provide an alternative view and analytic of the position of the unemployed resistance and its relation to neoliberal governing.

The Possibility of Resistance

The rise of local and transnational grassroots mobilisations against austerity policies, inequalities and socio-economic marginalisation have propelled many scholars to explore the causes, effects and forms of resistance in relation to neoliberal globalisation.[40] In particular, the conventional idea that unemployed people are unlikely to mobilise because of their lack of resources, opportunities and motivation has been challenged by the collective action that the jobless have organised against their precarious situation in neoliberal times. Studies on unemployed collective action in the US,[41] Europe,[42] Latin America[43] and the MENA region[44] have shown that unemployed protests 'are more probable than expected'.[45] The Arab uprisings in 2011 further demonstrated the importance of unemployed mobilisations, as the demand for the right to work was the very trigger of these events.

While a wide range of approaches and research questions as well as various analytical perspectives exist, many of these studies, particularly Marxist and post-Marxist approaches, tend to conceive resistance as external to and directly against domination. They also see resistance as a space constitutive of counter-hegemony or anti-neoliberal ideals.[46] From a perspective assuming a sharp divide between resistance and domination, Foucault's understanding of resistance has often been considered 'troubling', as it does not seem to provide any space for resistance outside neoliberal power.[47] Indeed, Foucault has not placed resistance outside of what he has called 'power' in the first volume of *The history of sexuality*.[48] For him, resistance does not also necessarily oppose power. Malmvig has further described this nature of resistance, noting that, '[r]ather than a transcendence of government, resistance is implicated in the very relationships of power it opposes. Subjects therefore do not cease to be governed when they resist'.[49]

Is there a possibility for resistance when it is immanent in power? And what can a Foucauldian understanding of resistance add to our knowledge of unemployed mobilisations? To answer these questions, the first issue that we need to understand is Foucault's differentiation of power from states of domination, 'which are what we ordinarily call power'.[50] Power, in his general use of the term, refers to relationships between individuals that involve an ensemble of actions upon actions to induce others.[51] This is to say that power is not something which certain institutions or groups possess; rather, it is a force which is always relational and exercised by individuals in order to 'influence and modify the actions of other individuals'.[52] Power is not a negative force, since influencing or leading others does not necessarily result in depriving the liberty of others.[53] Individuals 'are always in the position of simultaneously undergoing and exercising [...] power'.[54]

How is power exercised then? According to Foucault, power is exercised through discursive practices which in turn structure the ways in which individuals think and act or, in his terms, structure the 'possible field of actions of others'.[55] Discursive practices in his methodology of power are not textual or verbal communications only. Rather, they are a network of both linguistic and non-linguistic actions that form discourses – namely, patterned ideas that (re)shape the ways in which we see and make sense of particular subjects and objects. Take the global discourse of development in developing societies as an example: it is not only what is being said, but also what is being routinely *performed* by donors, governments, media, consultants, international and local staff and so on that, despite their varying foci and priorities, form a dominant discourse of development that structures our way of thinking of what are (and what are not) good development practices. Importantly, a discursive formation follows the logic of dispersion. By dispersion, Foucault does not mean a random scattering of things. Rather, it is a dispersion in *regularity* that loosely links pre-existing and divergent discourses to each other,[56] again much like the discourse of development which is constituted through the convergence of different discursive zones such as education, health, security, law, finance and environment.

The networked unity that arises from the intersections of heterogeneous discourses is not static or fixed.[57] As human interactions are by nature mobile and dynamic, the formation of discourses – that is, the exercise of power – is always in flux. What can be inferred from this dispersed power is that subjects are embedded in fields of possibility or discourses, which are historically constituted by complex power relations. What surrounds individuals is not so much a single dominant discourse that determines their subjects, but *multiple* discourses in which these discourses themselves are often contradictory. That no individual is free from the field of possibility means that the choices of both the governing and the governed subjects are constrained by fields of possibility. Moreover, subjects are not mere receivers who passively accept a set of rules or discourses imposed on them. They have the freedom given in multiple discourses. Dynamic and relational power therefore assumes that subjects actively participate in the construction of discourses.

Domination, however, is considered the effect or a 'simulacrum' that emerges from relations of power in which particular relations of subjugation are exercised.[58] The dichotomy between governing and governed (such as the relationship between global donors and recipient countries, or the relationship between employment policy-makers and job-seekers in the development discourse) is ostensibly fixed and stable, because the dominant group is likely to have more material and symbolic means than the subordinated group. It is in this sense that people usually perceive that one has power. Yet, while one can argue that certain individuals or groups occupy a dominant position, it does not mean that they possess power *per se*. A type of domination is also not permanent due to the nature of the dialectic between power and domination. One can think of critiques of the top–down development assistance approach and the growing call for a more horizontal, partnership-like relationship preferring terminologies such as 'international cooperation' to the term 'development'. Foucault, according to Widder, understands power and domination as immanent to and reciprocally conditioned to one another: whereas power constitutes relational networks which are constantly in flow, domination, as 'the overall effect' of power, seeks to arrest and fix their movements.[59]

The tension that arises from the dialectical relationship between power and domination is central to Foucault's understanding of resistance. The form of resistance that he has sought to grasp is a movement not against power relations, but against the *ways* in which dominant actors or institutions attempt to fix one's subject position in a particular fashion. And both domination and resistance perform and interact within power relations.[60] It is in this context that we can understand Foucault's argument that 'it is a form of power which makes individuals subjects'.[61] That power exists everywhere does not foreclose the possibility of resistance. To the contrary, it is the relations of power that become the very condition on which resistance operates.[62] If discursive practices and the formation of discourses are not only something that dominant groups can exercise upon others, but rather something that every subject can perform, albeit not equally, then resistance always exists in as much as power relations exist. Foucault's distinction between power and domination is crucial to the conceptualisation of resistance in the context of neoliberal governing. In particular, his notion of counter-conduct provides an alternative approach to resistance, which goes beyond the binary of domination and resistance.

Counter-conduct in Tunisia

In his 1978 lectures, Foucault introduced the term 'counter-conduct' in order to analyse a particular dimension of resistance the characteristics of which cannot be reduced to a resistance to economic exploitation or political subjugation. It is a form of resistance seemingly less spectacular than a revolt or a revolution seeking to overthrow a system. That being said, it also differs from movements that seek reform in a system. How is counter-conductive resistance different from what we generally conceive of as resistance? It denotes a form of struggle within and against relations of power that, like pastoral Christianity, governs by guiding and directing individuals towards certain goals. Rather than rejecting the status of being governed, this form of resistance aims at being governed and conducting the self *otherwise*. Rather than claim that 'we do not want to be governed', counter-conductive resistance revolves around the question of 'how not to be governed *like that*, by that, in the name of those principles, […] and by means of such procedures'.[63] If governmentality provides an analytic of neoliberal governing that operates by steering and guiding populations so as to be citizens of enterprise, then counter-conduct offers an analytic of how such government is challenged by and interacts with the various forms of dissent in neoliberal times. It does so by unpacking two peculiar elements in movements against *ways* of being governed as neoliberal citizens.

First, counter-conduct emphasises the inseparability of domination and resistance by locating the two within relations of power. As Death has elaborated in his appraisal of counter-conduct, it then 'looks within government to see how forms of resistance rely upon, and are even implicated within, the strategies, techniques and power relationships they oppose'.[64] Foucault has discussed this interiority of resistance in his analysis of counter-conduct in Christianity, noting that anti-pastoral struggles operated partly but significantly through the invocation of the return to Scripture or asceticism, which were by no means external to pastoral power relations.[65] By deploying and reproducing a set of tactics within governmental technologies, counter-conductive resistance has an aspect of sustaining and reinforcing the domination that they seek to challenge. This ambivalent position of resistance has been discussed in relation to neoliberal governing with empirical cases.[66] Applying counter-conduct to the case of the Occupy movements in London, for example, Bulley has argued that the occupiers' tactics not only challenged but also were implicated in global capitalism, in the sense that they relied on and literally bought into products of capitalism for their communication, shelter, food and drink while occupying a global city.[67]

The second and more important characteristic of the counter-conduct analytic is its emphasis on the 'ethical component' of resistance.[68] In the process of struggling to be governed and directed differently, counter-conducts also 'seek, possibly at any rate, to escape direction by others and to define the way for each to conduct himself'.[69] In this sense, they are 'not only about being led otherwise, but also about conducting the self and being otherwise'.[70] Analysing Syrian artists in the post-2011 context, for example, Malmvig has highlighted that their dissenting practices through the arts focused on *being different* from those producing traditional forms of visual practices (either for or against the regime) by producing more subtle, less political (in a narrow sense) but critical visual materials.[71]

As I have mentioned above, a key element of neoliberal technologies is conducting the conducts of individuals or groups through the formation of the self. While governing practices subjectify individuals in a particular way, counter-conducts can function as a space for the care of the self and others – namely, a space in which resisting subjects attempt to escape the ways of being subjectified and to invent new ways of being.

Foucault did not argue that this ethical dimension of resistance was separated from or superior to class struggles or political revolts. Rather, it is almost always part of them.[72] What he sought to emphasise with the notion of counter-conduct is that the struggle for alternative subjectivities is no less fundamental than resistance with explicit political and economic demands.[73] Perhaps this ethical dimension of struggle becomes more and more visible as neoliberal governments increasingly incite their populations to be empowered and autonomous subjects. The care for the self and others begins with the question of 'who am I, and how should I behave?' The desire of being and acting not in the way that one is told to be is found in global North and South alike, for example, through the occupation of global cities with bodies and counter-cultures in Europe,[74] or through the re-appropriation of the modern citizen subject by indigenous movements against the relocation policy for modernisation in Africa.[75] Taken together, counter-conduct directs our attention to what resisting techniques within governmental power are deployed by resisting subjects and to how, in the process of resisting socio-economic exploitation or political subjugation, they not only reproduce but also attempt to create new modes of being and care of the self.

Foucault's notion of counter-conduct is closely relevant to and can provide a distinct analytic to the study of unemployed mobilisations in Tunisia. While the ruling elites and the unemployed movements remained in an antagonistic relation to each other in terms of their visions and strategies for social and economic reforms, the newly implemented liberal democratic system obscured the previously sharp division between 'democratic' mobilisations and 'authoritarian' ruling. This is reflected in the fact that both the protesters and the elites came to rely on democratic values, means and languages (such as human rights and liberties) in order to legitimise their position while delegitimising the other side. Also, while Tunisian unemployed movements are more politically heterogeneous than one may assume, most of the visible protests organised by unemployed populations since 2011 did not demand the overthrowing of the regime as such. In many cases, their demands were oriented towards reforms *within* the newly established democratic system. More importantly, as the later chapters will illustrate in detail, the unemployed protesters' resistance for socio-economic justice marked by the right to work entailed struggles to escape and challenge subjectivities constructed by the elites in order to conduct the conducts of the unemployed as well as the struggles to invent and create alternative modes of being.

This indicates that, while the unemployed movements in Tunisia were socio-economic struggles in the most visible sense, there existed within such struggles 'some of the points of resistance, some of the forms of attack and counter-attack'[76] in the form of a struggle to be governed differently and to govern the self. Counter-conduct as an analytic of resistance can contribute to the study of the unemployed resistance, by illuminating and elucidating such points of resistance which cannot be grasped through binary understandings of domination and resistance. In doing so, it provides a more subtle and nuanced way of thinking about the relationship between neoliberal governing and the unemployed struggle in Tunisia, without romanticising or trivialising the potential of the unemployed as a resisting subject.

This book sees the unemployed movements as an ensemble of resisting practices in which both a struggle for socio-economic justice and a struggle for different ways of being governed and alternative modes of being coexist. In analysing the neoliberal management of the unemployed and counter-movements in Tunisia, I particularly focus on how the perceived threat of terrorism and the urgency of the War on Terror operated to conduct the conducts of the unemployed. The counter-terrorism discourse was arguably at the heart of the dialectic between the neoliberal attempts to conduct the ways in which the unemployed think and act, on the one hand, and the unemployed protesters' struggle to counter the process in which they were conducted, on the other hand. Applying the governmentality approach developed in this chapter so far, the following section will provide an alternative way of understanding terrorism, in which it is conceptualised not as a brute fact, but as a dominant security discourse mobilised for the purposes of neoliberal governing.

The War on Terror and the Securitisation of the Unemployed Subject

Terrorism has attracted considerable scholarly attention particularly since the attack on the World Trade Centre in the US in 2001. Dominated by the realist approach that conceptualises terrorism as an objective fact,[77] traditional studies have been increasingly subject to criticism, especially by scholars who have advocated a 'constructivist turn' in the study of security. Rainer Hülsse and Alexander Spencer, for instance, have proposed to turn to a discourse-centred approach to terrorism studies, arguing that terrorists and terrorism are essentially social constructions. This should not be taken to mean that constructivists deny the existence of real people purporting real actions. What they rather point to is 'what these people and their deeds mean is a matter of interpretation'; such an interpretation is not external to and affected by discourses, especially by the discourse of the global War on Terror.[78] It is in this sense that one can say that terrorism and terrorists exist only through discursive practices. Richard Jackson, a leading scholar in critical terrorism studies, has also pointed to the epistemic crisis of terrorism and counter-terrorism in political and academic discourses and conceptualised terrorism as a social fact, arguing that it 'lacks a clear ontological status – which actually makes an objective definition impossible'.[79]

Among the growing body of literature that challenges the realist approach to security, the Copenhagen School's securitisation theory is particularly influential in terms of which security issues are conceptualised not as objectified threats, but as the 'intersubjective establishment of a threat'.[80] According to the Copenhagen School, security is a 'speech act' that 'takes politics beyond the established rules of the game and frames the issue either as a special kind of politics or as above politics'.[81] Based on this definition of security, securitisation becomes a process in which a particular issue is labelled (through speech acts) as a security issue and, therefore, as existential threat to specific communities, allowing for the suspension of normal politics and the implementation of emergency measures in dealing with the issue.[82] Theoretically, the Copenhagen School's scholars have highlight the role of a relevant 'audience' or 'constituency' whose acceptance or rejection of narratives for making security determines whether a securitising move (a speech act that presents an issue as a priority that requires extraordinary measures) can turn into successful securitisation (such as the implementation of emergency measures).[83] In other words, a securitising move can lead to the securitisation of an issue only if and when that move is 'legitimised' by the audience. Scholars have argued that such a distinction between a securitising move and securitisation is critical in order to be 'precise about' the threshold of securitisation.[84] Finally, they focus on 'facilitating conditions', including the forms of speech acts, the speaker's position and the 'historical resonance of particular threats', among others, as the conditions that enable security-making to be successful.[85]

Taken together, the Copenhagen School's securitisation framework promises to provide the following: firstly, a unitary theory of securitisation which approaches it as discursive processes of making security and the intersubjective establishment of a threat; and, secondly, the analytical tools to address the questions of 'who securitises, on what issues (threats), for whom (referent objects), why, with what results, and not least, under what conditions (i. e., what explains where securitisation is successful)'.[86] The rejection of the understanding of security as a brute fact and the call for attention to discourses are a valuable move forward, not least because 'talking about security' is becoming more and more politicised in the already established liberal democracies in the post-9/11 era. The criticism of the positivist view on security and the re-focus on a self-referential aspect of security are also central to understanding the ways in which societies are governed in the MENA region. Most dictatorial regimes (including that of Ben Ali in Tunisia) maintained their regimes by securitising specific issues, such as radical Islamism. As I have pointed out, the close tie between the establishment of a new democracy and the political debates on terrorism in the post-uprising Tunisian context also reveals that governing through the making of existential threats has been an important dimension of democratisation.

Having contributed to the development of critical approaches to security, however, the Copenhagen School's securitisation theory is insufficient to analyse how the construction of a threat is closely linked to broader political, economic and social domination. According to Jacqueline Best,[87] the school tends to neglect the political and economic dimensions of securitisation because of its heavy focus on 'sovereign moments of decision between the rule and the exception'. Consequently, it does not grasp how exceptions are produced and reproduced through mundane practices, as well as how particular political economic decisions serve exceptionalist practices and vice versa. Several studies have pointed out that the global War on Terror has served to give states much flexibility to govern societies in the neoliberal era. For instance, Boukalas[88] and Lafer[89] have argued that the US authorities attempted to undo gains achieved by workers' movements by prioritising national security in the name of counter-terrorism. Lafer has also noted that the Bush administration's security measures under the rubric of the War on Terror deprived approximately 170,000 workers of previously enjoyed basic rights, including the right to form or join a trade union.[90]

The Copenhagen School's framework also falls short of explicating the convoluted process of securitisation due to its predominant focus on the state as securitising actor. Although it acknowledges the role of 'audiences' in the process of securitisation, it pays scant attention to their voices. This is because, as the choice of the word indicates, it recognises an audience as a securitiser's constituency that either accepts or rejects a securitising move to be securitisation, while focusing on the facilitating conditions which it believes to determine the choice of acceptance or rejection. In other words, those subjected to the securitiser's influence are reduced to a passive subject that is expected to respond submissively to dominant narratives and external factors. The securitisation framework's over-emphasis on dominant agents thus fails to understand the complex process of securitisation in which multiple actors (that cannot be easily dichotomised into a 'securitiser' and an 'audience') interact with one another for not necessarily the same purposes.

Empirically, this theory falls short of explaining the ways in which Tunisian unemployed protesters were constructed as a threat to democratisation, through the discursive association of unemployed protests with terrorism, as well as the effects of such construction. Whereas the key aim of the authorities in using the terrorism label was to directly restrict political freedom under the Ben Ali regime, now much of their focus has shifted to the regulation of and the management of freedom. As I will elaborate in Chapters 3 and 4, in the context of democratisation the War on Terror became increasingly involved in the securitisation of the unemployed as a technology of neoliberal governing. By means of this technology, the society as a whole and the unemployed protesters in particular were to be governed to discipline themselves as 'good citizens' who are vigilant against violent protest and patiently supportive of the nascent democratic institutions. Likewise, the actors involved in the production of terrorism-related discourses were diversified to include civil society and social movement actors. Human rights organisations' active participation in the process of the amendment to the anti-terrorism law and their anti-terrorism marches, several NGO reports regarding terrorism, as well as the secular activists' association of the Salafi movements with terrorism are notable examples of the involvement of non-state actors in the construction of knowledge on terrorism. These examples indicate the need to understand the current War on Terror in Tunisia, not merely as a continuation of the authoritarian tactic, but as an important part of neoliberal governing.

These conceptual limitations of the securitisation framework have been clearly pointed out by several scholars in the field of International Political Sociology. In particular, drawing on the Foucauldian approach, Aradau and van Munster and Bigo have provided alternative frameworks that overcome the Copenhagen School's interpretation of security and securitisation. Bigo has rejected the idea of security as a homogeneous and unified strategy monopolised by a dominant actor and instead conceptualised it as an 'effect of anonymous multiple struggles' in which heterogeneous professions are located in a 'field' of security and 'recognize themselves as mutually competent, while finding themselves in competition with each other'.[91] Bigo has also stressed the importance of routinised bureaucratic practices and institutional settings as constitutive elements of securitisation. Similarly, Aradau and van Munster have approached the War on Terror as 'a new form of governmentality', shifting attention away from the actors involved in the War on Terror and towards the ways in which the threat of terrorism serves to govern 'social problems'.[92] These studies have shown how the Foucauldian approach to securitisation can shed light on more convoluted and complex processes in which a network of multiple actors (not one dominant actor) with heterogeneous interests and practices contributes to the construction of a particular knowledge on security, whereby social problems and 'problematic' actors can be regulated and governed.

My approach is in line with these Foucauldian approaches to securitisation. Yet, it goes further than their interpretation of the relationship between securitisation and governmentality in that it incorporates the voices of those securitised into analysis. Applying this governmentality approach, counter-terrorism is conceptualised as a security discourse that is constitutive of and constituted by the contentious politics between those governing and those governed/resisting. While stressing the heterogeneity, rather than the centralised manifestation, of the construction of security, Bigo does not go so far as to consider the presence of resistance and its potential to engage in the process of securitisation. As I have emphasised, however, the role of resistance is central to Foucault's concept of governmentality and should be included in the analysis of securitisation. As far as securitisation is intersubjectively shaped and reshaped, it is not only the state and various professions in the field of security, but also those who are policed, regulated and disciplined to be silent, yet cannot be fully subjugated, who influence the formation of the discourse of counter-terrorism and its effects on society.

From the counter-conduct perspective, securitised subjects do not necessarily aim to reject or subvert securitisation as a whole. They may also resist the ways in which they are securitised. In this process, the contentious politics between conductive forces and counter-conductive forces, despite their heterogeneous interests and antagonism towards one another, can be mutually constructive. Also, that counter-conductive forces are located within governmentality does not mean that they are passive subjects. They can challenge the ways in which a dominant knowledge of security at a given time circulates, functions and delineates individuals' identities.[93] In doing so, they can intervene in the formation of a dominant security discourse and participate in the construction of their subjecthood.

When applied to the Tunisian context, this alternative approach guides us to ask not only how unemployed populations are securitised by the governing elites, but also whether and how such securitisation involves the interaction of multiple actors in competition, including the authorities, political and economic elites, civil society agencies and, importantly, unemployed protesters who challenge such a process.

Towards an Analysis of Discursive Practices

The above discussion leads us to shift our analytical focus toward discursive practices that (re)structure or contest patterned ideas about terrorism in the process of the (counter-)securitisation of the unemployed subject. To analyse discursive practices is first to investigate what forms of *competing* discursive practices are performed by those governing and resisting and how these practices are related to the formation of a distinct dominant discourse of security. This is to say that we need to analyse an ensemble of discursive practices (both linguistic and non-linguistic) that, while being performed by actors in competition with each other, 'follow directions' constituting a dominant discourse.[94] That discursive practices (re)shape a dominant discourse of security, however, does not indicate a simple linear causality between the two realms. Rather, the nature of their relationship needs to be understood as interdependent, because what is performed and what is unperformed are also partly the products of pre-existing discourses. In this book, I use the term 'discursive terrain' to refer to pre-existing dominant discourses (such as global terrorism, democracy, rule of law and development) in which the elites' and unemployed protesters' discursive practices are partially embedded. The embedding of discursive practices in discursive terrains indicates that both those dominating and those resisting are not fully external to one another. They share the discursive terrains that condition the ways in which they think and act at any given historical moment.[95] While discursive practices are embedded in discursive terrains, they also constitute new discourses by utilising and modifying the discursive terrains strategically.[96]

Secondly, my discourse analysis also pays particular attention to the dimension of subjectification, which makes it possible for free subjects to conduct others and the self.[97] It does so because the formation of the self as an autonomous, responsible and economically rational subject becomes central to the existence of the neoliberal regime. The formation of free subjects entails not only governing *through* freedom (such as empowering individuals' abilities and capacities for self-management), but also governing *for* freedom, through various sovereign and disciplinary

mechanisms. That discursive practices within neoliberal governing structure subjectivities does not mean that the dominant actor (such as the
state) determines their forms. Processes of subjectification always involve
resisting practices that, while partially reproducing the given subjectivities, simultaneously operate to unsettle and escape them and to invent and
create alternative modes of being.

Having identified the two aspects of discursive practices in a conceptual sense, applying these to an actual analysis of the securitisation of the
unemployed is not without challenges. How are we to empirically analyse
competitive and at the same time mutually constitutive relationships
between practices to conduct and practices to counter-conduct? How can
we capture whether unemployed protesters reproduce and/or challenge
the ways in which they are securitised? How do we know whether the
unemployed resistance takes an ambivalent position vis-à-vis the elites,
because both parties, as Foucault might argue, are indeed embedded in and
making use of the same discursive terrains?

For the purpose of this book, I draw on Laclau and Mouffe's critical elaboration of Foucault's conception of discourse and their analytical
tools.[98] Engaging with Foucault's conception of discursive practice, they
have suggested to see the formation of a hegemonic discourse not as
the result of a unitary and homogeneous will, but as the result of discursive struggles in which multiple actors with heterogeneous necessities
and goals compete to fix the meanings of subjects and objects. In doing
so, they have criticised the association of Foucault's discursive practice
with language acts, arguing that the distinction between linguistic and
non-linguistic is inconsistent with his notion of discursive formation.[99]
According to them, any seemingly non-discursive entities such as institutions or organisations as well as objects can only be themselves through
discursive practices insofar as their specificity is structured in their relation
to others. Therefore, seemingly linguistic practices (such as making claims
through interviews or chanting slogans) and non-linguistic practices (such
as deploying the military at the site of protest or arresting protesters) need
to be considered as equally constitutive of discourses.

Elaborating on Foucault's theory of discourse, Laclau and Mouffe also
offer several concrete analytical tools to investigate the contested process
of discursive formation. According to them, the formation of a hegemonic
discourse first and foremost requires what they call 'articulatory practices',
which refer to 'any practice establishing a relation among elements (such
as slave/master and men/women) such that their identity is modified as
the result of the articulatory practice'.[100] Any hegemonic discourse is only
partially fixed due to the presence of a surplus of meanings (in Foucault's

41

terms, the multiplicity of discourses). Articulatory practices that seek to provide an alternative hegemonic discourse become particularly visible when the pre-existing hegemonic discourse is unable to stabilise the field of discourse due to an operation of structural dislocation. What articulatory practices do is to build a 'chain of equivalence' in which various discursive elements – or what they call 'empty signifiers' – are articulated with each other.[101]

In order to build a hegemony, however, articulatory practices are not sufficient; they must take place as a form of antagonism.[102] An antagonistic frontier appears when a pre-existing relation of subordination (such as a master-and-slave relationship) is subverted and translated into a relation of oppression. According to Laclau and Mouffe, the slave is just a differential category of subject positions and does not necessarily designate itself as an oppressed subject until the subversion occurs through a discursive formation such as 'the rights inherent to every human being'.[103] They have suggested that it is 'only to the extent that the positive differential character of the subordinated subject position is subverted that antagonism can emerge'.[104]

Finally, Laclau and Mouffe's understanding of the formation of discourse as inherently contested takes the presence and role of disarticulation as a key element in discursive struggles. They note that, whereas articulation and the chain of equivalence work to establish antagonistic relations, the logic of difference operates to mitigate and subvert them, or to displace 'the frontier of antagonism to the periphery of the social'.[105] This indicates that discursive struggles to form a hegemonic discourse entail both articulatory practices, which operate through the logic of equivalence, and disarticulatory practices, which operate through the logic of difference. The logic of equivalence accounts for 'the simplification of political space' in which differences among discursive elements are reduced and the previously separate positions of subjects and objects are combined.[106] On the contrary, the logic of difference serves to increase complexity by 'dissolving existing chains of equivalence and incorporating those disarticulated elements into an expanding order'.[107]

Combining Laclau and Mouffe's theory of discursive struggle and analytical tools with Foucault's notions of governmentality and counterconduct offers a critical discourse analysis of the contentious and at the same time mutually constitutive relationship between neoliberal governing and unemployed protesters. However, such analysis must be situated in a concrete context to proceed. The next chapter will achieve this task by directing attention to the reconfiguration of power relations and the emergence of neoliberal governing in post-2011 Tunisia.

Notes

1. Foucault, *Power/Knowledge*, p. 156.
2. Foucault, *Foucault Live*, p. 187.
3. O'Donnell and Schmitter, *Transitions from authoritarian rule*.
4. Carothers, 'The end of the transition paradigm', p. 7.
5. Ibid. p. 7.
6. Diamond, 'Thinking about hybrid regimes'.
7. Karl, 'Dilemmas of democratization in Latin America'.
8. Diamond, Hartlyn, Linz and Lipset, *Democracy in developing countries*.
9. Pace and Cavatorta, 'The Arab uprisings in theoretical perspective', p. 127.
10. Asseburg and Wimmen, 'Dynamics of transformation, elite change and new social mobilization in the Arab World', p. 4.
11. Pace and Cavatorta, 'The Arab uprisings in theoretical perspective', p. 127.
12. For the discussion on variant forms of liberal democracy, see Hobson, 'Liberal democracy and beyond: Extending the sequencing debate'.
13. Dahl, *Polyarchy: Participation and opposition*; Zakaria, 'The rise of illiberal democracy'.
14. Berman, *The primacy of politics*, p. 211.
15. Berman, 'The roots and rationale of social democracy', p. 137.
16. Hobson, 'Liberal democracy and beyond', p. 449.
17. See, for instance, Rustow, 'Transitions to democracy'; Przeworski, 'Some problems in the study of the transition to democracy'; Diamond, 'Thinking about hybrid regimes'; Diamond et al., 'Reconsidering the transition paradigm'.
18. Schmitt, *The crisis of parliamentary democracy*, p. 13, emphasis added.
19. Hobson, 'Beyond the end of history', p. 639. See also Hobson, *The rise of democracy*.
20. Ibid. p. 643.
21. Teti, 'Beyond lies the wub', p. 7.
22. Foucault, *The essential works, 1954–1984*, vol. 1, p. 74.
23. Ibid. pp. 74–75.
24. Ibid. p. 77.
25. Dean, *Governmentality*, p. 174.
26. Foucault, *The birth of biopolitics*, p. 118.
27. Ibid. p. 121, emphasis added.
28. Ibid. p. 186.
29. Ibid. p. 138.
30. Ibid. p. 139.
31. Ibid.
32. Ibid. p. 140.
33. Odysseos, 'Governing dissent in the Central Kalahari Game Reserve', p. 443.

34. Kiersey, 'Neoliberal political economy and the subjectivity of crisis', p. 381.
35. Lemke, 'The birth of bio-politics', p. 201.
36. Dean, *Governmentality*, p. 175.
37. Dean, 'Liberal government and authoritarianism', p. 39. See also Hindess, 'Politics and governmentality'; Valverde, '"Despotism" and ethical liberal governance'; Dean, 'Liberal government and authoritarianism'.
38. Bourdieu, *Practical reason*; Chopra, 'Neoliberalism as doxa'; Kurki, 'Governmentality and EU democracy promotion'.
39. Foucault, *The birth of biopolitics*, p. 139.
40. Various ways of understanding resistance to neoliberal rule – such as the Occupy movement, the Arab Spring, the Green Movement and so on – have been developed in Social Movement Studies; see, for instance, Smith and Johnston, *Globalization and resistance*; Leitner, Peck and Sheppard, *Contesting neoliberalism*; Beinin and Vairel, *Social movements, mobilization, and contestation in the Middle East and North Africa*; Durac, 'Social movements, protest movements and cross-ideological coalitions'; Della Porta, *Social movements in times of austerity*; Hayes and Fominaya, *Resisting austerity*.
41. See, for instance, Lorence, *Organizing the unemployed*.
42. Perry, *Prisoners of want*; Baglioni, Baumgarten, Chabanet and Lahusen, 'Transcending marginalization'; Chabanet and Faniel, *The mobilization of the unemployed in Europe*; Lahusen, 'The protests of the unemployed in France, Germany and Sweden (1994–2004)'.
43. Rossi, *The poor's struggle for political incorporation*.
44. Bayat, 'Workless revolutionaries'; Badimon, 'From contestation to conciliation'.
45. Lahusen, 'The protests of the unemployed in France, Germany and Sweden (1994–2004)', p. 2.
46. Sean F. McMahon's study on the workers' movement in Egypt and Brecht De Smet's Gramscian approach to the Egyptian uprising provide two examples of (post-)Marxist approaches to resistance in the Arab region (McMahon, *Crisis and class war in Egypt*; De Smet, *Gramsci on Tahrir*). See also Darouiche, 'From the Asiatic mode of production to counter-revolution'; Gervasio and Manduchi, 'Introduction: Reading the revolutionary process in North Africa with Gramsci'.
47. Death, 'Counter-conducts as a mode of resistance', p. 207.
48. Foucault, *The history of sexuality, vol. 1*, pp. 125–27.
49. Malmvig, 'Governing Arab reform', p. 7.
50. Foucault, 'The ethic of care for the self as a practice of freedom', p. 19.
51. Foucault, 'The subject and power', p. 786.
52. Heller, 'Power, subjectification and resistance in Foucault', p. 83.
53. Lemke, 'Foucault, governmentality, and critique'.
54. Foucault, *Power/Knowledge*, p. 98.

55. Foucault, 'The subject and power', p. 790.
56. Widder, 'Foucault and power revisited', p. 416.
57. Foucault, *Power/Knowledge*, p. 98.
58. Widder, 'Foucault and power revisited', p. 414.
59. Ibid. p. 423.
60. The dynamic of domination and resistance can be further elaborated through the logic of intentionality and non-subjectivity. According to this logic, all subjects (whether those governing or being governed) are free, to the extent that they have multiple discourses to choose from and exercise them upon others in a more or less rational and calculated way. However, these subjects are equally unfree because their ability to speak and act is 'ontologically bounded by the discourses through which his or her subjectivity is constructed'. See Heller, 'Power, subjectification and resistance in Foucault', p. 91.
61. Foucault, 'The subject and power', p. 781.
62. The operation of this intentionality and unintentionality paradox is not only the key mechanism of the omnipresence of power, but it also guarantees the possibility of resistance with its limits.
63. Foucault, *Security, territory, population*, p. 44.
64. Death, 'Counter-conducts as a mode of resistance', p. 240.
65. Foucault, *Security, territory, population*, p. 125. See also Davidson, 'In praise of counter-conduct'.
66. Nişancıoğlu and Pal, 'Counter-conduct in the university factory'; Rossdale et al., 'Everything is dangerous'; Sokhi-Bulley, 'Re-reading the riots'; Death, 'Counter-conducts as a mode of resistance'; Meade, 'Foucault's concept of counter-conduct and the politics of anti-austerity protest in Ireland'.
67. Bulley, 'Occupy differently: Space, community and urban counter-conduct', p. 248.
68. Davidson, 'In praise of counter-conduct', p. 28.
69. Foucault, *Security, territory, population*, p. 195.
70. Malmvig, 'Eyes wide shut', p. 265.
71. Ibid.
72. Foucault, *Security, territory, population*, pp. 261, 264, 303–4.
73. Foucault, 'The subject and power'.
74. Bulley, 'Occupy differently'.
75. Odysseos, 'Governing dissent in the Central Kalahari Game Reserve'.
76. Foucault, *Security, territory, population*, p. 259.
77. While having a degree of variance among them with regard to their emphases, the scholars in the so-called 'traditional terrorism studies' have conceptualised terrorism as an 'objective threat' which involves the use of extreme violence against non-military civilians or symbolic targets by non-state actors or organisations with political and ideological motivations, in order to influence an audience; see Black, 'The geometry of terrorism'; Crenshaw,

'The causes of terrorism'; Drake, 'The role of ideology in terrorists' target selection'; Gibbs, 'Conceptualization of terrorism'; Hoffman, *Inside terrorism*; Martin, *Understanding terrorism*.

78. Hülsse and Spencer, 'The metaphor of terror: Terrorism studies and the constructivist turn'.
79. Jackson, 'An argument for terrorism', p. 28. See also Jackson, 'Constructing enemies'.
80. Buzan, Wæver and de Wilde, *Security*, p. 25.
81. Ibid. p. 23.
82. Ibid. p. 435.
83. Collective, 'Critical approaches to security in Europe'.
84. Buzan, Wæver and de Wilde, *Security*, p. 24.
85. Mcdonald, 'Securitization and the construction of security', p. 567.
86. Buzan, Wæver and de Wilde, *Security*, p. 32.
87. Best, 'Security, economy, population: The political economic logic of liberal exceptionalism', p. 379.
88. Boukalas, 'Class war-on-terror'.
89. Lafer, 'Neoliberalism by other means'.
90. Ibid.
91. Bigo, 'Globalized (in)security', p. 12.
92. Aradau and van Munster, 'Governing terrorism through risk'.
93. Widder, 'Foucault and power revisited'.
94. Deleuze, 'What is a dispositif?' p. 159.
95. Foucault, *Security, territory, population*, p. 93.
96. By strategic, Foucault means an 'urgent need' of subjects at any given moment to (re)produce discourses by manipulating and making use of the discursive terrains in a tactical way; see Foucault, *Power/Knowledge*, pp. 194–96.
97. Deleuze, 'What is a dispositif?' p. 161.
98. In their book *Hegemony and Socialist Strategy*, Laclau and Mouffe aimed at building a theoretical approach to the analysis of the formation of hegemony through which, they believed, the left-wing's struggles and strategies can go beyond the structural determinism and class essentialism of orthodox Marxist thoughts. While they found Gramsci's concept of hegemony innovative and useful for its emphasis on the 'materiality of ideology' and 'collective will' as political subjects, they also rejected his proposition of class as a unifying and ontological foundation. As an alternative, they offer a post-Gramscian hegemony in which the contingent nature of hegemony is highlighted through Foucault's notions of discourse and dispersion; see Laclau and Mouffe, *Hegemony and socialist strategy*.
99. Laclau and Mouffe, *Hegemony and socialist strategy*, p. 105.
100. Ibid. p. 105.
101. In Laclau and Mouffe, when one of the signifiers is able to represent this chain of equivalence as a whole, this privileged signifier becomes a

'nodal point'. Through this nodal point, previously separated signifiers are temporally identified as if they were a unified entity, thereby constituting a discourse; see Thomassen, 'Antagonism, hegemony and ideology after heterogeneity'.

102. Ibid. pp. 135–36.
103. Ibid. p. 154.
104. Ibid. p. 154.
105. Laclau and Mouffe, *Hegemony and socialist strategy*, p. 130.
106. Ibid. p. 130.
107. Howarth and Stavrakakis, 'Introducing discourse theory and political analysis', p. 11.

3

A Genealogy of Neoliberal Governing in Tunisia

This chapter revisits the contemporary history of Tunisia since the end of the Habib Bourguiba era to explore how neoliberal governing appeared in the process of democratisation. To this aim, it focuses on four junctures: first, the Ben Ali regime's rule that was upheld through the security syndrome and the economic miracle discourse; second, the emergence and development of the unemployed resistance; third, civil society and social movements' robust participation in the process of democratisation; and, finally, the reconfiguration of the pre-uprising elements of political economy through civil society's fear of Islamists and terrorism.

The process of liberalisation before 2011 took the form of centralised reforms towards democracy, through Ben Ali's authoritarian way of achieving stability and security, until the bottom–up resistance of unemployed youths, which previously could be ignored, turned into a revolutionary movement against the political and economic orders. While the moment of rupture during the revolutionary period opened up new possibilities for change, the very same possibilities were also utilised by the ruling elites. And it was particularly the notion of and the actors within 'strong and free civil society' through which Ben Ali's 'security pact'[1] reconfigured them, constituting the current form of neoliberal governing. These findings add nuance to the view that the currently dominant political and economic orders, which endorse the principles of a liberal market democracy, have been shaped solely by the old and new ruling elites and their international counterparts. To better understand the exercise of power in post-2011 Tunisia, close attention needs to be paid not only to the resilience of capitalist ruling, but also to the resilience of ordinary citizens' desire for consensus, national unity and the security pact against Islamists.

Two Pillars Upholding Ben Ali's Rule

Following a bloodless coup against Bourguiba in November 1987, Ben Ali swiftly implemented several reforms 'for democracy'. These included his 1988 National Pact with political parties, the release of political prisoners and the legalisation of opposition parties, which allowed them to enter parliament through periodic elections. His version of democracy, however, was closely associated with the construction of 'enemies' against democratisation. Like his predecessor, Ben Ali used the Islamist card and justified his repressive rule as necessary to protect Tunisia's democracy against what he called a 'reactionary ideology that rejects all democratic values' and against those who attempt to 'form a theocratic and authoritarian state'.[2] Both Bourguiba and Ben Ali exercised authoritarian rule over society, but the level of surveillance and oppression significantly intensified with the emergence of the so-called 'police state'. While security apparatuses were key institutions instrumentalised by both rulers, Ben Ali acted as a 'de factor Interior Minister', making the Ministry of the Interior 'presidentialised'.[3] Yet, it was not just violence and fear that made possible a dictator's reign over Tunisian society for nearly thirty years. A set of economic reforms and social development programmes was mobilised in the construction of the 'economic miracle' discourse claimed to ensure security and order, reduce poverty and inequality, and facilitate foreign investments and job creation.[4] These social and economic mechanisms were designed and implemented in a diffused manner so as to incorporate ordinary citizens into the exercise of domination.

COUNTER-TERRORISM AND THE SECURITY SYNDROME

Ben Ali's projection of Tunisia as a reliable partner in the 'Global War on Terror' was a key component of his authoritarian regime. However, his instrumentalisation of counter-terrorism started well before the emergence of the War on Terror. In the aftermath of the violent confrontations between police officers and Islamists in 1993, he amended the Panel Code introducing a broad definition of terrorism. According to the amended law, acts of terrorism were considered 'all actions relating to individual or collective initiative, aiming at undermining individuals or properties, through intimidation or terror' and 'acts of incitement to hatred or to religious or other fanaticism, regardless of the means used'.[5] The charge of supporting terrorist organisations was then actively used to repress and tame Islamist groups.

The anti-terrorism bill, which was drafted after a bomb attack on a synagogue in Djerba in April 2002 and adopted by the National Assembly on 10 December 2003, further intensified Ben Ali's dictatorial rule. The new definition of terrorism replaced that of the 1993 Penal Code, significantly expanding its scope to include acts of 'disturbing public order' and 'influencing state policy'.[6] This wide and vague definition of terrorism together with other ambiguous clauses in the 2003 law were then used by the authorities to randomly arrest those deemed dangerous to the regime. According to the United Nations Human Rights Council (UNHRC) report published in 2012, of a total of 8,700 political prisoners detained during the Ben Ali regime and released after the Uprising, around 3,000 people had been sentenced based on the 2003 law alone, and many of them were arrested for their perceived 'misconduct', such as 'growing beards and wearing particular clothing'.[7] And those convicted under the new anti-terrorism law were subject to draconian measures in prisons, such as torture and lack of access to medical assistance, often leading them to stage hunger strikes to protest mistreatment and violence.[8]

In fact, Ben Ali, much like his fellow dictators in the region, was under external pressure for democratisation, in line with George W. Bush's 'Greater Middle East Initiative' which presumed the promotion of democracy as one of the main elements of the War on Terror.[9] The rationale behind the democracy and counter-terrorism nexus was that repressive and authoritarian rules in the MENA region were providing a fertile ground for radical and extreme Islamic ideologies encouraging terrorist activities. The belief that spreading democracy and political freedom in the region would be necessary to prevent terrorism was concretised by the Bush administration in the aftermath of the 9/11 attacks.[10] When then US Secretary of State Colin Powell visited Tunisia on 2 December 2003, he delivered Bush's message to Ben Ali, encouraging him to respect freedom of expression and to promote democracy in Tunisia. According to Powell, Ben Ali positively responded to this call, noting that he wanted to 'move at a pace that he believed was consistent with the aspirations and expectations of the Tunisian people'.[11] What followed within the same month, however, was the adoption of the anti-terrorism law, several articles of which were far from any sort of freedom. He swiftly legitimised his repressive rule by introducing the new anti-terrorism law and repackaging it as part of the global community's efforts to combat terrorism.

Not only did Ben Ali effectively avoid the pressure for democracy and accusations of human rights violations, but he also positioned himself as an expert who had predicted the danger of global terrorism well before the international community had realised it, and he framed his ruthless counter-terrorism measures as a holistic approach beyond narrow security dimensions. This is well reflected in his interview with the Lebanese magazine *al-Hawadith* on counter-terrorism, which is worth quoting at length:

> What our world is witnessing today is the exacerbated dangers of extremism and terrorism, underscoring the need to redouble the international community's efforts to find common solutions to all these problems. We have warned of these consequences since the early nineties. Unfortunately, it took too long for many to realise that our approach to this phenomenon and the reality of what we had warned of were correct. […] We see the need to accelerate and bring all nations together for an international conference backed by the United Nations in order to develop a code of conduct to combat terrorism. […] What Tunisia offers to humanity as a whole in resisting this phenomenon is the awareness that confronting extremism and terrorism requires a holistic approach, which is not limited to security dimensions only, but also incorporates the economic, social, cultural, educational and political dimensions, because each dimension is a source that feeds extremism and terrorism.[12]

The importance of collective efforts to fight terrorism beyond security measures and Ben Ali's emphasis on Tunisia's leading role in this battle were reiterated by himself in the opening of the International Conference on 'Terrorism: Dimensions, Threats and Countermeasures' which was co-organised by the UN and the Organisation of the Islamic Conference (OIC) in Tunis in November 2007. His promotion of Tunisia as a country that respected international human rights obligations and contributed to the Global War on Terror was widely acknowledged and often praised by Tunisia's western counterparts. For instance, in his visit to Tunisia in April 2008, then President of France Nicolas Sarkozy applauded Ben Ali's counter-terrorism agenda, describing it as 'Tunisia's resolute determination to fight terrorism, which is the real enemy of democracy'.[13] The Western media also played a role in circulating Ben Ali's propaganda by, for instance, framing Tunisia as an important partner of the United States in the Arab world because 'democracy in Tunisia' was 'progressing successfully'.[14] The international actors' recognition of Tunisia as an important global actor in combatting terrorism in turn provided Ben Ali with legitimate credentials for his rule domestically. His speech on the nineteenth anniversary of his accession to power in 2006 is illustrative of how he mobilised the international acknowledgement of Tunisia's achievements in security and human rights to justify his successive rule over the country:

> Tunisia has always worked hard to uphold the value of justice, respect of the international law […] as well as the activation of dialogue between different cultures and religions. In this context, several initiatives have been launched,

and they have been appreciated and supported by the international community, in particular the World Summit on the Information Society and the call for the adaptation of a code of conduct against terrorism. […] The election of the Human Rights Council to have Tunisia as a member in 2006 was the renewed international recognition of the level of human rights in our country and of the important achievements made in this field.[15]

It is important to note that Ben Ali's abuse of the global fight against terrorism was not limited to targeting Islamist organisations or those who were 'Islamist-looking'. The threat of terrorism and arbitrary anti-terrorism measures facilitated the politicisation of security apparatuses in that it legitimised their illegal activities targeting human rights activists and regime-critical trade union members, bloggers, students, journalists and more.[16] However, many ordinbary citizens believed in the claim that Tunisia was successfully combatting terrorism while upholding human rights and other international norms. Moreover, a significant proportion of Tunisians participated in everyday surveillance and acted as *de facto* 'informants'. The ruling RCD (Rassemblement constitutionnel démocratique) party, in particular, played a key role in disciplining society. Approximately one-quarter of the whole adult population were members of the party,[17] and it consisted of a wide network of cells across the entire territory.[18]

THE ECONOMIC MIRACLE

The other important pillar of domination that upheld Ben Ali's authoritarian rule was the economic miracle discourse. Previously driven by a state-led economic development model, Tunisia's economic system began to shift towards a more liberal one in the 1980s. Facing the economic crisis as well as pressure from the World Bank and IMF, Ben Ali implemented dramatic reforms to liberalise the economic system and to integrate it into the global market.[19] State-led structural adjustment plans (SAPs) were designed to strengthen and stabilise macroeconomic performance, accelerate privatisation and foreign direct investment (FDI), and improve the international competitiveness of local industrial firms. To this aim, the first phase (the seventh development plan, 1987–91) of the reform focused on the control of budget deficits, for example, by aiming to reduce public investment from 25 to 21 per cent of gross domestic product (GDP) and to incentivise and diversify private investments through the revision of laws for industrial investment in key sectors, including agriculture, tourism, service and housing.[20] It was hoped that these measures would then be consolidated during the subsequent development phase

(the eighth plan, 1992–96) through further privatisation in the transporta-
tion, banking and communications sectors, increasing export capacity and
modernisation of the stock market, among others. For instance, the liberalisation of the banking and financial sectors involved the devaluation of
the Tunisian currency and allowed deposit money and development banks
to extend credits, over 90 per cent of which had gone to the private sector
by 1997.[21] The government also gradually reduced consumer subsidies in
the 1990s. By 1994, the state had managed to wholly or partially privatise
around forty-five small public enterprises in the service and agricultural
sectors and, from the late 1990s onwards, had expanded the target of
privatisation and restructuring into larger enterprises, including Tunisie
Telecom.[22] The Tunisian government announced that approximately 217
public enterprises had been restructured or privatised by 2009.[23]

The reforms for economic liberalisation turned out to be positive at
the macro level, with an average 4.56 per cent of GDP growth from 1987
to 1999 and an inflation rate below 5 per cent during the period from
1996 to 2010. While Tunisia's debt increased from 1985 to 1992, its
debt-to-GDP ratio dropped from 71 to 56 per cent during the same period,
and the current account deficit also fell from 8.5 per cent of the GDP
between 1981 and 1986 to 3.9 per cent between 1987 and 1992.[24] The
country's macro-level economic growth was also supported by an increase
in foreign direct investments and the development of sectoral capacity,
such as that in the mechanical, electrical and textile industries.[25] Ben
Ali's reforms for liberalisation and economic stability were applauded
by international financial institutions (IFIs). For instance, after its official
staff visit to Tunis between 27 May and 9 June 2008, the IMF praised
Tunisia's continued efforts to integrate its economy with the regional and
global markets, reporting that Tunisia was making significant progress
in terms of stabilising macro indicators and reforming its financial and
banking systems.[26]

As rapidly and widely acknowledged after the fall of Ben Ali, however,
Tunisia's outstanding economic performances and indicators had a dark
side. According to a working paper published by the World Bank in
March 2014, Tunisia's economy had been dictated by the Ben Ali family's businesses; the total value of their confiscated assets accounted
for more than a quarter of the Tunisian GDP in 2011 and appropriated
approximately one-fifth of all private-sector profits.[27] It also turned out
that the investment laws and regulations evaluated by IFIs as healthy and
progressive were manipulated by the regime in favour of the Ben Ali clan,
domestic crony capitalists and their international partners.[28] The severity
of poverty and other socio-economic problems was also revealed. The

World Food Programme (WFP) reported in April 2011 that the depth and scale of poverty in Tunisia was underestimated by IFIs due to their reliance on the data provided by the Tunisian state, and the southern and interior regions were particularly vulnerable to the problem of poverty and unemployment.[29] Systematically excluded from development opportunities, these regions have experienced what Larbi Sadiki has called 'multiple marginalisation' – that is, a state of being estranged from any sort of political, economic and social advantages.[30]

How was the Ben Ali regime able to maintain a strong grip on society and the economic miracle discourse, despite the negative side-effects of his liberal reforms? This was possible not least because of political repression, violence and everyday surveillance. Importantly, the liberal economic restructuring was accompanied by various institutions for social protection and redistribution, ranging from the tax system to investment and modernisation incentives such as the Tunisian Solidarity Bank (Banque tunisienne de solidarité BTS) and the National Solidarity Fund (Fonds National de Solidarité FNS). These mechanisms together constituted a fundamental element of the economic miracle. Ben Ali created the FNS, also known as '26-26', as a way to mitigate and manage the negative consequences of the liberalisation process. It was introduced as a social development programme with the aim to eliminate poverty by collecting donations (which, in fact, were closer to compulsory contributions) for the poor from registered businesses as well as ordinary citizens.[31] The BTS was also mobilised to support those excluded from the liberalised market by lending money for the purpose of financing small businesses.

As the below speech indicates, Ben Ali drew on these socioeconomic measures together with macro-economic indicators and positive international evaluations for the construction of the economic miracle discourse. The state-driven economic reforms were claimed to have contributed to the establishment of democratic values, stability and security, as well as economic development for the people, placing Tunisia 'at the forefront' of emerging countries in the world:

> Today, our country is at the forefront of emerging countries, as evidenced by the various indicators, experts as well as international institutions' reports such as the recent one published by the World Economic Forum. […] Our various forces have responded to our reforms with the support of the republican institutions and established the rule of law, the principles of democracy, pluralism and human rights. We have worked through these reforms, policies and programmes to exclude all causes of division, exclusion and marginalisation and to fortify our society against extremism and violence. [… We created] the National Solidarity Fund and a number of private programmes, so that we can

provide our people with a good life. A society with solidarity and balance is a society of dignity and stability.[32]

Ben Ali's social and economic policies were neither separated from nor spoiled by the authoritarian exercise of power.[33] On the contrary, they were 'at the heart of regime maintenance'.[34] The Ben Ali regime made the population dependent on the state's redistributive policies and utilised social development mechanisms as tools of discipline and surveillance. According to Béatrice Hibou, while social programmes such as the vocational training called 'Initiation to professional life' and BTS financing for young people were created to reduce unemployment, they equally provided 'new modes of control'[35] over university graduates who were reluctant to join the RCD party, by incorporating them into a supervisory system. Also, while data on how exactly BTS microcredit was distributed are not available, access to it was reportedly much easier for those connected to the RCD party or loyal to the regime, because the bank made decisions on the basis of the information provided by the police or the RCD cells.[36]

As Hibou has emphasised in her analysis of the exercise of power under the Ben Ali regime, it was not brutal repression alone that made the majority of Tunisians submissive and subordinated to the regime.[37] Rather, a set of mundane everyday mechanisms and administrative control in the economic field led ordinary citizens to participate in the construction and consolidation of the 'security pact' between the state and society. Yet, as we came to see over the course of the 2010 political upheaval, this pact was fragile and produced new possibilities for resistance. Among others, unemployed populations (and particularly those with higher educational background) became increasingly rebellious against the corrupt and authoritarian system.

Mobilisations of the Unemployed: From Everyday Struggle to Revolutionary Moments

Ben Ali's authoritarian governing through various political, social and economic mechanisms significantly deepened the regional disparities that already existed during the French occupation of Tunisia and the post-independence era. Political and economic resources had been unevenly distributed in favour of the coastal areas – such as Tunis, Sfax and Sousse – resulting in poor living standards and lack of social infrastructure in areas such as Gafsa, Sidi Bouzid and Kasserine.[38] This, in turn, led these marginalised regions to be the centre of various forms of social mobilisation against the authorities – from the Gafsa mining workers' strikes in the 1940s, over the revolts against French rule in the 1950s, to the bread riots in 1983–84.[39] However, despite the prolonged marginalisation, it was not until the 1990s that unemployment emerged as a major cause behind social mobilisation. While Bourguiba sought to liberalise the Tunisian economy in the 1970s and 1980s, the previous Keynesian type of economic system supported by Bourguiba himself during his socialist experiment still remained to some extent. He could maintain the public sector-driven development and even increase consumer subsidies until the early 1980s, thanks to favourable weather for the harvest and the high price of natural resources such as phosphate.[40] For instance, the state-owned phosphate company and its sub-contracting enterprises were able to employ most local males in the governorate of Gafsa, until the 'Plan to Rehabilitate the Gafsa Phosphate Company' as part of the SAPs was implemented in 1986.[41]

It was during the Ben Ali time that the economic system was rapidly liberalised, worsening the problem of unemployment, among others. The exact unemployment rate before 2011 does not exist due to the absence of official data produced by the authorities, for intentional or unintentional reasons. Yet, several conservative figures published before 2011 estimated a dramatic increase in the unemployment rate, particularly among those with higher education, since the 1990s. The unemployment rate for Tunisians with a higher education diploma rose from 3.8 per cent in 1994 to 21.6 per cent in 2008, whereas the rate of those with a lower level of education gradually decreased.[42] New data published soon after the Uprising suggest that the situation might have been worse. General director of the Observatoire national de la jeunesse Brahim Oueslati, for instance, has revealed that the youth unemployment rate (of those aged eighteen to twenty-nine) rose to approximately 30 per cent and that the rate of persons with higher education to 45 per cent in 2009, although these figures were not published during the Ben Ali era so as to maintain Tunisia's good reputation abroad.[43]

Considering the continued, if not increased, regional disparities, one can easily assume that the unemployment problem in the interior regions was much worse than in Tunis and the Sahel region at large. While Gafsa had been relatively better off than other interior regions due to the production of phosphate, Joel Beinin has provided an estimate that the number of employees working in phosphate mining in Gafsa dropped from 14,000–15,000 in 1980 to 5,000–5,800 in 2006.[44] Lacking opportunities to obtain decent jobs which had been more or less guaranteed for their parent generation, disillusioned youths in the interior began to challenge political, social and economic orders built over the previous two decades through their everyday resistance, and this evolved into the mass mobilisations that happened to end the rule of the 'strong man' in January 2011.

MAKING THE UNEMPLOYED A COLLECTIVE POLITICAL ACTOR

Compared to workers' strikes planned and organised through local or sectoral branches of the UGTT, protests mobilised by unemployed populations tended to be far more spontaneous and less organised, making it almost impossible for them to have meaningful significance until the mid-2000s. This began to change, however, with the emergence of unemployment mobilisations led by university graduates. While the increasing unemployment rate among those with higher education since the mid-1990s was clearly a factor behind the rise of the unemployed protests, it was the concept of the right to work that brought unemployed graduates onto the streets. The notion that university education guarantees jobs in the public sector emerged in the 1960s, when state-led development was implemented in Tunisia as a form of social contract and continued to operate in practice under Ben Ali.[45]

Despite the structural reforms under the Ben Ali regime, which disallowed the labour market to absorb all university graduates, the state rhetoric of social contract (and economic miracle) continued, raising the expectations of university graduates and at the same time fuelling their frustrations, as most of them chose to wait for years to enter the public sector.[46] In this sense, the main source of frustration among educated youth was less to do with a sense of exclusion than with the 'imposed situation of *waiting for inclusion*'.[47] Many unemployed graduates perceived that their right to work was violated, as they were 'forced to work in the informal sector' or had a job that did 'not correspond to their level of academic education'.[48] The nepotism and cronyism in the job search process furthered unemployed graduates' sense of injustice and grievance towards the authorities. It was in this context that an unemployed graduate organisation was established, called the Union of Unemployed Graduates (UDC).

Unable to become trade union members of the UGTT due to their unemployed status, about eleven graduates who had been active members in the General Union of Students of Tunisia (UGET) on university campuses established the UDC in 2006, in order to continue their political activities and collectively demand the right to decent work. The combination of the members' socio-economically marginalised position and their criticism of the lack of freedom was well characterised in the UDC's two main slogans: '*Shogul, hureiya, karamah wataniah*' (Work, freedom, national dignity) and '*Haqna fil hayah wa haqna fil 'amal*' (Our right to life and our right to work). Although it was an informal and illegal organisation, the UDC sought to maximise its presence on the streets by organising small-scale protests and supporting other social and economic mobilisations such as workers' strikes. It also utilised available online platforms in order to criticise the authorities and mobilise unemployed youths.

The first event that rendered the unemployed protesters visible as a collective political force was the revolt in the Gafsa mining basin in 2008. The production of phosphate in Gafsa has historically constituted one of the main sources of the Tunisian economy, but the region was largely excluded from the development process, and the unemployment rate in the region remained much higher than in the Sahel region. While the prolonged socio-economic marginalisation of the region and the local residents' perception that they were 'left behind' provided the context of the revolt, the trigger was the perceived injustice in the process of hiring mining workers.[49] Immediately after the result of the Phosphate company's employment exam was announced on 5 January 2008, several UDC activists in Gafsa protested the hiring list, which they thought to have been manipulated in order to employ those enjoying close relationships with the company management and local UGTT leaders.[50] While the initial target of criticism was the UGTT's regional head, Amara Abbasi, who at the same time was the owner of several enterprises sub-contracting for the public phosphate company and a representative of the ruling political party RCD,[51] the protest evolved with the slogan 'Work, freedom and national dignity'.

The unemployed protests were soon joined by other local populations, including the rank and file of the local UGTT branches, high school students, casual workers, and the widows and wives of Gafsa phosphate miners. Also, various protest tactics such as marches, setting up tents and burning tires to block the transport of phosphate were mobilised in the four mining towns of Radeyef, Oum El Araies, M'dhila and Metlaoui. The state repression escalated after the UGET members, leftist political parties and several middle-class opposition groups organised a solidarity march in the capital city of Tunis on 4 April, which gave the Gafsa movement 'a national character for the first time'.[52] The violent confrontation between the state and the protesters ended with the death of at least three protestors and the arrest of hundreds, including UDC activists and UGTT dissidents – and it also led to continued 'solidarity actions' in the coastal cities of Tunisia and abroad.[53]

The Gafsa revolt was a precursor to and part of the nation-wide mobilisation that toppled Ben Ali. It was the first mass protest in which the grievances and demands of unemployed youths were translated into a collective movement, resulting in a sense of solidarity across different parts of Tunisia. This event also led many unemployed youths to be politically active. With their experience of collective action, which had lasted more than six months, the unemployed protesters in Gafsa significantly contributed to the Uprising.[54]

Unemployed protesters were not the only leading force behind the revolutionary moments that Tunisia experienced between December 2010 and February 2011. Several already well-established civil society actors, such as the Bar Association and the UGTT, as well as young 'tech-savvy coastal dwellers', played crucial roles in one way or another. The UGTT's approval of regional general strikes in Tunis, Sfax, Kairouan and Tozeur in January was decisive for Ben Ali's decision to flee Tunisia.[55] That being said, it was the unemployed and precarious workers whose prolonged grievances and anger, embodied in two young men's suicide in December 2010, who through their revolutionary slogans made possible moments of unity among different segments of society. This does not mean that the unemployed protesters held a 'revolutionary vision' (as understood as a set of clear views and plans for an alternative political-economic system) before they took to the street. Rather, they, much like other segments of Tunisian civil society, became revolutionaries in the process of resistance, particularly through their experience of toppling Ben Ali.

The UDC's revolutionary legitimacy began to be widely acknowledged with the fall of the dictator. On the same day that Ben Ali left Tunisia, two founding members of the UDC were invited to a major Tunisian media channel called Nismaa, where the UDC's prolonged struggle under the dictatorship and its leading role during the revolutionary moments were acclaimed. The UDC's self-presentation as guardian of the revolution and as defender of the interests of unemployed populations in Tunisia also attracted a number of unemployed youths who held hope that the drastic political change could finally end the rampant inequalities that disadvantaged the interior regions and bring them opportunities to obtain decent jobs. The number of its supporters rapidly grew in 2011. For instance, when the UDC launched a public recruitment event in Maknassy, a small municipality town in Sidi Bouzid, almost 80 per cent of its entire unemployed population reportedly joined and showed interest in the organisation's visions and actions.

The UDC's increasing popularity among unemployed youths and revolutionary legitimacy positioned it as a mediator between the unemployed populations and the authorities during the initial phase of the post-authoritarian transformation. It established an official organisational body after holding a national meeting in the UGTT headquarter in Tunis on 5 February 2011. Similar to the UGTT, it formed an internal structure with a national board, twenty-four regional secretaries representing each governorate and local coordinators at the municipal level. In the process of building the organisation, the UDC also emphasised its democratic character, by announcing that it would elect the national office members every two years and that all decisions regarding its activism at different levels would be determined through bi-monthly executive bureau meetings consisting of the national office members and regional secretaries.

With this organisational body, the UDC operated as an important platform for unemployed protesters at the grassroots level. For instance, the Facebook pages of its national and regional branches were actively used by unemployed youths in different regions to organise and publicise their activities as well as to connect them to unemployed activists in other regions. Also, as Anna Antonakis-Nashif has noted, the UDC's activism went beyond the grassroots level, in that it attempted to push forward the unemployment issue by engaging in national coalition movements and the formal transitional process.[56] One such example is its participation in the Higher Commission for the Achievement of Revolutionary Objectives, Political Reforms and Democratic Transition (hereafter Higher Commission), which was formed as an *ad hoc* body on 23 March 2011 in order to structure and monitor the transitional period, until the National Constituent Assembly (NCA) was established.

More importantly, the UDC expanded its activism from raising the problem of unemployment to monitoring and directly challenging the transitional governments based on its rationale that the socio-economic marginalisation of unemployed populations cannot be resolved without fundamental changes in the political system. The organisation's active involvement in politics during the transitional phase is well-reflected in its role in the two Kasbah mass mobilisations against the interim government, which took place on Kasbah Square in January and February 2011. For the UDC, the government's decision to keep the members of the RCD party, which became a symbol of the old regime, in government positions was considered incompatible with transitional justice and the revolutionary path. The organisation's participation in the Kasbah Occupation and its continued intervention in political issues through street protests indicate that the unemployed movements represented by the UDC did not remain an issue-oriented movement and instead sought to maintain its revolutionary identity after the Uprising.

Democratisation and Contentious Politics

The revolutionary moments that brought all segments of society together in unity and successfully challenged the old regime gradually faded away. Key civil society actors such as the UGTT soon watered down their revolutionary rhetoric that emphasised the urgency of structural changes in the socio-economic system and shifted their efforts towards the transition to democracy, the normalisation of the economy and the process of reconciliation between previously opposite political camps.

During the transitional period, many perceived old folks of Ben Ali returned, under different names and in different forms. After all, Beji Caid Essebsi, a veteran politician who had served under the Bourguiba and Ben Ali regimes, restored himself as the new leader of the interim government on 27 February 2011. Mohamed Jegham who had served as the Interior Minister and then Defense Minister during the Ben Ali era, for instance, established a new political party, arguing that most RCD members were not involved in Ben Ali's businesses and thus should not be punished.[57] Following Essebsi's controversial 'Economic and Financial Reconciliation Bill', which was proposed in June 2015 and approved overwhelmingly by the Assembly in September 2017, those charged with economic fraud and corruption also became able to request amnesty in exchange for some form of restitution. Within a couple of months after its emergence, the reconciliation committee received thousands of applications, including that of Mohamed Slim Chiboub, Ben Ali's son-in-law, and Belhassen Trabelsi, Ben Ali's brother-in-law.[58] In the meantime, no meaningful progress in terms of social and economic reforms was made. The state's heavy reliance on the IFIs whose prescriptions for the socio-economic problems still revolved around the marketisation of Tunisia, as well as its top–down decision-making process regarding the distribution of wealth, remained largely *in situ*.

In parallel, civil society activists began to worry about the possible return of the police state amid the allegedly increasing threat of terrorism. They considered that a continuous state of emergency and the new anti-terrorism laws approved in 2015 were likely to further violate human rights and restrict their freedoms meant to be guaranteed after the Uprising. A new security bill submitted by the government in April 2015 and backed by the security unions to 'protect' the security apparatuses led domestic and international human rights organisations to denounce the state's attempts to justify and legalise the use of force against its citizens.[59]

These developments indicate that the old unjust political and economic systems remained in place. Since 2012, the sense of a lack of changes has led many youths, particularly those who are unemployed, to take to the streets again and raise the same slogan which they had chanted during the revolutionary moments. That corruption, marginalisation, repression and the state-led liberal economic policies in favour of international and domestic crony capitalists still existed, however, does not mean that post-uprising Tunisia was still governed by exactly the same authoritarian logics and tools that had operated during the Ben Ali era. Tunisia achieved a decent level of procedural democracy and pluralism at the level of high politics, as well as an increased presence and influence of civil society in politics since 2011, making the form of governance far more complex than before.[60] It is arguably through these changes that the pre-2011 political-economic orders came to reconfigure their relationship to others, as well as their strategies of governance within the newly 'democratising' society. In other words, what Tunisia witnessed after the Uprising was not so much a continuation of the old regime, but a set of transformation through which power relations within and surrounding state and society were re-imagined and re-constituted, producing a new form of governance.

INSTITUTIONAL DEMOCRATISATION

After the Uprising, Tunisia entered the phase of a 'transition toward democracy' amid continued bottom–up challenges that still held a strong revolutionary legitimacy. Following the announcement of a drastic change of the political-economic system on 3 March 2011, the ruling RCD party was dissolved; independent committees to plan and monitor the transition process were established; previously illegal political parties (including Ennahda) became legalised and new parties were created; largely free and fair parliamentary and presidential elections were held; a new constitution that highlighted the importance of the re-distribution of wealth across the country was approved in 2014. Many recognised these measures as signalling the end of dictatorial rule and the beginning of a new political order that would respect and promote democratic pluralism.

While the participation of youth and socially and economically marginalised groups was still limited, the initial transitional process was largely driven by the principle of inclusion. A notable example is the Higher Commission which was established to prepare and monitor the first Constituent Assembly election in October 2011. The interim government led by Essebsi created the Higher Commission by incorporating the two existing institutional bodies, the Committee for Political Reform and the National Council for the Protection of the Revolution (CNPR). While the Political Reform Committee was emblematic of the state's attempts to control the transitional process, the CNPR consisted of various opposition groups that represented the revolutionary sovereignty at the grassroots level. Initially composed of seventy-one members and then increasing to 155 members representing different segments of society, the Higher Commission discussed and made decisions on several sensitive topics regarding the new electoral law, such as gender proportion and the eligibility of former RCD members who could run for the upcoming election. Despite the internal tension and distrust among competing political forces, the Higher Commission through dialogue and negotiation managed to produce the electoral law and an independent electoral commission, the Superior Independent Instance for the Elections (ISIE). The role of this commission ranged from organising and monitoring the election, over educating the population, to guaranteeing the democratic quality of the election.[61]

It should be also highlighted that, with the presidential decree No. 88 announced in 2011 to protect the freedom of assembly, the number of civil society associations rapidly increased, and the newly given freedom led them to play a crucial role in transforming Tunisia. The UGTT, the Tunisian League for the Defense of Human Rights (LTDH), the Bar Association and other human rights organisations that were key actors of the CNPR continued to intervene in and sometimes lead the process of the institutionalisation of the new political system. For instance, the Tunisian National Dialogue Quartet (NDQ) was organised in 2013 as an *ad hoc* alliance of the UGTT, the Bar Association, the LTDH and the Tunisian Confederation of Industry and Trade and Handicrafts (UTICA) when the transitional government led by the Islamist Ennahda party was about to collapse due to mass mobilisations. This quartet's role in the peaceful negotiation with Ennahda was evaluated as a decisive step that protected Tunisia's transition from falling apart. Civil society actors also participated in the process of law-making, by suggesting and pressuring the state to reform laws based on the principle of liberty and equality. Gender equality was one of the most pressing issues in this regard. Feminist organisations such as L'Association Tunisienne des Femmes Democrates (ATFD) directly contributed to the enactment of the gender parity principle on the electoral list in 2011, as well as the protection of women's rights in the new constitution.[62] Moreover, civil society was now able to openly monitor and challenge state policies and the elected democratic institutions by exercising their freedom of expression and assembly. Non-governmental associations organised by youth, such as Al-Bawsala and IWATCH, effectively monitored political and economic corruption and scrutinised the governmental agencies and legislations to hold the post-uprising authorities to account. Their activism involved multiple channels and means, including social media, street protests and legal procedures.

POLITICAL ENGAGEMENT OF THE MOBILISED PUBLIC ON THE STREETS

One issue became clear in the process of democratisation: Tunisian civil society was not monolithic, and heterogeneous actors and movements had significantly different demands and priorities. The diverse and divergent characteristic of civil society was more visible in street politics than in institutional politics; in the latter, there still was a limited number of traditional organisations existing before 2011 that exercised dominant influence and played the legitimate representatives of 'the people'. Institutional democratisation opened up public space for previously less visible segments of society, including women workers,[63] LGBT communities[64] and grassroots Islamist movements.[65] New demands and mobilising strategies also emerged. For instance, various forms of environmental protests that took place after 2011 utilised political freedom in order to express fears, dissatisfaction and demands regarding the environment, a topic that 'previously could not be addressed openly, without being repressed'.[66] The transitional justice process also engendered new victim movements, including that organised by people who had been injured during the revolutionary period as well as families of martyrs.

In addition to the diversification of street politics, some notable features in the typology of protests appeared in the process of democratisation. Immediately after the fall of Ben Ali, Tunisia started witnessing the polarisation of a mobilised public over the increasing visibility and influence of Islamist forces. Ennahda's win in the October elections to the NCA and the following coalition government, the 'Troika', led to a wave of anti-government protests. Civil society groups – including UGTT, UDC, secular and leftist political parties and movements, feminists, as well as supporters of the old regime – mobilised against what they perceived as Ennahda's 'hijacking' of the revolution. This, in turn, brought about counter-movements denouncing the secular front. When anti-Troika protesters mobilised in 2011 and 2012 based on the claim of 'popular legitimacy', they encountered an opposition movement consisting of a 'heterogeneous crowd' of football fans, Salafists, the League for the Protection of the Revolution (LPR) and Ennahda party youth who defended the government based on the claim of 'electoral legitimacy'.[67] The tension between pro- and anti-Islamist protests also escalated over other political and religious issues, such as women's status in the new constitution and the establishment of mosques on campuses. Highly polarised political visions and narratives coexisted on the street in the initial phase of democratisation.

Also notable is that mobilisations with social and economic demands, which had never ceased to exist since the Uprising, dramatically increased after the establishment of the coalition rule between Ennahda and Nidaa Tounes. Whereas the period between 2011 and 2014 witnessed protests organised by unionised workers and unemployed youths relatively evenly, in 2016 the latter accounted for the largest group in socio-economic protests.[68] Two events in particular contributed to the sudden increase in protests for employment: the unemployed mobilisations that erupted in Kasserine in January 2016, which then became intensified and spread into other regions after an unemployed youth named Ridha Yahyaoui was electrocuted; and the sit-ins organised by the inhabitants of Kerkennah in April of the same year, against Petrofac's failure to meet its promise to initiate an employment programme and to provide social benefits for local inhabitants.[69] Precarious workers demanding better working conditions and job security were also a leading force in socio-economic protests. For instance, local protests and sit-ins organised by the so-called 'site workers' (*'umal hadha'ir*), who were hired by the state under a social programme for unemployed populations, began to evolve into collective action at both regional and national levels from 2015 onwards. The main source of their grievances was that, while their workload was similar to that of many formal employees in public institutions and ministries, they remained casual workers with no job security and could not even earn minimum wage.[70]

Street protests for social and economic justice increased as the successive governments failed to meet their promises to improve the living conditions of the majority and to resolve the problem of unemployment and regional disparities. The growing number of mobilisations was also the result of the gradual marginalisation of youths and revolutionaries from the formal process of democratisation. Over time, the 'liberal-associative'[71] category of actors in accordance with liberal democracy became dominant, while the more 'oppositional-resistance' category of actors that challenged it became excluded. A notable example of the disparities between the former and latter categories of civil society is provided by Antonakis-Nashif's analysis of how the feminist movement ATFD working for gender justice managed to gain more access to the governmental decision-making process than the UDC, whose demand for the right to work the governing elites did not necessarily perceive as a fundamental element of liberal democracy.[72]

It should be mentioned that, whilst protests based on socio-economic motivations are often analytically distinguished from those with more political demands, they are closely linked to each other, at least in the Tunisian context. In many cases, political demands (such as security reforms) and economic demands (such as employment and better working conditions) are raised simultaneously in protest events, as marked by the mass mobilisations in 2010 and 2011, as well as youth protests against police brutality in January 2021. The inseparability of the political and the socio-economic was pointed out by protesters who believed that one 'cannot achieve his economic rights and dignity without changing the political system'.[73] This was also the case with many unemployed activists throughout the process of democratisation. For instance, UDC members who were active in unemployed mobilisations at local and national scales were well-connected with other civil society and social movement groups – such as IWATCH and the *Manish Msamah* ('I don't forgive', in the Tunisian dialect) campaign – and actively participated in protests based on issues and slogans that were not explicitly economic.

The Neoliberal Reconfiguration of Democracy

As we have seen, the robust participation of various non-state associations and social movements in the name of 'civil society' suggests that they played a key role in defending and enabling the transition to democracy. The crucial role of Tunisian civil society in democratisation has been highlighted and acknowledged by scholars, policy-makers, as well as civil society and NGO actors themselves. Less focus, however, has been given to the contested meaning and role of civil society and to the question of which actors/actions came to be included in (and excluded from) the category of Tunisia's 'strong' civil society. Also, given that the majority of Tunisians saw resolving socio-economic issues as the post-2011 state's priority[74] and that Tunisian civil society obtained political opportunities and tools for changes, we are left wondering why it failed in pushing them forward in the context of democratisation. The strong civil society thesis quickly disappears when one is asked to make sense of the continued market hegemony that renders the economisation of state administration and public sectors, foreign investments and (social) entrepreneurship as the most feasible solutions through which to climb out of existing political, social and economic problems. The state-society relationship is then described as being still highly imbalanced in favour of the former. I am not attempting to rebut the claim that the resilience of the old system and the weak and fragmented civil society contributed to the *status quo*. But this claim needs to be much more nuanced based on closely studying the reconfiguration of the exercise of governance and Tunisian civil society's role in it.

Soon after the interim government was set in motion, the discourse of civil society began to revolve less around the notion of revolutionary and more around a liberal conception of freedom, citizenship and democracy. According to this logic, the revolution was over, and individual liberties and citizen's rights now had to be exercised in such a way as to keep the process of democratisation stable and peaceful; in order to do so, a national consensus between the state and civil society was necessary. The successive governments emphasised participation of civil society in decision-making processes as a key democratic value, but they limited its form and purpose of participation in dialogue and consensus, while disregarding more direct and radical forms of participation. One such example can be found in the 2015 Development Plan report in which the government noted the following:

> It becomes necessary that various actors including the state, political parties, pro-fessional organisations, civil society institutions and citizens with an awareness of responsibility adopt a negotiational democracy approach based on consulta-tion and dialogue instead of confrontational democratisation, narrow factional demands and disputes that do not take into account the national interest.[75]

According to this logic, criticism of government institutions and the problem within the system is tolerated, but any acts against the system itself are not tolerated because they 'lie outside the liberal-democratic con-sensus'.[76] This liberal notion of civil society and consensus was mobilised in holding heterogeneous segments of society together during and after the period of the increasing Islamist-Secularist conflicts.[77]

Also, for democracy to be consolidated in a peaceful way, national security had to be the priority. In his television interview held on 31 March 2011, then President Essebsi noted that the security chaos at the time of the revolution was 'normal' given the long period of state repression that Tunisian citizens had experienced. The absolute priority now, however, was security, which would require citizens to respect the state and law by practising their freedom in a 'civilised manner until the revolution achieves the desired democratic path and does not slip into chaos and failure'.[78] Throughout the transitional period, the citizen-subject exercising one's individual liberties and rights in a civilised manner was constituted through the construction of a 'non-civil' category of actions signifying any practices deemed radical, illegal, violent and destructive. Against this non-civil category, values such as national unity and consensus based on dialogue became the norm and the moral requirement that would guide Tunisians and lead them to learn how to think and behave as free and empowered citizens. In this context, counter-terrorism served as an important political tool to discipline some segments of civil society, by penalising and educating actors whose appearances and behaviours the authorities considered radical, illegal and extreme. Between 2013 and 2014, around 4,100 individuals were arrested under the 2003 anti-terrorism law.[79] In the first half of the following year, the police detained around 100,000 individuals, nearly 1 per cent of the entire Tunisian population, because of their Salafi appearance.[80]

Ben Ali's rule based on the security syndrome and the economic miracle discourse, as illustrated earlier, suggests that there is nothing new about the state's abuse of counter-terrorism and the notion that Tunisian civil society should be united against 'enemies' while whoever threatens the national consensus and democracy must be excluded. They served as political tools upholding the Ben Ali regime. Both before and after 2011, the state utilised these tools for nurturing docile citizens and punishing those deemed to challenge the system.

An important change made in the process of democratisation, however, was the following: whereas counter-terrorism practices and the construction of a national consensus were performed predominantly by Ben Ali and his security apparatuses for the purpose of maintaining the centralised system in the authoritarian context, now civil society actors became key agents voluntarily involved in the fight against Islamic extremism and terrorism. One may argue that Ben Ali's counter-terrorism was also possible, significantly due to the role of opposition political parties and civil society actors. Indeed, many secular-minded civil society organisations appreciated Ben Ali's crackdown on Islamist movements because of their anti-Islamist sentiments.[81] Some of them held the perhaps genuine belief that Ben Ali's social and political reforms to some extent met their democratic vision for Tunisia. The head of the Tunisian Women Association, Hayat Rais, explained why she voted for Ben Ali in the 2005 presidential election:

[Ben Ali] carries out an enlightened reform that has brought us to modernity. [...] The reform project of the president is based on the universal values of the notions of democracy, pluralism and human rights while preserving the country's specificity and belief in dealing with these values. [...] So, I voted for Ben Ali whose reform project will bring Tunisia to the class of developed countries.[82]

As I noted above, however, the unprecedented level of political freedom, empowered civil society and social movement actors, as well as their opportunities, abilities and experience of critiquing, influencing and intervening in high politics, clearly differentiated the post-2011 political context from Ben Ali's rule, even if we appreciate that the latter heavily relied on ordinary citizens' desire for the solicitude of the state and 'permanent negotiation'.[83] How can we make sense of the upsurge of civil society organisations' involvement in anti-terrorism and, more broadly, the Countering Violent Extremism (CVE) agenda in a 'politically' liberalising context? On the one hand, civil society's active role in CVE is closely related to the international donors' increasing attention to local actors as important partners in combatting terrorism and in security reforms in post-2011 Tunisia. While continuously providing the government with security assistance, external forces – such as the United States, the European Union, EU Member States, as well as the UN – have started offering funds for civil society actors' participation in preventative measures; this is based on the logic similar to that of liberal peace-building, according to which (liberal) civil society is considered essential to local legitimacy and thereby to making international intervention more effective.[84]

While being critical of the lack of autonomy and suspicious of the international community's focus on counter-terrorism itself, many civil society organisations considered their 'agenda adaptation' a strategic decision to receive the funds necessary for their survival.[85] A local NGO researcher who attended a civil society-led conference on counter-terrorism at a five-star hotel in Gammarth said: 'Is counter-terrorism or refugees a priority for Tunisian people? I don't think so, but they [civil society organisations] work on these issues anyway because donors are interested in them'.[86] His narrative suggests that civil society's active participation in CVE was partly the consequence of the 'marketisation' of a civil society characterised by increasing competition among civil society organisations over projects and their dependence on external funders.[87]

On the other hand, there indeed existed more genuine bottom–up efforts to fight violent extremism and terrorism with the motivation to protect individual liberties and rights from anti-liberal and anti-secular forces, particularly Salafi movements. Since the fall of the Ben Ali regime, the freedom of expression and assembly had allowed Salafists to publicly practice and promote their religious and social values, something that Tunisian society had not witnessed before. *Ansar al-Sharia* in Tunisia (AST), which represented this emerging Salafist trend, utilised political opportunities in order to promote its own version of Islamic democracy. AST actively used streets, universities, workplaces and other public spaces for *da'wah* ('Calling to Islam') and holding its National Congresses. Although it publicly announced its rejection of armed struggle and partly accepted liberal democratic rule, controversy around the influence of the Salafi movements and the suspicion that Ennahda was involved in AST's activism gradually increased in Tunisian society. In parallel, the escalating tension between secularists and Salafists involved several physical confrontations – including the Manouba incident on 7 March 2012, during which a Salafist replaced the Tunisian flag on the roof of Manouba University with the black flag symbolising Salafism, and the confrontation between the Tunisian Association for Drama Art and some Salafi protesters in downtown Tunis in March 2012. These events were widely publicised in the media and frightened secularists and liberals.[88] Ennhada's perceived tolerance for some extreme Salafists also led many secular-minded civil society actors to believe that Ennahda was intentionally neglecting the increasing influence of jihadi Salafism for its own political and ideological goals.

The notion that the freedom practised by radical Islamists posed a great threat to the transition to democracy, individual liberties and rights prevailed in the secular and liberal-associative community, leading it to function as 'liberal police'.[89] Various civil society organisations, unions and opposition political parties stood at the forefront in the War on Terror and the association of the Salafi movements with terrorism, playing a key role in designating AST as a terrorist organisation in August 2013. For instance, after the Manouba incident, five leftist political parties announced a joint statement accusing militant Salafism of violence, terrorism and sedition.[90] Also, in June 2012, a march against Salafist groups under the slogan 'No to extremism, violence and terrorism' was organised by a number of non-governmental organisations, including the National Union of Tunisian Journalists (SNJT) and the Association of Women and Dignity.[91] A month before this march, LTDH also called on the Troika government to take full responsibility for Salafist violence, accusing the militant Salafist groups of 'perpetrating terrorism and spreading horror', as well as 'material and moral violence against women, intellectuals, journalists, artists, trade unionists, politicians and human rights activists'.[92]

REFOLDING THE IDEAL CIVIL SOCIETY INTO THE EXERCISE OF DOMINATION

Liberal and secular civil society actors' fear that Tunisia's nascent democracy was under threat due to the rise of radical Islam and terrorism unwittingly contributed to the rise of Essebsi's right-wing secular party Nidaa Tounes ('Call for Tunis', in Arabic) and, ironically, the following establishment of the coalition between Nidaa Tounes and Ennahda. On 20 April 2012, Essebsi warned that Tunisia's social security was deteriorating due to terrorism and the resulting economic crisis.[93] Two months later, he officially declared the establishment of the Nidaa Tounes party; according to him, its aim was to unite all secularists and to counter Ennahda's hegemony.[94] Despite suspicions about the return of the old regime, many secular-minded civil society activists and, importantly, the leftist coalition Popular Front, which by that time enjoyed the support of grassroots revolutionaries, accepted Essebsi's party as a strategic partner in order to deter the perceived Islamic hegemony.

The Popular Front's tactical compromise with Nidaa Tounes significantly fragmented and weakened leftist political forces. For many grassroots revolutionary activists, its decision to establish a secular coalition – called the 'National Salvation Front' (NSF) – against Ennahda during the Bardo Occupation was considered a betrayal of the revolution. The decreasing popularity of the Popular Front, in turn, provided Nidaa Tounes with more space to manoeuvre. Essebsi quickly excluded the leftist political parties from the process of negotiation with Ennahda, by having a secret meeting with the Head of Ennahda, Rachid Ghanouch, in Paris on 15 August 2013. After the Paris meeting had been leaked, several revolutionary activists and NSF supporters in the Occupy movement criticised this meeting as a product of the intervention of Western countries and local businessmen.

The suspicion that Western agencies were involved in this meeting grew stronger because several foreign delegates – including the EU special delegation, the German foreign minister and the US ambassador to Tunis – visited Tunisia for meetings with major politicians only one week before the Paris meeting. The detailed contents of the meeting were not revealed, but Ghanouch's speech in the press conference on the same day of the meeting made the public believe that there was a trade-off between Nidaa Tounes and Ennahda. From the view of several critics, it was the Paris deal that produced the *de facto* roadmap for the future political compromise between Islamists and liberal democrats, with at least three consequences: Ennahda's continued position as the legitimate governing force, Nidaa Tounes' growing role as the most plausible counter-weight to the Islamic hegemony, and the marginalisation of the leftist parties and revolutionary movements.[95]

The notion that Tunisia needed a 'national consensus' to protect its democracy from extremism and terrorism served as a neoliberal rationale for state institutions. In January 2014, the National Assembly nominated Mehdi Jomaa, known as a non-partisan figure, as Prime Minister of the caretaker government, and this government was soon filled with technocrats who had worked in international organisations, including the UN and the African Development Bank (ADB). Through his visit to the US and the European and Gulf countries in March and April of the same year, Jomaa solicited financial assistance and investment in Tunisia, while expressing his commitment to the War on Terror and the economic structural reforms prescribed by the international money lenders. Domestically, he promoted in an outspoken manner his vision of economic development based on consumption and investment, proposing several austerity plans, such as 'a twenty-percent salary reduction'.[96] At the same time, the government carried out several counter-terrorism operations in the interior regions, widely broadcasting the violent scenes through local media channels. Although pessimistic voices and suspicion about the government's performance existed, the strong support from both the international agencies and domestic elites provided the care-taker government with a legitimacy that the former administrations had not enjoyed. The following Nidaa Tounes and Ennahda coalition government in 2015 further stabilised the process of liberal democratic consolidation and the integration of Tunisia into the global market. The two ideologically distant parties easily cohabited with one another based on their mutual preference of a market-driven economy and liberal democracy over a more state-centric economy and social democracy.

Consequently, while the earlier political turmoil caused by the confrontation between Islamists and secularists was mitigated, the tension between the newly established technocrat government and the protesters who demanded radical socio-economic changes gradually escalated. In particular, the authorities' continued neglect of the problem of unemployment and regional disparities based on the idea that procedural democratisation should come first led many unemployed youths in the interior regions to take up more radical and disruptive modes of action. It is in this context, together with secular and liberal civil society actors' increasing fear of radical Islam, that unemployed protesters became discursively linked to terrorists and regarded as a threat to the process of democratisation. As the next chapter will discuss in detail, the securitisation of unemployed populations was different from that of Salafists, in the sense that the former took a much more subtle and less repressive form than the latter. The dominant securitising practices focused on accusing particular modes of action deployed by unemployed protesters and their potential role in facilitating terrorism, while expressing sympathy and support for the protesters' *political* right to demand employment. Their concern had less to do with the presence of unemployed mobilisations as such and more with the protesters' often radical ways of being, thinking and behaving.

Notes

1. Hibou, *The force of obedience*.
2. President Ben Ali's speech on 4 August 1994; *Le Figaro*, 2 August 1994 (cited in Hamdi, *The politicisation of Islam*, p. 74).
3. Lutterbeck, 'Tool of rule'.
4. Hibou, *The force of obedience*, p. 181.
5. Translated by Amnesty International: Article 52 bis, amended by Law 93-112 of 22 November 1993; see Amnesty International, *New draft 'anti-terrorism' law will further undermine human rights*, p. 3.
6. Amnesty International, 'In the name of security', p. 8.
7. United Nations Human Rights Council (UNHRC), 'Report of the special rapporteur on the promotion and protection of human rights and fundamental freedoms while counter terrorism'.
8. Alfajrnews, '400 Sujun Tounisi yadrabun 'an al-Ta'am'.
9. Hobson, 'A forward strategy of freedom in the Middle East'.
10. Ibid.
11. US Department of State, 'Press availability in Tunisia'.
12. Alwasat, 'al-Ra'is Ben Ali fi Hadith lil-Majlah "al-Hawadith" al-Lbnaniyah'.
13. Amnesty International, 'In the name of security', p. 3.
14. Alchourouk, 'Washington Times: Tunis Bilad Namudhaji Tataqadam fihi al-Dimoqratiah bi Najah'.
15. Alwasat, 'Nas Khitab al-Ra'is Ben Ali bil-Munasiba al-Dikri 19 lil-Saba' min November'.
16. Lutterbeck, 'Tool of rule', p. 822.
17. Ibid. p. 818.
18. Hibou estimated that the RCD party during Ben Ali's time had 7,500 local cells and 2,200 professional cells across the country; see Hibou, *The force of obedience*, p. 86.
19. Kaboub, 'The End of Neoliberalism?' p. 535; Radwan, 'The impact and influence of international financial institutions on the Middle East and North Africa', p. 115.
20. Murphy, *Economic and political change in Tunisia: From Bourguiba to Ben Ali*, pp. 104–5.
21. Ibid. p. 145.
22. Alexander, *Tunisia: Stability and reform in the modern Maghreb*, p. 80.
23. Ibid. p. 81.
24. Ibid.
25. Ayadi and Mattoussi, 'Scoping of the Tunisian economy', p. 20.
26. IMF, 'Concluding statement of the article IV consultation mission'.
27. World Bank, 'All in the family state capture in Tunisia', p. 24.
28. Ibid. p. 4.
29. Murphy, 'Under the emperor's neoliberal clothes!' p. 41.
30. Sadiki, 'Regional development in Tunisia'.

31. Tsourapas, 'The other side of a neoliberal miracle', p. 28.
32. Alwasat, 'Nas Khitab al-Ra'is Ben Ali bil-Munasiba al-Dikri 19 lil-Saba' min November'.
33. Hibou, 'Domination and control in Tunisia', p. 187.
34. Baumann, 'A failure of governmentality', p. 471.
35. Hibou, *The force of obedience*, p. 192.
36. Ibid. p. 190.
37. Ibid. p. 9.
38. See, for instance, Ayeb and Bush, *Food insecurity and revolution in the Middle East and North Africa*.
39. Beinin, *Workers and thieves*, p. 83.
40. Alexander, *Tunisia*, pp. 76–77.
41. Beinin, *Workers and thieves*, p. 84.
42. Haouas, Sayre and Yagoubi, 'Youth unemployment in Tunisia'.
43. Hibou, Meddeb and Hamdi, 'Tunisia after 14 January and its social and political economy', pp. 37–38.
44. Beinin, *Workers and thieves*, p. 84.
45. Pfeifer, 'Parameters of economic reform in North Africa'; World Bank, 'Employment, development and the social contract in the Middle East and North Africa'.
46. Achy, 'Tunisia's economic challenges', p. 10.
47. Weipert-Fenner, 'Unemployed mobilization in times of democratization', p. 57, emphasis original.
48. Ibid. p. 57.
49. Gobe, 'The Gafsa mining basin between riots and a social movement', pp. 6–7.
50. Ibid. p. 7.
51. Allal, 'Becoming revolutionary in Tunisia, 2007–2011', p. 189.
52. Beinin, *Workers and thieves*, p. 87.
53. Ibid. pp. 88–89.
54. Allal, 'Becoming revolutionary in Tunisia, 2007–2011'.
55. Ibid. pp. 84, 105.
56. Antonakis-Nashif, 'Contested transformation', p. 138.
57. El-Khawas, 'Tunisia's jasmine revolution', p. 15.
58. Truth and Dignity Commission, 'Tunisia'.
59. See the reports published by Human Rights Watch on Tunisia (HRW, 'Drop or amend security bill' and 'Draft law could return Tunisia to a police state').
60. Cavatorta, 'No democratic change ... and yet no authoritarian continuity', pp. 142–43.
61. Murphy, 'The Tunisian elections of October 2011'; Zemni, 'The extraordinary politics of the Tunisian revolution'.
62. Antonakis-Nashif, 'Contested transformation', p. 134.
63. Debuysere, 'Between feminism and unionism'.

64. Huber and Kamel, 'Arab Spring'.
65. Torelli, Merone and Cavatorta, 'Salafism in Tunisia'.
66. Pepicelli, 'People want a clean environment', pp. 39–40.
67. Boubekeur, 'The politics of protest in Tunisia', p. 2.
68. This observation was made in Vatthauer and Weipert-Fenner's study on the typology of socio-economic protests in Tunisia (Vatthauer and Weipert-Fenner, 'The quest for social justice in Tunisia', p. 9).
69. Chomiak, 'The revolution in Tunisia continues'; Feltrin 'The struggles of precarious youth in Tunisia'.
70. Han, 'Precarious public sector "site" workers denounce new union agreement'.
71. Martin, 'Do Tunisian secular civil society organisations demonstrate a process of democratic learning?' p. 800.
72. Antonakis-Nashif, 'Contested transformation'.
73. Interview with Ben Mahmoud, political activist, Tunis, 2 December 2020.
74. Arab Barometer.
75. Ministry of Development Investment and International Cooperation, 'Mukhatit El Tanmiyah 2016–2020', p. 58.
76. Martin, 'Do Tunisian secular civil society organisations demonstrate a process of democratic learning?' p. 801.
77. Ibid. p. 801.
78. Alhiwar, 'Essebsi: al-Amni Awalan'.
79. Tamburini, 'Anti-terrorism laws in the Maghreb countries', p. 1245.
80. Aliriza, 'Tunisia at risk'.
81. Dalmasso and Cavatorta, 'Reforming the family code in Tunisia and Morocco'; Haugbølle and Cavatorta, 'Will the real Tunisian opposition please stand up?'
82. For the entire interview, see Alchourouk, 'Jam'yun I'lamiyun wa Muthaqafun Yaktabun: li-hadha Nantakhab Ben Ali'.
83. Hibou, *The force of obedience*, p. 202.
84. Letsch, 'Countering violent extremism in Tunisia'.
85. Ibid. p. 182.
86. Interview with Abou Salem, Human rights activist, Tunis, 28 December 2016.
87. Letsch, 'Countering violent extremism in Tunisia', p. 182.
88. See, for instance, Attounissia, 'Kiliya al-Adaab bi Manoubah: Tawatur wa Mutaalib bi Rahil "al-Qajdughli"'.
89. Dean, 'Liberal government and authoritarianism'.
90. Tap, 'Ahjab Siyesiya Ta'tabir Injaal al-'Alam al-Tunisi Ta'adiyan 'ala Ramj al-Siyedah al-Wataniyah'.
91. Alwasat, 'Uzarah al-Dekhaliyah al-Tunisiyah Tamna' Taẓaharah Da'y al-Layha al-Sabt bi Shara' al-Habib Bourguiba'.
92. LTDH, 'Bayan al-Rabitah al-Tunisiyah lil Difa'a 'an Huquq al-Insen'.
93. Infosplus, 'al-Nas al-Kamil lil Mubadrah Essebsi'.

94. Alfajirnews, 'al-Beji Essebsi Ya'aulan T'asis Harakat "Nidaa Tunis" lil-Tasdi li Haimanah "Ennahda"'.
95. This observation was made during the author's conversations with local journalists and political activists in Tunisia.
96. Szakal, 'One hundred days of lentitude: Jomâa on his work in office'.

4

The Securitisation of the Unemployed Subject

If we now start preparing and organising a protest for tomorrow, from this midnight onwards, the media will talk about the threat of terrorists and fear of terrorist infiltration into the country through Kasserine. Do terrorists enter Kasserine only when there are protests?![1]

The exercise of domination since 2011 was neither a simple continuity nor a total discontinuity with the Ben Ali regime. What Tunisia has witnessed since the political upheaval in 2010 and 2011 was rather a form of reconfiguration of old and new power relations across multiple domains including social, economic and political, in such a way that norms and principles of liberal democracy were practised by multiple actors to construct and govern 'problematic' subjects. In particular, as the above quote from my interview with Abdul Ahmed who introduced himself as a casual worker and unemployed protester illustrates, the unemployed youth increasingly became subject to social control in the name of the 'War on Terror' with the emergence of the technocrat government in 2014.

In this chapter, I will illustrate in detail how speech and non-speech acts were mobilised to securitise the unemployed as a threat to Tunisia's democracy. I do so by deploying the governmentality framework discussed in Chapter 2 and by investigating what discursive terrains, signifying narratives and subjectivities were constructed, while the authorities, political and economic elites, experts and media discursively articulated the unemployed as having links to terrorism and counter-terrorism. The analysis of their narratives shows that the dominant securitising acts served as a way to regulate and govern the conducts of the unemployed so as to be able to think and act in conformity with a neoliberal modality of liberal democracy. They did so by building a chain of equivalence between the unemployed and terrorism, through their use of multiple discursive terrains and the construction of the meta-narrative that 'the unemployed must be self-governable and self-responsible to counter terrorism' (hereafter the self-governable unemployed).

This argument proceeds in two steps. This chapter firstly illustrates how the discursive terrain of global Islamist terrorism was mobilised in the association between the unemployed and terrorism, through the logic of equivalence as well as logic of difference, and how these securitising practices were implicated in the process of subjectifying the unemployed as naïve, deviant and (maybe) terrorist. This will be then followed by an analysis of how this chain of equivalence between the two separated subjects was elaborated through two additional signifiers, by deploying two other discursive terrains – that is, democracy and economic development. Building on the investigation of the three signifying narratives, it elaborates how these narratives operated to regulate the conducts of the unemployed in general and the protesters in particular. Thus, it examines the ways in which commonly perceived liberal democratic values – such as rule of law, human rights, and free and fair elections, as well as the notion of economic development – served the governing elites in both liberal and illiberal ways, shaping the unemployed as self-governable and entrepreneurial democratic citizens.

The Inevitable Islamist Terrorism and Unemployed Protests

The first signifying narrative and pillar of the meta-narrative of 'the self-governable unemployed' is that the terrorist threat in Tunisia was an inexorable and imminent phenomenon, given the presence of religious extremists, and that they can easily manipulate the social unrest caused by unemployed protests. In building this narrative, the ruling elites heavily drew on 'Islamist terrorism'[2] as its discursive terrain. Given that a vast majority of Tunisians present themselves to be Muslim, the elites' association of Islam with terrorism entailed much more 'careful qualifications'[3] (such as 'terrorists are not real Muslims') than that observed in many non-Muslim societies. However, a series of assumptions, labels and categorisations produced by the elites to describe the Islamic State (or Daesh) or Al Qaeda indicate that their securitising practices were to a great extent dependent on global ideas of Islamist terrorism; consequently, terrorism is considered irrationally and religiously motivated, with fanaticism or hatred, and more dangerous than conventional forms of terrorism, since, according to them, it operates in a decentralised global network structure and causes casualties among civilians as well as mass destruction.[4] The increasing visibility of the Salafi movements in the post-uprising context also discursively served to render Islamist terrorism as a taken-for-granted reality that threatened Tunisian democracy.

The portrayal of Tunisian circumstance as fragile and vulnerable because of its geographical proximity to Arab countries such as Libya and Syria, where 'global jihadi networks' operate, as well as the existence of Salafists on Tunisian soil was, in turn, connected to the unemployed protests, promoting the idea that protests could be a devastating and disastrous acts that might easily provide a gate for the infiltration of terrorists. In the process of securitising the unemployed, the elites used both the logic of equivalence and the logic of difference.[5] Firstly, the logic of equivalence operated to establish an equivalential chain between terrorism and unemployed protests in two stages. Constructing Islamist terrorists as the enemy of Tunisia, the elites created social antagonism between Tunisians and the terrorist enemy, thereby building solidarity among different social segments (including the regime and unemployed protesters) in conflict in the field of job creation and development. This enemy category was then expanded to incorporate some 'problematic' unemployed protests, by creating and associating some naïve and/or deviant unemployed individuals with terrorism.

The below news report published by *Assabah*, a leading Tunisian news outlet previously owned by Ben Ali's son-in-law Sakr Al Materi,[6] provides an illustrative example of a rhetoric that resonated with politicians, security experts and media commentators in constructing 'foreign terrorists' as the enemy of Tunisia. The association of unemployed protests with terrorism intensified after several negotiations between key secular and Islamist elite forces had reached an agreement to establish a new technocrat government. The first target of such an articulation was the unemployed mobilisation that had started in Kasserine on 5 January 2014 based on the demand for employment and regional development. The protests organised by unemployed youths and supported by several civil society organisations and local populations in Kasserine rapidly spread to other marginalised regions in Southern Tunisia. The level of urgency of this bottom–up threat to the stability of the newly established government, as perceived by the elites at that time, is well-reflected in the fact that fifteen out of the total 109 securitising claims were produced during the period between 9 and 24 January 2014. These claims directly targeted the Kasserine unemployed protests and their aftermath in other regions:

Assabah news was informed by sources that the foreign department of the Tunisian Intelligence Service in the National Security received very important information this week, from a foreign intelligence service that previously predicted the political assassination of Mohammed Al-Brahimi in Tunisia. According to the sources, it is likely that this information included the infiltration or the suspected infiltration of 450 of those who were described as 'mercenaries' and who were believed to be religiously extreme and terrorists, from different nationalities, most likely Tunisians, Libyans, Malians, Mauritanians and Algerians. There was no additional information about the reason for their infiltration. But our sources have confirmed that those described as mercenaries are likely to be terrorists or religious extremists linked to Al-Qaeda in the Islamic Maghreb and may have infiltrated, most likely, from the Libyan border and perhaps from the Algerian border to our country, with the intention to commit terrorist acts in coordination with some settled sleeper cells in Tunisia. The same sources reported that, while it is for sure that these terrorists infiltrated Tunisian territory in recent days, they took advantage of the preoccupation of the security forces and the army to counter social protests, especially riots, sabotage and attacks on security headquarters and public facilities in different regions.[7]

While *Assabah* did not use the term 'Islam', it portrayed those thought to have infiltrated Tunisia as religiously extreme mercenaries drawing on and thereby reproducing the global notion of Islamist terrorism. Its deployment of the discursive terrain of Islamist terrorism was further specified by describing those mercenaries as being linked to Al-Qaeda, invoking the 'mythology'[8] that there exist thousands of jihadists who are linked to global jihadi terrorist networks and waiting to enter Tunisia. Building on the global Islamist terrorism discourse, *Assabah* associated terrorism with the Kasserine unemployed protests through several rhetorical techniques.

Firstly, the lexical choice of words such as 'riots', 'sabotage' and 'attack' reduced the protests to violent events, rendering invisible multiple actors involved in the protests and their demands. Secondly, the use of numerical information (as in '450 mercenaries') depicted the given information as if it were accurate and highlighted the negative impact of the protests. Also, by portraying the origin of the information as a reliable intelligence service that had correctly predicted the 2013 assassination of Mohamed Al-Brahimi, the speaker enhanced the authenticity of the information, even though the direct source from which *Assabah* had obtained this information remained vague and unknown. Lastly, it is also notable that most information about the profiles of terrorists and their exploitation of the protests were described by using a mixture of lexical presuppositions such as 'most likely' and 'perhaps' with factive verbs such as 'confirm', thereby blurring the boundaries between facts and assumptions about the infiltration of terrorists from outside.

These rhetorical techniques provide a representative example of how Islamist terrorism in Tunisia was discursively formed as 'the object of which they speak'[9] and how the pre-existing discourse of global Islamist terrorism was mobilised in the criminalisation of the unemployed protests. Also, they show how the securitising speech acts used the logic of equivalence constituting a new 'political frontier between two opposed camps'.[10] While unemployed protests remained the target of criticism by the speaker, the articulation of terrorists as enemies that infiltrated and threatened Tunisia discursively shifted the antagonistic frontier from that between the authorities and the protesters to that between the enemy-terrorists and the Tunisian nation as a whole.

In addition, the construction of the 'terrorist-enemy' category served to create a new chain of equivalence between terrorism and the unemployed. This was done by producing both 'well-meaning but naïve' and 'ill-meaning and deviant' unemployed subjectivities. The below comment made by a security expert and former colonel on the unemployed protests in Dehiba in February 2015 provides an illustration of how Tunisian security experts, through the use of their authoritative position, intentionally or unintentionally contributed to the construct of the naïve unemployed subject who might have good intentions but can easily be misguided and deceived by terrorists. The protests in the town of Dehiba in Tataouine were the second unemployed mobilisation that became subject to the elites' intense criminalisation and policing in the name of the War on Terror. It should be noted that, in addition to the large scale of the Dehiba protests and the escalation of tensions between the protesters and the security forces, the establishment of the Ennahda and Nidaa Tounes coalition government in February 2015 might have played as an important political context in bringing together various competing elite groups to condemn the unemployed protesters.

> The severe blows that the terrorists experienced because of the army and security made them try to do anything that would restore their presence and achieve the outcomes they seek, such as provoking the 'creative' chaos in which the south is currently living, [...] some of the local people are deluded and do not realise this reality, and they are paid for a living without knowing what that lobbying money for smuggling and terrorism seeks.[11]

In an interview with the news channel *Hakaekonline*, the security expert framed the protest events in Dehiba as 'the south' with reference to 'creative chaos', which is a term often used in Arab countries to refer to the 'US-Israeli conspiracy' to weaken Arab countries by promoting democracy. With these negative connotations, the specific conditions based on which the Dehiba protests had occurred as well as their demands disappeared, and the protests were constructed as being suspicious and dangerous. Further, by using an assertive tone, these negative descriptions of the protesters were constructed as if they were objective facts rather than the speaker's assumption or opinion. The use of 'expert tone'[12] to strengthen their authoritative position was one of the recurring rhetorical tactics found in the speech acts of Tunisian security experts, whose discursive effect not only re-contextualised unemployed protests but also rejected the protesters' agency. The re-construction of the protest events in Dehiba was then used for framing the protesters as 'local people who do not realise the reality' and being 'deluded' by terrorists and 'paid for a living', without being aware that terrorists were exploiting them. Again, the construction of the naïve protester subject position served to subjectify the speaker as being knowledgeable and qualified to diagnose what was 'really' happening, establishing a hierarchical relation of power between the experts and protesters. Discursively, the elites' subjectification of the unemployed as naïve served to identify them as being vulnerable to terrorism and to manipulation for other political interests, even if their initial intention and modes of protest were legitimate.

With this well-meaning but naïve subject position, unemployed protesters were also often constructed as colluding with terrorists and therefore being ill-meaning and deviant. In particular, the protesters in the border areas were frequently subject to the accusation that they fabricated protests in the name of employment, but actually helped terrorists cross the borders. For instance, Habib Essid who served as prime minister in 2015 described the unemployed protests in Medenine and Tataouine located near the border with Libya as 'fabricated' with the intent to facilitate smuggling and terrorism, giving the impression that the protesters intentionally helped terrorists commit crimes:

> Regarding the protests in the southern regions and Haoudh Al-Manjimi, as well as the recent social tension in Kebili governorate, Essid revealed that many protests in the border areas in the two governorates Medenine and Tataouine were fabricated to cover up the smuggling of weapons and to allow the passage of terrorists after the security force's commitment to calm the security situation and maintain public facilities, and this is what has been proven by the security investigations.[13]

Instead of being framed as passive agents that were misguided, the unemployed protesters living in the border areas were constructed in Essid's speech as active agents, through the use of the action verbs 'to cover up' and 'to allow'. Although the speaker did not explicitly equate the protesters with terrorists, his description of the protesters as intentionally helping smugglers and terrorists blurred the boundary between these two different subjects, leaving the audience with the suspicion that the protesters in the border areas might be colluding with terrorists and, thus, might also be terrorists. As with the case of the naïve protester subject, this 'deviant and might-be terrorist' subjectivity was constructed in relation to the state subject as being well-informed with knowledge about the protests and terrorist activities in the South. While the speaker did not provide any concrete information regarding the 'terrorists' and the 'weapons' purportedly within Tunisia, their presence was constructed as if it were an objective fact, through a hierarchy of knowledge between the state and the audience, as epitomised by Essid's claim that 'this is what has been proven by the security investigations'.

Interestingly, these two supposedly contrasting natures of unemployed protesters, as naïve and deviant subjects, were reconciled with each other in the elites' securitising speech practices, through the construction of the categories of good and bad protesters. In most cases, protesters were not directly labelled as terrorists. Instead, their speeches created a category of strange, suspicious and deviant individuals among protesters, whose goal was to instigate otherwise peaceful and innocent citizens to violence, to cause chaos and carry out terrorist attacks, casting 'reasonable doubt' that any protesters might fall under these suspicious/threatening categories. In Laclau's terms, the construction of the two contrastive categories of the unemployed served as a logic of difference through which the unemployed subject as a collective identity was broken down into 'contrasting' segments of the unemployed with their own 'particularities'.[14] The below comment of Mohamed Fadhel Ben Omran, a former head of Nidaa Tounes, on the unemployed protests in Southern Tunisia provides a clear example of how the negative category of unemployed protesters was constructed and set against the positive one:

> I am really afraid of the situation in my country, because Daesh is only a few kilometers away from the Tunisian border. There is the possibility that these events [the unemployed protests] become a pulse for the extremist terrorist groups […] The general opinions in the South and Kebili governorate are against violence, burning the [police] station and attacks on public institutions. Strange individuals who are not living in the governorate were observed among the protesters, […] unknown and strange parties blocked the road and prevented the deputy from meeting the [local] families.[15]

What is notable about the speaker's claim is that it established two contrasting categories of unemployed protesters, in which normal and abnormal protesters emerged. The positive category of protesters with the descriptive reference 'against violence, burning and attacks' was set against the negative one marked by those who 'blocked the road', by framing the latter as unknown and strange parties that attempted to prevent any peaceful resolutions from taking place. The portrayal of the former as 'general opinions' and of the latter as 'strange individuals' further enhanced the antagonistic distance between peaceful and violent protesters by attributing the legitimate characteristic to peaceful protesters. This way of breaking down the unemployed subject into contrasting sub-identities followed the logic of difference that unsettled the tie among unemployed protesters, whose modes of protesting varied from hunger strike to more radical and directly disruptive acts such as blocking roads, thereby weakening and displacing 'a sharp antagonistic polarity'[16] between the state and the protesters.

The above examples illustrate how the dominant securitising practices associated unemployed protesters with terrorism by drawing on the pre-existing discursive terrain of Islamist terrorism. Laclau and Mouffe's analytical tools help to elucidate what specific mechanisms operated in the process of such securitisation. First, the construction of Islamist terrorists as the enemy of Tunisians and the establishment of a chain of equivalence between terrorists and gullible and/or deviant unemployed protesters served to build the signifying narrative that naïve and deviant unemployed protesters contribute to terrorism. Second, the construction of this narrative also entails the logic of difference by which peaceful and violent categories of unemployed protesters are constructed and differentiated. This discursively weakened the antagonistic frontier between the unemployed protesters as a collective subject and those against whom they protested, while enhancing the antagonistic frontier between the Tunisians – peaceful protesters – and the enemy terrorists – unruly protesters. This way of dislocating the unemployed subject recurred in the elites' securitising speech acts.

Dangerous Unemployed Protests against Democracy-building

The first narrative, which posited that naïve and deviant unemployed protesters contributed to terrorism, was elaborated through the elites' use of another discursive terrain – that is, democracy. Their emphasis on a liberal notion of democracy constructed the protesters' 'unarmed violence'[17] as being incompatible with democratic values such as individual liberties and rights, rule of law, and belief in free and competitive elections. In particular, the elites' rhetoric was framed around the 'illegality' of violence committed by the protesters and the 'legality' of the state violence against protesters. This then facilitated a particular understanding of rule of law and citizen's liberties in which national security and protecting personal and public properties were presumed as the supreme values for democracy while mitigating the value of the constitutional rights claimed by the protesters. For instance, commenting on the Kasserine unemployed protests in January 2016 in a news interview, Ennahda's then Vice President Abdul Hamid Jalasi said:

> In the democratic system, the right to protest is guaranteed and legitimate. But, in the democratic system, it is also necessary to protect properties, public assets and state institutions […]. We must distinguish between peaceful civil protest guaranteed by the constitution and acts of vandalism and riot, because vandalism is unacceptable constitutionally politically and morally.[18]

According to the logic of democracy promoted by Jalasi, unemployed protesters had the right to protest for their right to work, but their rights needed to be exercised in accordance with the existing legislation and procedural understanding of democracy. Disruptive actions were described as no longer acceptable and deviant, based on the idea that Tunisia was now ruled by democratic institutions.

While the Ben Ali regime also often invoked democratic values to justify its rule in response to social mobilisations, the workings of the democracy discourse in post-uprising Tunisia needs to be distinguished from that of the authoritarian context. When it comes to the notion of the rule of law, a subtle but important change was made in terms of the question of 'how autonomy is problematised and opened up for intervention'.[19] Whereas under the Ben Ali regime the rule of law was invoked mainly to constrain or remove space for autonomy, the problem in the post-authoritarian political landscape in Tunisia became more about an 'excess of irresponsible autonomy',[20] as in the case of more advanced liberal democracies in the global North. In other words, the exercise of the state sovereign power in an authoritarian way did not disappear, but it became a constitutive part of democratising (and regulating) Tunisian society. The governmentality analytic is useful for explicating this changing function of the democracy discourse in Tunisia. It shows how the post-uprising regime's self-proclaimed commitment to the establishment of democracy with the continued domestic and external pressure expanded the role of the state and the function of the rule of law from the punishment of those challenging the regime to the 'regulatory'[21] management of resistance in the name of the people rather than of state sovereignty.

Army deployment at protest sites and arbitrary detention were among the various 'pre-emptive' measures in the name of the rule of law, as instrumentalised in the association of the unemployed subject with terrorism.[22]

Any forms of disturbance or petty crimes committed by certain individuals during protests were easily termed terrorist or terrorist-like acts, rendering them a sort of quantifiable evidence of the great threat of terrorism. The most notable example of the deployment of the rule of law to govern unemployed protests, however, can be found in the ways in which the state of emergency operated in the post-uprising context. The imposition of a state of emergency in Tunisia was not an extraordinary measure that resulted from the success of securitising speech acts, as the Copenhagen School theorises. As of 2017, the most recent state of emergency had been in place in Tunisia since November 2015, following an attack on the Presidential Guard in Tunis. However, it was only during a short period of time (from March 2014 to July 2015 and from October 2015 to November 2015) that Tunisia had *not* been under a state of emergency since 2011. Rather than being in contradiction to each other, Tunisia's democratisation process coexisted with a prolonged state of exception. From a governmentality perspective, the creation and management of exceptions is an essential component of the neoliberal attempt 'to govern free individuals'.[23] The exercise of domination since 2011, in this sense, was closely linked to the neoliberal governing intended to nurture autonomous and self-responsible citizens.

While the necessity of a state of emergency in Tunisia during this period was framed around the threat of terrorism and the importance of the War on Terror, a key concern regarding its implementation was the unemployed protests, as explicitly expressed by then Prime Minister Habib Essid in a parliamentary meeting in July 2015. In this meeting, he discussed the possibility of declaring a state of emergency, based on the justification that social mobilisations were disrupting the efforts of the security forces to win the War on Terror; therefore, they needed to be limited through emergency measures.[24] A week after this meeting, then President Essebsi approved a state of emergency and justified it as a necessary measure given the instability caused by strikes and social movements.[25] As indicated in the excerpt below, the purpose of a state of emergency with regard to unemployed protesters was framed around the necessity of nurturing (rather than banning) the protests which otherwise might cause damage to properties and contribute to terrorism:

Interviewer: How do you see the movement that is happening now? Is it a second revolution?

Moro: The demands made by the protesters are legitimate. They have been waiting for the answers for years, especially the unemployment of university graduates, which is rising by large numbers. [...] Everyone stresses the need to overcome the difficulties and to respond to the demands of the Tunisian people, but not at the expense of the stability of the country, because the chaos will cause disruption and even open the door to the infiltration of terrorists.

Interviewer: Is this not an excuse to intimidate citizens by claiming its [unemployed mobilisation] rights, which it described to be legitimate?

Moro: Mobilisations on the street can begin, but they need to be nurtured, and no one can mobilise a large number of protesters and guarantee them not to be exploited by terrorists. I have warned that many of those who mounted the wave of protests are criminals.

Interviewer: Have the authorities done well by declaring a state of emergency?

Moro: The state must protect individual and collective property. Many criminals have taken advantage of the chaos. Given that our army and police are in the fight against terrorism, I think it is difficult to secure all areas, and that is why the state of emergency was announced, to guarantee stability.[26]

The *Assabah* news interview with Abdel Fattah Moro, a former deputy speaker of the parliament and the head of Ennahda, came amid increasing tensions between the unemployed protests organised in Kasserine and the security apparatus in January 2016. When asked about his view on the Kasserine mobilisations, Moro first positioned himself as a supporter of the protesters' right to work, by describing it as a 'legitimate' demand that had to be addressed urgently. However, with the use of the conjunction 'but', the protesters' actions were soon framed as 'chaos' that threatened the stability of the country. Further, he discursively linked the Kasserine unemployed mobilisations to terrorism, in that he framed the chaos as having the potential of opening the 'door to the infiltration of terrorists'. Rather than rejecting the legitimacy of the unemployed protest as such, this articulation was founded on his distinction between the protesters' legitimate demands and their illegitimate modes of actions. In Foucauldian terms, his association of the unemployed with terrorism was involved in the neoliberal governing by which to govern the protesters through their capacities for 'regulated freedom'.[27] This is marked by his claim that mobilisations can happen, but that they need to be 'nurtured' in order to guarantee 'stability'. In this context, the function of a state of emergency became less about countering terrorism as such, and more about protecting a capitalist way of life by regulating and guiding the conduct of the unemployed protesters.

Moro's invocation of exceptions to guide the behaviours of the protesters shows how the neoliberal notion of democracy operated hand in hand with the construction of exceptions in Tunisia. Interestingly, his immediate response to the question of the necessity of a state of emergency revolved around 'property' rather than rights, democracy or even stability. This rationality echoes Foucault's view on liberal democracy, which posits that it not only requires maintaining the 'normal everyday frame' through the creation of exceptions, but that it also actively uses the emergency to criminalise those challenging the neoliberal power structure (the unemployed protesters, in this particular case) by which to 'secure and extend the power of corporations and the control of capital'.[28] The state of emergency in Tunisia did not directly thwart 'ordinary' protests. Rather, it first and foremost served to create conditions for a 'new normal' in which exceptional measures could operate not as exceptions but as the *rule*.[29] Exceptional measures such as the declaration of a curfew were then deployed against stigmatised subjects, including unemployed protesters, blurring the distinction between them and terrorism.

During the 2016 Kasserine protests, a curfew was declared after the anger of many unemployed youths exploded following the death of Ridah Yahyaoui, an unemployed graduate in Kasserine who committed suicide after discovering that his name had been deleted from the list of unemployed graduates to be hired in the public sector. In this context, the emergency measure, rather than stopping unemployed youths from mobilising, operated to set a limit to and control the scope of their actions. The authorities' illegalisation of night protests was then used by media commentators to discursively link the unemployed protests to terrorism, as illustrated in this quote from a news article published by *Attounissia*:

> Considering its deviation from the natural course and the presence of destructive and criminal parties entering the previously peaceful movements of the unemployed youths of the marginalised class in Kasserine, was the wave of the recent protests in the country, albeit legitimate given their demands for development and work, pre-planned to open up an opportunity for the infiltration of terrorists from neighbouring countries, particularly from Libya? Numerous readings of the events indicate that the acts of vandalism and looting that affected several public properties were not spontaneous [...] given the high number of those who attacked public and sovereign institutions. [...] This indicates that these groups were already ready to carry out riots and looting. [...] The evidence would be their determination to violate the curfew law.[30]

In describing the Kasserine unemployed protests, the speaker discursively associated them with terrorism, with reference to the 'curfew law'. What is notable here is that, instead of directly equating the protests with terrorism, the speaker highlighted the destructive and criminal characteristics of the previously peaceful and legitimate unemployed protests. While a positive category of protest is constituted by a choice of words such as 'legitimate', 'natural course' and 'peaceful', the general tone and focus of the text indicates that these positive words function to emphasise the negative category of protest, as marked by delegitimising language such as 'criminal', 'terrorists', 'vandalism' and 'looting'. This negative category of protests was distinguished from the positive one through the portrayal of the former as a 'pre-planned' infiltration of terrorists into previously peaceful protests. More interestingly, the contrasting relationship between peaceful and dangerous protests constructed by these lexical choices became vague and equivocal through the framing of the violation of the curfew law as the indicator based on which a protester can be labelled either a rightful protester or a terrorist suspect. The effect of blurring the distinction between protesters and terrorists in reference to the curfew, from the governmentality perspective, is that it demarcated the boundaries as to what were, and what were not, legitimate forms of unemployed mobilisation. In the case of the state of emergency, the invocation of the curfew for categorising modes of protest as either legal or illegal shows how these exceptions operated not as a mere suspension of the rule of law, but rather as an instrument of the law or its 'periphery' through which particular modes and tactics of protest (night protests, in this case) became subject to '"illegal" policing operation for "law" enforcement'.[31]

Even in the absence of a publicly declared state of exception, the War on Terror formed one of the 'different loci of decision on what constituted the exception'[32] rendering state violence against unemployed protesters as normal and legitimate. The anti-terrorism legislation in Tunisia, in this sense, discursively served to normalise a state of emergency, or what Giorgio Agamben has called a 'zone of indistinction'[33] between law and exception. The comment below made by a former Interior Ministry spokesman, Mohammad Ali Arawi, shows how the security apparatuses deployed their expert positions with reference to the War on Terror in order to justify the exceptional measures marked by the use of police violence, shifting the responsibility for violence away from the police and towards unemployed protesters. This statement came right after the police had fired guns at the protesters in the town of Dehiba in the governorate of Tataouine in February 2015, killing Sabri Milyan, a twenty-year-old unemployed man, and injuring several unemployed protesters.

The use of violence by the security forces was to repel the attacks of some unknowns to storm the headquarter of the border guard battalion in Dehiba. The security forces tried to prevent the burning of the centre by all means to repel any infiltration of terrorist groups from Libya to Tunisia or vice versa. What is happening is very dangerous and threatens national security. The protests in the region led to the burning of all security offices and the National Guard on Saturday.[34]

In his comment on the death of Milyan caused by the security forces, Arawi portrayed the police violence against the protesters as a necessary pre-emptive action to prevent terrorist attacks, with exaggerated terms such as 'very' dangerous and 'all' security offices. According to him, the security forces were forced to use violence to defend themselves, and they were the victims of the protesters' act of violence. Through his truth claim, the excessive deployment of security forces and a random police house raid – which, according to a report published by an independent committee investigating the Dehiba event, occurred a day before the violent confrontation – was muted.[35] The exercise of police violence at the sites of unemployed protest in Tunisia was not simply an authoritarian tool. From the governmentality approach, the police's exercise of armed violence against the protesters' unarmed violence in Dehiba operated as a technique of *democratic* rule, by demarcating what are and what are not acceptable acts in conformity with procedural democracy[36] and by regulating unemployed protesters' actions that 'deviate from formal democratic procedures'.[37]

Unemployed Protests and Terrorism are Obstacles to Economic Development

Building on the first and second narratives that link unemployed protesters to terrorists, the last signifying narrative performed through the dominant securitising practices renders terrorism and protests as two key obstacles to stability, democracy and development. In doing so, they drew on market-driven economic development as their discursive terrain in which the market was constructed as the only available model for development in Tunisia, while other possible alternatives were excluded. In particular, investments from domestic and international businessmen, entrepreneur mentality and private-sector-driven initiatives were seen as the necessary step towards economic progress and social well-being. Whether intentional or not, the elites reproduced the assumed causal relationship between these market mechanisms, on the one hand, and job creation and regional development, on the other. This neoliberal logic, which in practice functions to naturalise 'a reserve of unemployment' from a Foucauldian understanding, was drawn to reject the state's direct intervention in the economy and to idealise the role of the state as a facilitator for investment and production, as indicated in the excerpt below. This text is part of a lengthy interview by *Attounissia* with a member of the People's Assembly for the Ennahda party, Moez Bel Haj Rhouma, regarding an upsurge of unemployed mobilisations in January 2016. Having served as chairman of the Employment and Investment Committee in the governorate of Nabeul, he was also a businessman who owned three industrial firms reportedly employing more than 800 workers in Nabeul. When asked his opinion about the protests and the state's solutions to resolve the problem of unemployment, Rhouma responded as follows:

> I understand these protests as chairman of the Employment and Investment Committee. I have held many meetings with youth groups, especially those unemployed in Nabeul. We try hard so that every meeting can give hope to them and make every effort to support them, so that they can launch small projects. […] Of course, it is necessary to develop radical solutions, but not through the public sector. Unfortunately, the state today is no longer capable of operating the public sector. Today, the public sector is 2.5 or 3 times of that of world average. Let me give you an example. […] Today, a big portion of the state budget, more than 40 per cent was allocated to the public sector […] which is catastrophic. The conclusion is that the state is no longer the incubator that absorbs university graduates, nor the vocational training centre for their employment, except for some sectors such as the military or the security forces to counter terrorism. In my view, the state needs to provide a climate for investment and employment. […] The state is no longer able to build factories and employ citizens. The evidence is that the state has given away many institutions and factories, and building and running factories and employing young people have become the tasks of the private sector.[38]

By choosing the title 'Chairman of Employment' instead of others, such as businessman or member of the Ennahda party, Rhouma projected himself as an expert who possessed good knowledge about the issue of employment. The additional information about 'many meetings', marked by terms such as 'every effort' and 'support', also gives the sense that he was well-aware of the reality of unemployed youth, as well as of what they needed and wanted, and he was working hard to address the unemployment problem. Such expert-activist position conveys the idea that what he claimed was an objective and realistic prescription coming from someone deeply concerned about the unemployed youth. Yet, the rest of his interview revolved around his key argument that young people's voluntary participation in private sector businesses was *the* solution to the problem of unemployment. To build this argument, he first highlighted the public sector's inability to serve as engine for employment, by using a mixture of factual information and negative connotations. He mentioned the budget required to maintain public employees to emphasise the magnitude of the financial burden. He also supported his value claim that the state must remain a facilitator rather than a leading actor in the process of economic development, by framing the privatisation of public assets and services as 'evidence' of the state's inability to employ young people. This rhetoric rendered his prescription of 'letting the private sector do its job' unavoidable and inevitable.

This minimalist model of the state was particularly emphasised in 2014 under the technocrat government, which was then followed by the Ennahda and Nidaa Tounes coalition government in 2015. Interestingly, as this 'facilitating' role of the state was proven ineffective in terms of boosting investments and reducing unemployment, the responsibility for these failures was directed away from the state and towards the unemployed mobilisations and terrorism. The following statement from the same interview illustrates how the unemployed protests, which resulted from the lack of distributive economic policies and uneven development, were construed as reason for the lack of economic development:

> The state needs to provide infrastructure in the interior areas of Kasserine, Sidi Bouzid, El Kef, Jendouba, Siliana, Tataouine and other governorates, which have been marginalised throughout history, marginalised from the development plans during the era of Bourguiba or Ben Ali, [...] but we must not forget what the country has gone through in 2013 and 2014. That was mobility paralysis, as a result of protests and sit-ins, especially at the company in Gafsa, in addition to the blow to the tourism sector, especially after terrorism arrived in Tunisia in a new style. [...] For sure, the people who came out to demand their right to work are sincere in their demands and peaceful. However, we must be aware that, whenever there is social tension created by certain organisations or people, there are some parties that are involved [...] including terrorist gangs that seek to inflame Tunisia's current situation in order to create a security vacuum and repeat what happened in 2011. [...] Therefore, those who target us by burning are firstly smuggling gangs, secondly deviants and thirdly terrorist groups, which are the greatest danger threatening Tunisia.[39]

His description of the interior regions as marginalised in the development plans, combined with the suggestion to supply infrastructure to these regions, built a solidarity claim, giving the impression that the speaker and the protesters in the marginalised regions share an urgent need for the state to provide those areas with employment and development. By associating the regional marginalisation with the 'era of Bourguiba or Ben Ali', he also separated the post-uprising from the pre-uprising regime. His solidarity claim and his separation between the pre- and post-uprising regimes (re)created and stabilised the particularities and differences of each regime. This discursively subverted the equivalential chain between the two regimes, as it had been based on the unemployed protesters' claim that the current regime was exactly the same as the previous one in terms of its neoliberal socio-economic agendas. Likewise, the state's responsibility to provide infrastructure was re-contextualised through the association of the unemployed protests with terrorism, so as to establish a victim image for the state and a perpetrator image for the protesters. By using the conjunction 'in addition to', the protesters and terrorism are placed on the same level as the main causes that impeded the efforts of the state to develop their regions; thus, the protesters, previously projected as victims of marginalisation, were now constructed as those who contributed to the deteriorating economy.

While the above interview illustrates the role of the state as the guarantor and facilitator of market capitalism in an abstract way, the following excerpt provides an example of what the ruling elites often meant by 'creating a favourable climate for investment and employment'. This statement was made in July 2015 by the Tunisian Association for Governance, a civil society organisation led by Nidaa Tounes party member and economist Moez Joudi, to support the Economic Reconciliation Bill initiated by President Essebsi and intended to pardon the businessmen involved in financial crimes under the Ben Ali regime.

> The deterioration of the economic and financial situation in Tunisia [is] due to several factors, perhaps most notably terrorism and social protests, in addition to the reluctance of the most important economic actors, especially business owners, management and banks, to take initiative or to make decisive decisions for fear of prosecution, makes it urgent to decide on the president's initiative regarding economic and financial reconciliation and to bring it into force as soon as possible, to serve as gateway to a comprehensive process of national reconciliation. This process will improve the business climate and drive investment and regional development towards growth.[40]

While 'terrorism and social protests' emerged as the main obstacles to the economy through the additive paratactic relation, the focus of his statement was directed at the business sector's 'fear of being prosecuted' as the main issue that needed to be addressed for economic development. The clause 'the reluctance […] for fear of prosecution' indicates that the possibility of being prosecuted under the corruption charge was impeding the capacity of businessmen to boost the economy. Combining this latter cause with terrorism and protest by using the expression 'in addition to' discursively establishes an interesting relationship of hierarchical equivalence between the three causes. These three elements are constructed as equivalent when it comes to their negative impact on the economy, conveying the idea that the fear of the corruption charge was as harmful as terrorism and protests, and therefore had to be addressed urgently. With the attribution of positive qualities to the bill, such as to 'improve the business climate' and 'drive investment and regional development', the speaker's expert position as an economist and his authoritative voice are also marked by the future simple tense 'will'; hence, providing amnesty to corrupt businessmen is projected as an inevitable and urgent solution for economic development. Joudi's reasoning was shared by the majority of politicians within Nidaa Tounes and Ennahda, as indicated by the fact that this bill was eventually passed by parliament in September 2017, with 117 deputies' votes in favour of the bill. Selim Azzabi, then President Essebsi's chief of staff, for instance, asserted in parliament that this law would 'liberate the energies [of government to] restore investment and get the wheels of the economy turning'.[41] After the bill had been approved, Rachid Ghannouchi also said that the voting result reflected 'Islamic virtues of forgiveness and tolerance'.[42]

The Unemployed as Self-governable and Entrepreneurial Citizen

We have seen how the ruling elites' association of unemployed protests with terrorism based on their construction of the naïve and/or deviant subject position of the unemployed served to encourage protesters to exercise their political freedom in particular ways. An analysis of the dominant securitising practices also indicates that disciplining and policing unemployed protests through their notion of the rule of law (and the rule of exception) were 'implicated in a more general logic of neoliberal subjectification' of the unemployed as free but self-disciplined and vigilant citizen.[43] The free but self-regulatory protester subjectivity was promoted through the construction of the unemployed as rightful, but whose rights can be heard only if and when their modes of action remain lawful. Also, in the context of the War on Terror, the boundary of what was legal and what was illegal was often determined based on 'expert knowledge' produced by various security professionals.

As Louiza Odysseos has pointed out in her analysis of *homo juridicus* as part of neoliberal governmental technologies, the language and framework of rights often 'regulate freedom' and 'displace prior lexicons and frameworks, such as revolution, wealth redistribution and structural change', in order to (re)shape individuals as mature subjects in conformity with a new political, economic and social system.[44] This type of 'structural ontogenesis'[45] is also found in the ways in which the Tunisian elites (re) deployed the language of revolution in order to mitigate the unemployed protesters' revolutionary motivations and goals. In a media interview, for instance, former President Essebsi fragmented the notion of revolution into two sub-categories, in which 'good' and 'bad' categories of revolution emerged, and these, in turn, served to mitigate the tension between unemployed protesters and the authorities:

> The Tunisian revolution has not yet achieved its main demands, dignity and work. It is never possible to imagine dignity without guaranteeing the right to work. [...] But there were those who tried to hijack this protest movement and spread terrorism. And there are also those [who] tried to employ this protest by adopting the speech that talks about 'the second revolution' or completing 'the revolutionary path' that started on 14 January 2011. This discourse is political and not realistic. The current political system is a democratic and elected one, and this system cannot be overthrown, except through elections.[46]

In this interview, Essebsi shaped the first category of the (Tunisian) revolution as a process to achieve dignity and work. As marked by his appropriation of the protesters' slogan 'no dignity without work', this positive category of revolution was rendered as 'our' – that is, the 'Tunisian' – revolution. And he implicitly positioned himself as part of 'our' revolution by taking the slogan as his own value claim, establishing a relationship of solidarity between himself and the unemployed protesters. Having acknowledged the incomplete nature of the revolution for dignity and work, however, he repudiated the protesters' demand for a second revolution and for the completion of the revolutionary path by categorising it as 'political' and 'unrealistic'. By using the adversative conjunction 'but', he juxtaposed his solidarity with the protesters within 'our' revolution against the protesters described as those who tried to hijack and exploit the protest, thereby creating the category of an illegitimate revolution (the second revolution). The construct of the two categories of revolution thus re-subjecified the protesters as citizens of a 'democratic and elected' political system where dignity and decent work can only be achieved through procedural democracy.

Also, the desirability of conducting others and the self revolved around a liberal notion of 'citizen' who is responsible for the well-being of the country, for being vigilant and for cooperating with the security apparatus in the context of the War on Terror. From the perspective of governmentality, the elites' subjectification of unemployed protesters as patriotic and vigilant citizens can have the effect of regulating the protesters to behave as 'liberal police'[47] who voluntarily join and participate in daily surveillance and sanctions for the purposes of the development and security of the country (thereby becoming part of the governmentalisation of society). The excerpt below illustrates how this particular notion of citizenship was employed to (re)construct and regulate the conduct of unemployed protesters.

[The] citizen is an active partner in the process of development by means of pressure and contribution, not burning and sabotage. [...] The security responsibility is entrusted to all of us, to prevent the recurrence of the terror machine which seeks to continue this situation and attacks the security centres to relieve the pressure on smugglers, bandits and armed terrorist groups, [...] all of which require firm vigilance and support for the security and military establishments, because development and security are two parallel tracks in the process of achieving the objectives of the revolution.[48]

The above statement belongs to Amna Mansour Al-Qarawi, president of the Democratic Movement for Building and Reform party, in response to the protests organised by Kasserine's unemployed youth in January 2014, against the new budget law and the following violent confrontation with police forces. In the first sentence, a category of 'citizen' emerges as an active partner in the process of development. The term 'active partner' is then used to demarcate which actions are civil and which are not: pressure and contribution are constructed as 'civil', while burning and sabotage (the elites' common description of unarmed violence exercised by unemployed youth) are narrated as 'uncivil'. Thus, the construction of an adversarial relationship between civil and uncivil operates to encourage protesters, who want to be seen as civil, to behave in accordance with the given category of citizen and to reject actions that are categorised as uncivil. Secondly, the War on Terror is constituted as the context in which all Tunisian citizens are bound to live, requiring them to take responsibility for national security. By describing terrorists as persons who want to exploit unemployed protests, the speaker constructs the threat of terrorism as another rationality based on which protesters were to behave in the sites of protest. Protesters are encouraged to remain aware of the terrorist threat and therefore to be vigilant, in order to prevent terrorists from exploiting any moment of instability during their protests. Instead of being unwillingly and passively policed, they are encouraged to be actively cooperating with and supporting the security apparatus – in other words, behaving like the police while protesting against the authorities.

The regulation of individuals' conducts takes the form of a 'structural ontogenesis' that shapes their subjects and integrates them 'into *new structures* that allow for their better (in the sense of less direct and cost-effective) government'.[49] Several Foucauldian scholars have considered the individualisation of social problems (such as unemployment) as a key feature in advanced western societies.[50] An analysis of the securitisation of the unemployed in Tunisia shows how the self-responsible and entrepreneurial unemployed subject position is promoted in non-Western contexts as well. In addition to promoting the image of a new democracy that protects political rights and empowers its citizens, the governing elites projected Tunisia as a new actor on the global market. Accordingly, Tunisia's economic development and democracy are dependent on as well as contributing to the global market, and the state needs to act as a facilitator of economic development. Notable in this development logic is that the responsibility for the failure to achieve the *goals* of development is shifted onto unemployed protests and/or terrorism. Building on the promotion of the patriotic and self-governable democratic citizen subject position of the unemployed in the context of the War on Terror, shifting the responsibility to the unemployed operated as a way to encourage unemployed individuals to conduct themselves as pro-active and entrepreneurial citizens. In the remainder of this section, I will look at how the unemployed became subject to neoliberal attempts at producing entrepreneurial citizens on the global market.

The below comment belongs to Jalasi, Ennahda's then vice president, on the Kasserine unemployed protests in January 2016. It provides an exemplary narrative of how the economic logic which posits that boosting the private sector and shrinking the public sector will automatically enhance the economy and enrich all Tunisians constructs the proactive and self-responsible citizen as ideal and necessary for the well-being of citizens. Within this economic logic, the promotion of the entrepreneurial citizen-subject operates to shape unemployed protesters who demand work as 'having some type of deficit that could be remedied through teaching and instruction'.[51]

> *Interviewer*: Was Tunisia the target of 'creative chaos' during recent protests, as some parties have confirmed?
>
> *Al Jalasi*: The country has gone through a difficult situation due to the protests, and some tried to employ and deviate from them, providing an incubator for terrorist acts to collapse the political process. [...]
>
> *Interviewer*: What practical solutions does Ennahda propose to solve the social crisis?
>
> *Al Jalasi*: The solution is political first, in the sense that political parties and major organisations must be convinced that they are interested in responding to the citizens' demands. Secondly, the solution is substantive in the sense that our country does not have great natural resources. Therefore, it must work to provide an attractive environment for domestic and foreign investment and encourage tourism, as well as international partners to invest in our country. The cultural solution is to convince [people] of the value of work and production and to encourage the culture of initiative in a society that for a long time has lived with the culture of the public sector, the mentality of the 'nail in the wall', fear of risk and waiting for the role of the state, which

exhausted and burdened the state because most ministerial budgets tend to [be used to] pay wages instead of going towards development. We also consider that the solution lies in educational reform, which builds a smooth and direct relationship between the course of education and the needs of the labour market.[52]

Firstly, the association of unemployed protests with terrorism appears in Jalasi's answer to the interviewer's question; in this context, he elaborates on 'creative chaos' as a situation in which some deviants intentionally exploited the unemployed protests for the purpose of committing terrorist attacks. More remarkable in this interview, however, is that the neoliberal logic of economic development serves to transform the 'mentality' of the unemployed so as to conform to the value of work and production. While the significance of the domestic elites to respond to the demands of the protesters (who are framed here as 'citizens') is highlighted, practical solutions are reduced to providing an attractive environment for investment and encouraging the values of production and entrepreneurship through cultural and educational means. With regard to the cultural dimension, he presents the 'culture of initiative' as ideal and positive, by attributing to it the 'value of work and production', while juxtaposing this value against the 'culture of the public sector'. The culture of the public sector is further elaborated on as lazy, irresponsible and incompetent, by using the Tunisian idiom 'a nail in the wall' which, in the Tunisian context, refers to the status of getting a monthly salary and preserving one's position while doing nothing – it is mostly used to pejoratively describe people working in the public sector. The desirability of work in the private sector is then linked to what he calls 'educational reform', which the speaker considers necessary to guide and train students so that they will be able to meet the needs of the labour market. By portraying the unemployed as being in need of help, encouragement, education and support by the state so as to be able to be a productive labour force, he discursively articulates being dependent on the state as a personal deficiency, while he applauds being dependent on the labour market as a mark of freedom.

Jalasi's evaluation of the unemployment problem and his prescription echo that of his fellow Ennahda member Rhouma who, while rendering the state the facilitator of a market-friendly enviroment, also claimed that 'we seek to change the mentality of Tunisian citizen and convince him that the public job is no longer able to help him to live and that further employment in the public sector is a sabotage of the state'.[53] According to their logic, the state's budget and efforts should not be given to employing more unemployed youth (except for employment in the police and military forces); instead, they need to be expended to *transform* and *restructure* the mentality of the unemployed, so that they can become independent of the state and be able to conduct themselves as autonomous and creative labour in micro-enterprises. The invocation of the values of work, productivity and entrepreneurship in post-2011 Tunisia did more than just project them as good and important values. The elites often drew on them in such a way as to create, regulate and make responsibilise those deemed to lack these qualities. This was also the case with the 2016–20 development plan produced by the government; in this plan, immediately after it acclaimed the values of work and production, the government pointed out that 'too many illegitimate protests' negatively contributed to a lack of productivity and development.[54]

The analysis of the dominant securitising practices throughout this chapter has shown that the association of the unemployed with terrorism was mobilised in the subjectification of the unemployed person as a 'worker in transit',[55] whose ways of thinking and behaving need to be modified to adapt the logic of the market and to maximise productivity. In this sense, the securitisation of the unemployed as a threat to national security, development and democracy, as well as the association of the unemployed with the value of work, did not merely aim to punish and marginalise problematic and deviant actors within unemployed protests. Rather, these securitising practices partly served to manage and govern unemployed protesters and, more generally, unemployed populations so as to become *homo oeconomicus*.[56]

Concluding Remarks

This chapter has discussed in great detail the ways in which the government, politicians, businessmen, security experts, as well as some of the 'independent' media discursively linked the unemployed mobilisations, particularly those in the interior regions, to terrorism. The dominant securitising practices analysed in this chapter suggest that they were not merely a re-utilisation of the authoritarian measures or the 'divide-and-conquer' technique deployed by the Ben Ali regime. Rather, it was a constitutive part of the neoliberal governing that regulates the conduct of the unemployed as self-helping and disciplined entrepreneurial citizens, in accordance with the norms of (neo)liberal democracy.

Throughout the democratisation process, civil society and human rights organisations expressed their concern over the possible return of authoritarian practices in the name of the War on Terror. That being said, they took an ambivalent position when it came to the securitisation of the unemployed. On the one hand, influential civil society actors (such as the UGTT and LTDH) explicitly criticised the government's excessive use of violence against unemployed protesters, calling for urgent action to address the problem of unemployment and the continued marginalisation of the interior region. On the other hand, their support of the protesters' demands was often accompanied by their strong condemnation of protesters' modes of action and the fear that they could be easily exploited by terrorists. For instance, when the Kasserine unemployed protests were evolving into a large-scale and cross-regional protest wave in January 2016, the UGTT Executive Office issued an official statement, part of which is as follows:

> [The UGTT] also called for the government to open constructive and serious dialogues and listen to the concerns of the people of Kasserine and other marginalised interior regions, stressing the importance of civil society's actual participation in the search for immediate, medium or long-term solutions. The Executive Office of the Labour Union urged the protesting youth to demonstrate in peaceful, civilised and organised ways, staying away from all forms of violence, destruction, damage to public and private property and disruption of activities. In the same context, it warned that terrorists and saboteurs are waiting for these opportunities and an attempt to exploit them and infiltrate them to divert the direction of the protests to sabotage, arson and murder, as well as to spread chaos, which is the most appropriate situation for terrorist activity.[57]

The UGTT's narrative is illustrative of how some civil society actors came to be involved in the 'management' of unemployed protesters by discursively linking them to terrorism. Also, the UGTT often (unwittingly) reified what it sought to denounce – that is, the state blaming socioeconomic protests as an obstacle to stability and economic development, by categorising the protesters' 'uncivil' modes of action not only as acts that damaged public and private property, but also as acts of disrupting production. Commenting on the unemployed protest organised against the Gafsa Phosphate Company in May 2016, for instance, former UGTT Assistant Secretary General Bouali Mubarki raised his concern over the possibility of the protest being exploited by terrorists and claimed that 'the protesters can protest, but they do not have the right to stop phosphate production', stressing 'the need for the Phosphate Company to return to the maximum level of production'.[58]

As the next chapters will show, many unemployed protesters felt that the discursive association of their protests with terrorism was the strategy of the state (and of the media colluding with the state) to prevent the possibility of sporadic unemployed protests from evolving into another revolutionary moment. If, as the protesters claimed, the authorities' construct of a causal link between the two distinct subjects was *intended* to direct public attention away from the cause and demands of unemployed protests and towards national security, it was not unsuccessful. Unemployed protesters' radical forms of action were to some extent mitigated by the invocation of the threat of terrorism, particularly in the period extending from two attacks on tourists in March and June 2015 to the end of that year. FTDES's report on the socio-economic protests also suggests that a significant decline in what it called 'random' protests in October 2015 was due to a fear of terrorists and their potential exploitation of social movements.[59] Yet, the dominant securitising practices to manage and direct the unemployed populations did not remain unchallenged. The following chapters will show how unemployed protesters as the securitised subject resisted the process of being securitised.

Notes

1. Interview with Abdul Ahmed, casual worker and independent unemployed protester, Kasserine, 3 February 2017.
2. The concept 'Islamist terrorism' has developed within studies on religious terrorism as a 'new' type of terrorism distinguished from the 'old' one in terms of its apocalyptic motivation, global organisational structure and, importantly, its potential of mass destruction. This so-called 'new terrorism paradigm' became increasingly popular with the emergence of the notion of the global War on Terror after 9/11. While the concept of the new terrorism is not limited to Islam, it has been predominantly used by politicians, security experts, academics and journalists to define, describe and counter Islamist organisations, such as Al Qaeda and Daesh. For more discussion on religious terrorism and new terrorism, see Rapoport, 'Fear and trembling'; Hoffman 'The confluence of international and domestic trends in terrorism'; Laqueur, *The new terrorism*.
3. Jackson, 'Constructing enemies', p. 402.
4. Ibid. p. 409.
5. For a discussion of Laclau and Mouffe's logic of equivalence and logic of difference, see Chapter 2.
6. *Assabah* is an example of several news outlets that operated as pro-regime media under the Ben Ali regime and have become independent and progressive media since 2011. For more information on the relationship between the Arab media and the state, see Owais, 'Arab media during the Arab Spring in Egypt and Tunisia'; Joffé, 'Government-media relations in Tunisia'.
7. Assabahnews, 'Istaghalu Inshghal al-Amni wa al-Jeysh bil-Tasdi li Ahdath al-Shaghab ... Tasalul 450 "Murtazqah" ila Tunis ... li Tanfid A'mal Irhabiyah!?'
8. Jackson, 'Constructing enemies', p. 408.

9. Foucault, *The Archaeology of Knowledge*, 49.
10. Howarth, 'Introducing discourse theory and political analysis', p. 11.
11. Hakaek, 'Hal Takun Ahdath Dhahbah Ghata' li Tahrib al-silahah ila Tunis?!'
12. Chiapello and Fairclough, ''Understanding the new management ideology'.
13. Hakaek, 'Fi Liqa' Jam'ah bihim S'aten: Essid Yunaqsh ma' al-Sahafeen 'Adeed al-Mlafat ... wa Yakshf 'an B'ad "al-Israr"'.
14. Howarth, 'Space, subjectivity, and politics', pp. 113–14.
15. Tuniscope, 'al-Fadl Ben Omran: Ahdath Qibali Jas Nabd min Qibal al-Jama't'.
16. Howarth, 'Introducing discourse theory and political analysis', p. 11.
17. The term 'unarmed violence' is used in this book to refer to protesters' use of improvised weapons such as throwing stones, or any (unarmed) actions deployed by protesters for causing social damage or disruption. While these actions are often described as 'non-violent' in social movement and protest studies, the distinction between non-violent action (as understood as non-disruptive) and unarmed violence is made here in order to take into account the different rationalities, calculations and effects that they involve. For a discussion of unarmed violence in protests, see Paret, 'Violence and democracy in South Africa's community protests'; Pressman, 'Throwing stones in social science: Non-violence, unarmed violence, and the First Intifada'.
18. For the entire interview, see Attounissia, 'Abd el Hamid el Jilasi (Naib el Ghanouch) li "Attunissia"'.
19. Kienscherf, 'Producing "responsible" self-governance', p. 178.
20. Ibid. p. 178.
21. Foucault, *The history of sexuality*, vol. 1, p. 144.
22. Han, 'Securitization of the unemployed and counter-conductive resistance in Tunisia'.
23. Dean, 'Liberal government and authoritarianism', p. 39.
24. Attounissia, 'Khubra' Yajiboun: Hal anna al-Auen lil I'elan al-Tawari'?'
25. Hakaek, 'al-Muhami Naaman Mazid li Essesi: Sayedah al-Rai's, al-Harb 'ala al-Irhab Taftard Aidan Rijel Harb'.
26. Assabahnews, 'Mourou: Nakhsh Idkhal Tunis fi al-Fauda ... walla A'taqid an Hunalik Hilal Sahriyah Anye lil-Mashakil'.
27. Rose and Miller, 'Political power beyond the state', p. 174.
28. Dean, 'Power at the heart of the present', p. 464.
29. Agamben, *State of exception*, p. 6; Dean, 'Power at the heart of the present', p. 464.
30. Attounissia, 'Hal Tafadat Tunis "al-Fauda al-Khalaqah"?'
31. Tosa, 'Anarchical governance', pp. 416, 421.
32. Dean, 'Power at the heart of the present', p. 470.
33. Agamben, *Homo sacer*, p. 41.
34. Babnet, 'al-Aroui: Ist'amal al-Quah Kana li Himeyah Maqr al-Hars al-Hudoudi al-Mukalif bi Man'a Tasalul al-Irhabeen'.

35. Assabahnews, 'Taqrir li Lajnah al-Tahqiq fi Ahdath al-Dhahbah: al-Ihtijajat Silmiyah wa Mashroua'ah wa Tariqah al-Ta'ati Kanat 'Anifa wa Ghair Mutanasibah'.
36. Oksala, 'Violence and neoliberal governmentality', p. 479.
37. Paret, 'Violence and democracy in South Africa's community protests', p. 119.
38. Attounissia, 'Mouz bil Haji Rouhmah "Ennahda" li "Attounissia": Barounat al-Tahrib Wara' al-Harq wa an Nahib'.
39. Ibid.
40. Hakaek, 'al-Jama'iyah al-Tunisyah lil Hukumah: Min Sha'n Mubadrah al-Masarah al-Eqtisadiyah al-Dfe'a bil-Istithmar wa Tanmiyah ... wa Lekin ...'
41. Financial Times, 'Tunisian parliament passes controversial economic reconciliation law'.
42. Ibid.
43. Binkley, 'Happiness, positive psychology and the program of neoliberal governmentality', p. 372.
44. Ibid. p. 763.
45. Ibid.
46. Assabahnews, 'El Beji: Lan Aourath Ibni ... wa Mutamasak bil-Sayed Rai'sa lil-Hukumah'.
47. Dean, 'Liberal government and authoritarianism'.
48. Attounissia, 'al-Harakat al-Dimoqratiah lil-Israh wa Bina' Tahadhr min al-Inzlaq fi Muraba'a al-'unf'.
49. Odysseos, 'Human rights, liberal ontogenesis and freedom', p. 762, emphasis added.
50. See, for instance, McDonald and Marston, 'Workfare as welfare'; Dean, 'Liberal government and authoritarianism'.
51. McDonald and Marston, 'Workfare as welfare', p. 386.
52. Attounissia, 'Abd al-Hamid al-Jilasi (Nai'b al-Ghanouch) li "Attunissia": Ennahda D'd Taghir Essa'id wa al-Intikhabaat al-Mubakrah'.
53. Attounissia, 'Mouz bil Haji Rouhmah "Ennahda" li "Attounissia": Barounat al-Tahrib Wara' al-Harq wa an Nahib'.
54. Ministry of Development Investment and International Cooperation, 'Mukhatit El Tanmiyah 2016–2020', p. 59.
55. Foucault, *The birth of biopolitics*, p. 139.
56. Odysseos, 'Human rights, liberal ontogenesis and freedom', p. 752.
57. Radiotunisienne, 'Itihad Shogul Yada'u il-Hukumah ila Itkhadh Ijra'at 'Ajilah'.
58. Alchourouk, 'al-Mubaraki Yaḥmal al-Hukumah Masuw'liya al-auda' fi Gafsa'.
59. Alchourouk, '81Taharoka iḥtijajiya shahr October al-ma'di fi 16 Wilayah'.

5

The UDC's Counter-securitising Practices

As I have discussed in Chapter 3, the UDC's visible role in the 2008 revolt in Gafsa and during the revolutionary moments in 2010 and 2011 placed it as an important player in the initial process of democratisation. While its influence on the actual policy-making decisions was limited, the UDC's revolutionary legitimacy and commitment to the problems of unemployment and social justice attracted a number of unemployed youths, after it had officially established an organisation for the unemployed in February 2011. Yet, its popularity as a national organisation representing the Tunisian unemployed population began to dwindle, particularly due to the perception that leftist political parties were controlling its agenda and activism. This chapter turns to the story of the UDC in the context of its decreasing popularity from 2013 onwards and of the elites' systematic association of the unemployed with terrorists. Despite its limited resources, the UDC still remained the sole organisation representing the interests of the unemployed. In particular, with its self-positioning as expert on the unemployment issue, it sought to challenge the ways in which the unemployed youth were securitised in the name of the War on Terror.

For the purposes of this book, I will focus on the ways in which UDC activists navigated the elites' association of the unemployed with terrorism. I do so by analysing whether they attempted to produce any alternative nodal point or meta-narrative to challenge that of the elites and, if so, to what extent the competing narratives constructed by the two parties were conflicting with one another and/or mutually constitutive. I will also assess to what extent the organisation reproduced and/or challenged the subjectivities promoted by the elites to conduct the conducts of the unemployed. The analysis shows that the organisation produced three counter-narratives re-appropriating the discursive terrains used by the elites. This process involved the association of those governing as terrorists, the dissociation of the UDC's struggle from terrorism and, finally, the re-articulation of unemployment as terrorism. I will highlight that the UDC's resistance to the process of being securitised entailed an ethical dimension of struggle – that is, a struggle to escape the given sub-jectivities and to re-define ways of governing the self. The UDC attempted to subjectify the unemployed as 'victim of Islamist terrorism' and 'victim of and revolutionaries against state terrorism'.

The UDC in the 'Post-Uprising' Context

> There has been ups and downs in the UDC's activism. Now it's weak because there's division within the UDC structure because of [its relationship to] political parties. There's tension within the structure of the organisation. The members who are connected to political parties say that the UDC is independ-ent, but it's connected to them. […] But the UDC doesn't fail because of its name. Even if the UDC is weak, even if the UDC cooperates with the regime, I need to be a part of the UDC in order to continue my revolutionary activism.[1]

The above comment made by a UDC activist, Chahed Mohamed, on the reality of the UDC after the Uprising suggests that its affiliation with political parties was not only a perception that undermined its legitimacy and representation of the unemployed population from outside, but also a factor that weakened the internal structure of the organisation. Yet, the UDC's controversial relationship with leftist political parties and its negative impact should be understood in relation to the organisation's 'undemocratic' decision-making process and the decreasing influence of the leftist forces in general from 2013 onwards.

From the very establishment of the UDC, it was no secret that leftist parties had close ties with the organisation, as the public could observe several joint statements and mobilisations. However, the left-wing image started to affect the UDC's reputation negatively after the Popular Front, a political front that incorporated nine leftist parties, established an *ad hoc* coalition with the Nidaa Tounes party during the Bardo Occupation against the Ennahda-led government. After Essebsi had established Nidaa Tounes in April 2012, the secular segments of Tunisian society witnessed a polarisation between revolutionary-minded leftist groups who strongly criticised his call as a return of the old regime and those who supported Nidaa Tounes, considering it a counter-weight to increasing Islamist influ-ence. The decision of the Popular Front to work with Nidaa Tounes under the banner of 'National Salvation Front' in July 2013 was for many activ-ists within the UDC a 'catastrophic' and unacceptable compromise that directly contravened the revolutionary process.[2] The UDC's executive board, however, officially announced its support for and participation in the NSF, ignoring inside voices against the coalition movement. This event and the following political reconciliation between Ennahda and Nidaa Tounes resulted in a decreasing popularity of the leftist political parties, while increasing the skepticism of many activists within the UDC regarding its revolutionary legitimacy. Also, it led some unemployed youths, who considered themselves apolitical but supported the UDC due to its role in the struggle for the right to work, to turn their back on the organisation.[3]

Another important factor that contributed to the UDC's decreasing popularity was the perception that it worked only for the employment of university graduates and marginalised those who did not have university degrees. While this negative perception is in part a reflection of the general distrust towards the organisation resulting from its involvement in the NSF campaign, its increasing focus on the employment of a group of university graduates who called themselves *Mafrouzeen Amniya* (in Tunisian dialect, 'those blacklisted by the Interior Ministry') in 2015 and 2016 amplified the image of the UDC as an organisation whose demands were exclusively for those with university degrees and leftist activists. Referring to those excluded from public-sector employment opportunities due to their political activities in the UGET under the Ben Ali regime, Mafrouzeen claimed that their struggle for jobs in the public sector was not just a narrow demand for its members, but one of the most important conditions for transitional justice.[4] The Mafrouzeen movement initiated its own online platform to publicise their hunger strikes and street activities in November 2015. However, because many UDC activists were also members of the movement, Mafrouzeen became one of the main issues covered on the UDC's official Facebook pages. The UDC attempted to articulate the Mafrouzeen problem as the broader demand for structural reforms around employment; however, pushing this issue in the absence of any tangible structural reforms achieved by its activism since 2011 led many unemployed youths without degrees to perceive it as impotent and selfish.[5]

As Mohamed's reflection on the UDC indicates, however, the importance and potential of the organisation in the unemployed struggle at large cannot be underestimated. After all, the UDC remained the only organised political force that constantly challenged the ruling elites' attempt to render the problem of unemployment less imperative than the consolidation of the democratic political system and to domesticate the unemployed resistance. The organisation sought to act as an expert on the unemployment issue through its active online and offline activities. More importantly, the fact that the UDC, thanks to its partnership with more resourceful civil society organisations, provided the protection and logistics necessary for street protests still encouraged many unemployed youths to maintain their ties to the organisation for purposes of protection. Although the post-uprising governments largely tolerated bottom–up challenges, political activists were still often subject to repression and intimidation if they did not belong to well-known civil society organisations. As Chapter 4 has elaborated, this was particularly the case when, in the context of the War on Terror, unorganised unemployed protesters performed radical forms of political action or raised slogans that implicitly or explicitly demanded regime change. Facing the elites' frequent association of unemployed protests with terrorism, the UDC, as the only national and legally accepted organisation for the unemployed, sought to play a significant role in resisting such articulation through its multiple forms of counter-securitising practices.

The UDC and Counter-terrorism

Counter-terrorism as such was not on the agenda of the UDC, but it was nevertheless an important concern of the organisation, given the perceived negative impact of the War on Terror on socio-economic protests organised by the unemployed. This is indicated in the fact that the number of the UDC's terrorism-related narratives on its Facebook pages dramatically increased in 2015, the year that witnessed two violent attacks on foreign tourists and one against the Presidential Guard. Its main concern was that the fear of terrorism and the imposition of emergency measures were operating against unemployed protesters. As illustrated in the below interview with Ahmed Murad, one of the UDC leaders in Tunisia's capital city, the motivation behind its intervention in the counter-terrorism discourse first and foremost rested in the organisation's awareness and critique of the state's attempts to securitise the unemployed through such discourse:

> The government is well aware that it cannot control the social movements, but it can delay their intifada [in Arabic, revolt or uprising], delay the unity of social movements. There are a number of tools... such as creating secondary problems, I mean, the fear of terrorism. This is one of the behaviours of the government. I am not talking about this government only, but all of them. They talk about fears and create discussion in the media to shut their eyes to the economic and social policies that they implemented.[6]

When asked about how the authorities had responded to unemployed mobilisations and their demands since the Uprising, Murad pointed to the 'fear of terrorism' as a tool utilised by the authorities to undermine the scale and influence of social mobilisations. According to him, the authorities' fear-mongering in the name of the War on Terror was also intended to distract from socio-economic policies that otherwise would face bottom–up resistance. Considering the UDC's active involvement in defending the political rights of the unemployed populations, as well as its vocal criticism of the elites' social and economic policies, Ahmed's view on the terrorism discourse, which was shared by most UDC activists interviewed, explains why the organisation's resistance against the dominant securitising practices became an important part of its struggle for work, freedom and social justice.

The elites' securitising practices not only became subject to the UDC's criticism, but they also affected the ways in which some radical activists within the organisation engaged with the unemployed struggle in the context of the War on Terror, as indicated in the below comment made by Mohamed. Elaborating on why he chose to remain within the organisation despite his view that it did not necessarily represent the unemployed populations at large, he noted:

> The reason is obvious. The regime will consider activists outside [civil society] organisations as terrorists terrorising institutions. You need an organisation that protects you from any security assaults or harassments, because if you lead a revolutionary movement, some organisations should exist to protect you, or provide lawyers and defenders for you.[7]

Mohamed was one of the UDC activists who presented themselves as revolutionaries 'distinguished' from the organisation's leaders and key members who, according to those revolutionaries, were partisan and in favour of gradual reforms rather than radical changes. Having been dissatisfied with the internal structure of the organisation, some of them chose to be part of it in order to protect themselves from the terrorist label. His narrative reflects how the subjectification of the unemployed as deviant and/or terrorist affected (and at the same time was resisted by) part of the UDC. They searched for a 'legitimate space' where they could exercise their political rights and challenge the regime with less worry about being charged under the anti-terrorism law and emergency measures.

More importantly, the UDC actively re-appropriated the dominant counter-terrorism discourse because terrorism, from the UDC's perspective, reflected the reality of the unemployed in Tunisia. It did so in the sense that 'terrorism, marginalisation and corruption' were 'closely related to each other, and there's no counter-terrorism without countering unemployment'.[8] Mohamed Salmi, a UDC activist in Gafsa, also noted that the organisation's position concerning the War on Terror can be represented by the following slogan: 'If you want to eliminate terrorism, then eliminate unemployment first'.[9] As elaborated in detail in the following sections, the governmentality approach helps us to interpret the UDC's resistance to the elites' securitising practices, not as a mere rejection of such securitisation, but as a form of counter-securitisation of the self, in which it resisted the process of neoliberal governing of the unemployed so as 'not to be governed *like that*, by that, in the name of those principles'.[10] The UDC activists produced counter-narratives to alter the meaning of counter-terrorism and counter-subjectification of the self, some of which were not external to the securitising practices performed by the elites.

The Elites are Behind the Rise of Islamic Extremism

The first counter-narrative produced by the UDC posits that those governing are responsible for terrorism due to their role in the rising Islamist extremism. In building this narrative, the activists used a logic of equivalence to identify the state with the increasing influence of Islamic ideology, by framing the state as not only incapable of countering but also encouraging terrorism in Tunisia. Remarkable in this narrative is that, in the process of resisting the dominant securitising practices through their alternative signifier, the UDC deployed the discursive terrain of Islamist terrorism elements which were also used in elites' speech and non-speech securitising acts. In most cases, the UDC activists presented terrorism as an objective fact that began to emerge after the Uprising and terrorists as those motivated by extreme Islamic ideology and travelling to Syria or attacking state institutions, reproducing the elites' truth claim of 'the inevitable threat of Islamist terrorism'.

The ambivalent location of the UDC in regard to its counter-securitising practices shows how its attempt to 'subvert' – in Laclau and Mouffe's sense – the meaning of counter-terrorism as constructed by the elites entailed a counter-conductive aspect in which their resistance was intrinsically connected to the rationalities and techniques of those governing. The following quote from an interview with Ahmed provides an exemplary narrative of how the UDC activists built a chain of equivalence between terrorism and the state, by utilising the discursive terrain of Islamist terrorism. After arguing that terrorism was one of the tools by which state institutions distracted public attention from the unemployed mobilisations, he was asked to what extent the terrorism discourse had affected public perception. He answered:

Even in the terrorism case, we should agree that we talk about Tunisia. Things might differ in other countries such as Western countries or Arab countries such as Syria or Libya. Tunisia has its unique conditions. In Tunisia, terrorism does not operate isolated from the state. This means that we will find, if we open real investigation, we will find the state guilty in one way or another, we will find a number of media guilty, we will find a number of individuals, big capitalists, ministries and, on top of the list, the ministry of the interior guilty. In Tunisia, it is not possible for individuals, even if they have terrorist orientations, to practice terrorism out of sight of those organisations. They can't. They should find political protection from a ruling party [...] media and security coverage [protection]. Otherwise, he will not be able to do anything. Whoever thinks that it is possible in Tunisia that thousands can go to Syria without the knowledge of the ministry of the interior and without a political and security protection is an idiot. This is not feasible, it is impossible. You cannot smuggle arms in Tunisia without political protection.[11]

While Ahmed labels the threat of terrorism as one of the authorities' strategies to mitigate the influence of the unemployed protests, terrorism, at the same time, is framed as an objective fact. Also notable in his claim is the category of actions and characteristics on which he draws to define terrorists. He describes terrorism in general terms, as an issue that goes beyond the Tunisian context and exists in other places, too. By adding Western and Arab countries to the list of areas subject to terrorism, he implies that terrorism has become a global phenomenon and that Tunisia is part of it. What he means by terrorism is then elaborated through his portrayal of individuals who, so he considers, have the inclination to practise terrorism. According to him, terrorists are those who travel to Syria to participate in the civil war and smuggle weapons into Tunisia. This way of illustrating terrorism echoes the elites' narrative of the threat of terrorism in which global jihadi networks are portrayed as operating inside and outside of Tunisia. The importance of Ahmed's claim from the governmentality perspective is that the UDC's resistance to the elites' fear-mongering is 'implicated in the very relationships of the power it opposes', rather than a 'transcendence of government'.[12]

This does not mean that the UDC merely reified and justified the elites' construction of the threat of terrorism to govern the unemployed. As the body of the quote indicates, Ahmed's main target of criticism is not terrorists, but those governing the country, and this is found in the ways in which he associated the ruling elites with terrorists. His rhetoric builds such an association through the construction of the terrorist as a passive subject who cannot operate in their own capacity and, therefore, needs help and protection from the state, government ministries, media and businessmen. The impossibility of terrorists' presence on Tunisian soil without the 'approval' of the state is described as an undisclosed but real feature that distinguishes terrorism in Tunisia from that in other countries. This way of promoting the passive terrorist subject position accentuates his claim that the elites are responsible for the perceivably growing threat of Islamist terrorism.

Ahmed's narrative is indicative of how the UDC re-appropriated the dominant notion of terrorism used by the elites in the process of countering the elites' securitising practices. On the one hand, the fact that the UDC's counter-narrative is embedded in the discursive terrain (of global Islamist terrorism) used by the elites suggests that the discursive terrain of global terrorism partially conditioned the ways in which the elites and the UDC (and Tunisian society at large, as I have discussed in Chapter 3) thought of and acted on the other party. The post-uprising context in which both political and militant Islamic movements became increasingly visualised operated as a form of a 'possible field of actions'[13] that structured what the elites and unemployed protesters said and did, mitigating the antagonistic relationship between the two parties. Yet, the UDC worked on the notion of Islamist terrorism *strategically* (as the elites perhaps did) to delegitimise the other party. In particular, as reflected in the below Facebook post by the UDC, its most frequent target of criticism among the categories of elites was Ennahda, given its Islamic orientation and the allegation that it was closely involved in the Salafi movements that emerged right after the Uprising:

> Employment and development, the two burning issues of the people, are not of the concerns or interests of the Troika. All its concern is to ensure the seats of government and its continuation and control over the state, the sources of wealth and channels of money. All its interests are to plant its feet in the government and to transfer strange schemes to Tunisia and its people, which have brought into the country political crime and assassinations. Terrorism became a real thing in its era.[14]

This post was written in November 2013, when the 'Troika government', the Ennahda-led triple coalition government with two secular political parties, was still governing Tunisia, despite an upsurge of public criticism of Ennahda's inability to resolve the social and economic problems, as well as increasing security concerns in Tunisian society. Firstly, the UDC portrayed the Troika government as being indifferent to people's demands for employment and development and as desiring only political and economic power. It soon becomes clear that the target of the UDC's criticism is Ennahda, as the negative portrayal of the Troika is elaborated on by relating it to the two assassinations committed by radical Salafists against Leftist leaders in 2013. In doing so, 'real' terrorism – that is, the political violence carried out by Salafists – is constructed as the result of the 'strange schemes' that Ennahda purposely spread to the Tunisian people.

The following quote from an interview with Yousef Hamdi, an UDC activist based in the governorate of Gafsa, provides a more detailed elaboration of what the organisation meant by 'strange schemes':

> Who created terrorism in Tunisia? This is a question that needs to be answered. It is the government that created terrorism in Tunisia, the governments after 14 January 2011, and mainly the Ennahda government that is linked to the international brotherhood organisation. [...] Terrorism will not come by itself to Tunisia, there are those who allowed it to come to Tunisia, there are those who fed terrorism in Tunisia, and we are not afraid to announce that the Ennahdha movement in Tunisia, even after Nidaa Tuonis, did not present anything that fights terrorism. Ennahda feeds terrorism based on its ideology and international orientation.[15]

When asked whether he was satisfied with the general anti-terrorism agenda in Tunisia, Yousef raised a counter-question about the source of terrorism. Similar to the above Facebook post, he identifies terrorism as being created, facilitated and fed by Ennahda after 2011. Most notable in his claim is that he constructs terrorism as an ideologically driven act, and this ideology is, according to him, connected to the International Muslim Brotherhood, one of the most influential political and social Islamic movements today. While Ennahda's intimate relationship with the Muslim Brotherhood is not a contested issue, as it has been publicly acknowledged by both sides, it remains controversial whether and to what extent Islamic extremism is linked to their political orientation and initiatives. Particularly after the political upheaval in 2011, there emerged at least two competing views regarding the subject position of Ennahda in Tunisia and the Muslim Brotherhood in Egypt: one that highlights the compatibility between modern democracy and its socio-political role, and the other that postulates their democracy language as a temporal and tactical move in order to hide their real ambition – that is, the Islamisation of the Arab region by taking advantage of the newly given political freedom. Arguably, it is the latter perspective that was often used in the international media discourse to support the scenario of rising religious terrorism around the world.[16] Yousef's narrative reifies and reproduces the notion of global Islamist terrorism, part of the dominant security logic in Tunisia, by associating Ennahda with terrorism and international Islamic networks, while excluding an alternative view of the role of Islam in politics.

The UDC's articulation of the Ennahda-led government as linked to the rise of Islamist extremism was also constituted by its involvement in the anti-terror and anti-Ennahda movements. An illuminating example is a nationwide mobilisation calling for the end of the Ennahda government on 25 October 2013, in the aftermath of a reported violent confrontation between the Tunisian army and unknown 'terrorists' in the governorate of Sidi Bouzid. The UDC's decision to take part in the mobilisation and its slogan 'Down with the terrorist Ennahda' was followed by random attacks on several Ennahda party offices across the country, despite the absence of any concrete evidence that Ennahda was behind the event. This indicates how the declaration and punishment of Ennahda's role in terrorism were self-referential and how the UDC contributed to the 'enemisation' of Ennahda. It might be the case that the organisation's idea of Ennahda as helping and facilitating religiously motivated terrorism while ignoring socio-economic problems was intended to present the unemployed resistance against the state as necessary for a better life, not only in terms of socio-economic conditions, but also regarding security. However, its deployment of Islamist terrorism to accuse the authorities had the unintended effect of reproducing and normalising part of the elites' securitising logic. Insofar as the narrative of the inevitable threat of Islamist terrorism operated as a constitutive part of the art of neoliberal governing in Tunisia, the UDC did not cease to be governed when they resisted, and they were 'embedded into the interaction between the art of governing and the practice of resistance'.[17]

State Institutions Violate Constitutional Rights

Building on the first counter-narrative, the UDC activists elaborated on the chain of equivalence between those governing (mainly Ennahda) and terrorism, by producing another narrative in which they highlighted the 'illegality' of the state repression of the unemployed mobilisations, as well as the undermining role of the state in counter-terrorism. Whereas the first narrative was based on the logic of equivalence, the second one was constructed partly through the UDC's use of the logic of difference, disarticulating 'equivalential chains'[18] between terrorism and the UDC-led unemployed protests. Particularly notable is that the values and norms of liberal democracy, such as civil and political freedom, which the elites deployed to create and criminalise 'deviant' protesters, emerged once again as a discursive terrain for the UDC. The organisation drew on this terrain to present itself as a legitimate and civil force, while rendering the state institutions as incompatible with constitutional laws and incapable of fighting terrorism.

Interestingly, the UDC's distinction between terrorism and unemployed protesters through the use of the language of democracy often entailed the creation and discursive association of a negative category of unemployed protests with terrorism; by doing so, it could distance itself from both terrorism and violent protests. The below example shows how the UDC reproduced the elites' construction of the violent/peaceful protest divide. This excerpt is part of an official statement by the UDC, which came amidst the escalation of the unemployed mobilisations in Kasserine in January 2016. Although the January event was not initially organised by the UDC, it announced a statement to express its solidarity with Kasserine youth, as well as to criticise the authorities' use of force and its attempts to criminalise the protests:

> The UDC and the majority of civil forces called for peaceful movements and demanded not to engage in the 'suspicious night movements', which were accompanied by acts of looting and deliberate and systematic acts of cutting off roads, giving the wrong impression that many terrorists are infiltrating the movements. Accordingly, the UDC demands that the government respect the right to peaceful demonstration and calls on the government and its security services to ensure marches and sit-ins, rather than confronting them violently. We disapprove of any deliberate confusion between the peaceful movements organised by the unemployed and the looting and theft behind which there are groups who have no interest in the unemployed and the marginalised attaining their right to development, employment and welfare, and who have no interest in the country to overcome the current state of instability. We call for the highest degree of vigilance and awareness in managing and organising the resistance movements and [we call for] not leaving room for those parties that are working to sabotage the protesters and to bring violence and chaos.[19]

The main purpose of this statement was to counter the 'wrong impression' of the unemployed mobilisations as being exploited by terrorists. The UDC also accused the authorities of using violence when dealing with the protests, through their 'deliberate confusion' between crimes and unemployed protests. Yet, in the process of challenging and resisting the top–down articulation of the two separate subjects as linked, the organisation relied on 'the strategies, techniques and power relationship' mobilised for the securitisation of the unemployed subject.[20] It did so by drawing a line between peaceful movements and 'suspicious night movements', the division of which was (re)produced by the elites in governing the unemployed subject. Its rhetoric approved of, supported and encouraged the peaceful/ legitimate category of protest, whereas it disapproved of and rejected the violent/fake protest category. Reproducing the dominant securitising practices, the organisation also criminalised the negative category of protest by conflating crimes such as looting with blocking roads, a protest tactic commonly used by unemployed protesters and casual workers in the interior regions of Tunisia.

Also notable is that the UDC's creation of the divide between peaceful/ legitimate and violent/fake unemployed protests, as well as its criminalisa-tion of the latter as being against the interests of the unemployed popula-tion and Tunisia as a whole, was used to encourage the former category of protesters to be 'vigilant' of the latter's attempt to sabotage the former and to cause violence and chaos. As the first sentence of the text indicates, it became the unemployed protesters, and not those who conflated social movements with terrorism, that must bear the responsibility for not 'giving the wrong impression' that terrorists can manipulate their protests.

The discursive divide between peaceful and violent protests constructed by the UDC's rhetoric was also performed through its protest strategies. Although the organisation supported locally mobilised unemployed protests in the interior regions in general, it often distanced itself from the so-called 'random' (often violent) protests, especially those in the regions where the organisation's national bureau had no actual influence.[21] According to its members, most of the UDC-led street politics also took an 'organised form', by officially announcing their planned modes of action with a clear purpose and clear demands. In performing well-structured and peaceful protests and rejecting random and violent actions, the UDC's intention was to place itself in a position conforming with modern and civilised democracy; yet, while doing so, it also unwittingly reiterated the divide between legitimate and illegitimate categories of unemployed protests. The above statement and the UDC's protest tactics indicate how, rather than rejecting the status of being securitised, it challenged the *ways* of being governed by the elites, particularly the state's use of sovereign violence. In doing so, it partially justified sovereign violence against unemployed protests, by reproducing and criminalising the violent cat-egory of unemployed protests and by reifying the elites' responsibilisation of the unemployed protesters.

The ambivalence of the UDC's resistance characterised as a 'struggle against the *processes* implemented for conducting others'[22] also resided in the ways in which it invoked liberal democratic norms to criticise the authorities' counter-terrorism policies. This was particularly the case when the UDC attempted to render the state's abuse of emergency laws and violence as not only being incompatible with human rights, rule of law and democracy, but also being less effective in countering terror-ism. A representative example is the Facebook post below, part of a joint statement made by various civil society organisations, including the

UDC, the UGTT and the UGET on 17 December 2015. This statement came amidst increasing concern among civil society and social movement actors regarding both so-called 'homegrown terrorism' and a potential return of authoritarian rule in the name of the War on Terror. The text aptly illustrates how the UDC framed the state approach to terrorism as illegitimate and ineffective, while attempting to reconcile the necessity of countering terrorism and protecting their political rights:

> More than sixty organisations issued a statement about the repeated violations in Tunisia today, which are incompatible with the values and principles of the democratic state. We condemn the systematic targeting of national and inter-national civil society organisations engaged in civil and modern democratic projects, the use of the War on Terror as an excuse in order to raise suspicions about their funding and objectives. [... We condemn the state's] campaigns to question the system of human rights and public freedoms which are guaranteed by the constitution and international treaties ratified by the Tunisian state in order to undermine the rule of law and institutions. We condemn the employ-ment of the state of emergency in order to carry out abuses and violations during the conduct of random raids. Emphasising the importance of a steadfast fight against terrorism at all levels, security, military, cultural, social, political and media, we stress that the effectiveness of the counter-terrorism policy remains hostage to the respect for human rights, the promotion of fundamental freedoms and the involvement of civil society forces and their efforts to protect the citizens' right to security.[23]

In this statement, the UDC and other organisations present the state as a violator whose practices are frequently incompatible with democratic norms and institutions, while describing civil society actors as a legitimate force upholding these values. The image of legitimate civil society is also amplified by referring to the 'constitution' and 'international treaties'. By invoking and relying on the authority of these abstract norms, the UDC characterises civil society (of which it is a part) as the agent that protects and serves 'values and principles of the democratic state', thereby rendering the state's act of challenging civil society as a violation and systematic attack on democratic initiatives and rule of law. Also, lexical choices – such as 'excuse' and 'abuse', as well as the use of the purposive clause 'in order to' – are made to emphasise the intentionality of the state's violation of global/liberal norms, conveying the idea that the ruling elites manipulated the War on Terror and the emergency law for the purpose of undermining civil society.

Notable in this lengthy joint statement is that the construct of the antagonistic relationship between the state as a violator and civil society as a guardian of democracy discursively places civil society in an authoritative position from which it can prescribe a more 'effective' way to counter terrorism. The UDC's construct of the fight against terrorism as requiring not only security measures but also the involvement of civil society at 'all levels' reflects that the ways in which the elites and the UDC strategically used democratic and security values as discursive strategies were 'not external to each other', even though they articulated as linked to each other 'on the basis of their difference'.[24] The UDC's criticism of the government's emergency measures through its support of more effective counter-terrorism entailed ambivalent implications for the operation of sovereign violence. On one hand, its emphasis on the protection of human rights and political freedom as a necessity for counter-terrorism served as civil pressure to increase transparency in the process of implementing emergency measures, thereby holding the authorities more accountable for their use of violence. On the other hand, the UDC's endorsement of the necessity of counter-terrorism and of the importance of involving civil society in confronting terrorism simultaneously operated to approve and normalise the liberal civil police.

If Terrorism is a Battle, Work is the Mother of the Battle!

Importantly, the UDC's counter-securitising practices to be securitised differently operated for its struggle over the right to work. This is indicated in the way in which the organisation re-articulated unemployment as linked to terrorism, by producing an alternative meta-narrative claiming that 'the elimination of the unemployed is the most effective way to counter terrorism'. This narrative emerged as one of the UDC's key slogans especially since the beginning of 2015, the year when most media attention was given to the establishment of the Ennahda and Nidaa Tounes coalition government in February and then to three violent attacks on foreign tourists and security forces. UDC activists, however, have recalled this year as a critical but frustrating period for unemployed mobilisations, because their socio-economic resistance was being revitalised and could possibly have been shifted to another revolutionary moment.[25] Indeed, the UDC's online campaign as well as its strategic engagement with the issue of terrorism was most active in 2015. The below excerpt from an official statement by the UDC illustrates how the organisation chained the inevitable threat of Islamist terrorism and the right to a decent life as a fundamental human right to the problem of unemployment, by constructing unemployment as causing the expansion of terrorism:

Unemployment is currently one of the fundamental problems that affects most regions. [...] A number of the country's regions have been living in a period of social unrest that has begun to surround different marginalised areas and is gradually expanding, especially in the interior areas that are living in poverty and marginalisation. Both poverty and unemployment are the major causes of the expansion of terrorism and smuggling, and they are dangerous social plagues that threaten the citizens. Many unemployed people in Sidi Bouzid, who spoke to us, thought that the terrorism cancer was caused mainly by unemployment and poverty. As is well known, the plague of terrorism takes the marginalised and poor regions as its shelter, and it may be noticeable that sleeper cells and terrorist Takfiri cells enter the regions that are experiencing social crises. This is not an accusation against the marginalised youth of rural areas, but a reality that we live, see and analyse. Some considered that the most appropriate solution for Tunisia to flourish was to combat unemployment and in particular guarantee young people the right to a decent life.[26]

The beginning of the post indirectly associates unemployment with social unrest, by identifying unrest as being spread into most of the interior regions, which have suffered prolonged unemployment, poverty and marginalisation. Yet, this implicit link between the two elements is soon translated into a more direct causality between unemployment and terrorism, as marked by the following sentence: 'Both poverty and unemployment are the major causes of the expansion of terrorism and smuggling'. Emphasising the importance of resolving the problem of unemployment, the UDC renders counter-terrorism an urgent and necessary task through several metaphors. The first metaphor of 'plagues' assigns to terrorism a contagious nature, thereby emphasising its great threat, its negative impact on Tunisia as a whole and the urgency of counter-measures. The metaphors of 'cancer' and 'shelter' also function in a similar way. Framing terrorism as a cancer and the marginalised regions as its shelter in which it hides and feeds itself conveys the impression that terrorism is a social disease that needs to be eradicated before it grows any further; what needs to be done first and foremost is the elimination of its sources – that is, unemployment, poverty and marginalisation.

Furthermore, the above post written by the UDC draws on 'expert knowledge', the discursive effect of which can enhance the objectiveness and credibility of the causal link between the two subjects and render the 'right to decent life' the 'most appropriate solution' for the well-being of Tunisia. Unemployment as the cause of terrorism is not presented as what the organisation views in the first-person perspective, but as what it has heard from 'many unemployed people in Sidi Bouzid'. The use of the third-person perspective here can be interpreted as having the effect

118

of projecting its claim as less biased and less emotional. With this expert tone, the UDC is discursively placed in an authoritative position where it produces factual and credible information as well as a diagnosis.

Whereas the above excerpt illustrates how Islamist terrorism has been chained to the right to a decent life under the meta-narrative (the elimination of unemployment), the below excerpt provides an example of how the importance of the eradication of unemployment also acquired its meaning 'through its positioning relative to' the state's responsibility for terrorism, while simultaneously 'assigning meaning to' it within the counter-terrorism discourse:[27]

> The struggles of the unemployed have proven and are still proving that what the previous and current governments are saying about being busy fighting terrorism is just a 'righteous word used for an ill purpose'. Ever since the revolution started, people have been asking for creating employment opportunities and undertaking some effective strategies to reduce the poverty rate and marginalisation, because these [poverty and marginalisation] are the incubator of violence and terrorism. Any strategy to eliminate this danger will not succeed if it is limited to security measures only.[28]

In this Facebook post, the UDC first portrayed terrorism as an objective threat that needed to be combatted, as indicated in the choice of the term 'righteous word' and in its general description. The body of this text, however, indicates that the terrorism reference is used mainly to criticise the governing elites whom the UDC considered as abusing the War on Terror as an excuse for 'ill purpose' – that is, to ignore the reality of unemployment. More importantly, by using the metaphor of 'incubator', it directly articulates the situation of unemployment (marked by poverty and marginalisation) as violence and terrorism. As the last sentence of the text clearly shows, the UDC's construction of unemployment as the fundamental cause of terrorism – albeit neglected until today because of the state institutions' reliance on security measures – makes it the state's responsibility to provide employment as the way to succeed in the War on Terror.

In addition to public statements on its online platform, the UDC utilised multiple methods to associate unemployment with terrorism. For instance, a UDC-led unemployed protest was organised in the governorate of Jandouba on 2 April 2015, in order to criticise the state's unwillingness to fight corruption and nepotism, which the activists recognised as pervading employment in the public sectors. In this protest, the UDC mobilised public support under the slogan 'Elimination of unemployment is the first step to eliminate terrorism'. As the following section will elaborate, a number of unemployed youths on the streets chanting this slogan could convey two seemingly contradictory meanings about their relationship to terrorism. On the one hand, the activists victimised themselves as the 'prey of terrorism' by highlighting the close ties between terrorism and the status of being unemployed. On the other hand, they presented themselves as fighters against terrorism, by performing the act of protesting for the elimination of unemployment and against the state which, according to them, nurtured terrorism by ignoring marginalised youth.

Taken together, these examples show how the UDC's narrative about the elimination of unemployment as the most efficient way to fight terrorism, which aimed at challenging and criticising the ruling elites' securitising practices, did indeed 'adopt and invoke the tactics of government', sustaining and at the same time challenging them.[29] The use of expert knowledge and metaphors such as 'incubator' and 'creative chaos' are frequently found in the dominant securitising acts that often over-exaggerate the threat of terrorism and the potential of unemployed protests to be exploited by terrorists, thus justifying the authorities' acts of policing the unemployed through liberal and illiberal means. As the governmentality approach emphasises, however, that the UDC's resistance was implicated in securitisation simultaneously reflects its potential for diverting securitisation from within. Not only did the UDC's association of unemployment with terrorism operate to deflect the responsibility for terrorism from the unemployed protesters towards the state, but it also served to present resolving the problem of unemployment as the most urgent task for Tunisia's security and stability.

We are the Victims of Terrorism

The previous section has shown how the UDC projected unemployment as the main cause of terrorism and, in doing so, utilised various discursive terrains to promote the elimination of unemployment as the most efficient way of fighting terrorism. The UDC's reaction to the securitisation of the unemployed was counter-conductive in that, rather than fully rejecting its status as being securitised in the name of the War on Terror, it sought to be governed differently by articulating, disarticulating and re-articulating the discursive elements performed by the ruling elites. Importantly, the UDC's counter-securitising practices were not only a struggle to be governed differently, but they also entailed a struggle for the care of the self to 'seek, possibly at any rate, to escape direction by others and to define the way for each to conduct himself'.[30] Particularly notable is that, while escaping the state's responsibilisation of the unemployed, the UDC constructed the unemployed subject as a victim of terrorism. The 'victims of terrorism' signified the unemployed youth who ended up being 'terrorists' due to their experience of deprivation, alienation and injustice, as reflected in the following excerpt:

> The thing that opens the doors to brainwashing and religious extremism is poor social infrastructure. When he is unemployed at the age of twenty-nine or thirty years and does not even have money for coffee or cigarette he finds someone that brainwashes him in a way. […] Religious speech is profound speech, and with his psychological situation that reflects his life, its effect will be deeper.[31]

This part of my interview with Mohamed illustrates how the subject position of an unemployed person as a potential terrorist and victim of terrorism was promoted through the UDC's counter-securitising acts. When asked about the effectiveness of the state's approach to counter-terrorism, his answer is 'neither yes nor no, because the root cause remained unsolved'. He then associates the unemployed with terrorists, by describing poor social infrastructure as a factor that leads unemployed youth to be subject to 'brainwashing' and religious extremism. On the one hand, he reproduces the elites' narrative that unemployed youths are easily deceived by Islamist terrorists. Yet, whereas the elites emphasised the unemployed people's naïvete or deviance, Mohamed re-appropriates the elites' narrative to emphasise the victimhood of the unemployed. His subjectification of the unemployed as being forced to become terrorists is elaborated through his portrayal of the conditions in which the unemployed are living. Notably, he utilises references to both age and lack of basic commodities (coffee and cigarette) that characterises low socio-economic status to illustrate the psychological impact that deepens the effect of already profound religious speeches on the unemployed.

The victim subject position of unemployed youth is also constructed through the UDC's responsibilisation of the state, for its systemic failure to address socio-economic insecurity which may force many unemployed youths to become terrorists. The UDC's statement below provides an example of how it frames the unemployed subject as a passive object, by directing the responsibility of terrorism towards those governing society:

> The union [UDC] has provided recommendations and alternatives to all groups that have governed the country over time, all these recommendations were prioritised and classified according to their short and long-term importance, and despite all that, 'they fell on deaf ears'. According to numbers and indicators, the situation of those unemployed was aggravated under the governance of the Troika. Until today, there are a lot of youth that die in the sea, commit

suicide and set themselves on fire, or they enter the world of crime, prostitution and deviation, and others fall victim to the recruitment of terrorists when their ignorance makes them think they are jihadists for Islam […].[32]

In this statement, the UDC portrays the unemployed as being involved in illegal migration, suicide, crime and terrorism. In doing so, as with the case of Mohamed, it reifies the image of the unemployed as being deceived by 'jihadi terrorists'. Notably, the passivity of the unemployed is particularly emphasised in the case of terrorism, with the clause 'and others fall victim to the recruitment of terrorists'. As the first two sentences indicate, this victim subject position of the unemployed is framed around the ruling elites' deliberate negligence and manipulation of the problem of unemployment. The victimhood of the unemployed and the guilt of the elites are also constituted through the UDC's positioning of itself as an expert that 'has provided recommendations and alternatives' to resolve the problem of unemployment. From the perspective of governmentality, the coexistence of the passive subject (the unemployed in general) and the active subject (the unemployed signifying the UDC) in its narratives indicates an ambivalence embedded in its resistance with respect to the question of 'who we are'. As I have discussed in Chapter 4, the securitisation of the unemployed contributed to shaping and governing the unemployed as self-governable and responsible individuals, by simultaneously differentiating between legitimate and illegitimate unemployed protesters and discursively associating the latter with terrorism. On the one hand, the UDC's identification of the self as an active subject can be understood as an attempt to distinguish the self from the majority of the unemployed whom the elites projected as an abstraction of the vulnerable and/or deceived subject. On the other hand, the UDC's resistance also entailed a struggle against the ways in which the elites' securitising practices dislocated the unemployed as a collective identity and subjectified them as individuals able to exercise their freedom for the well-being of the self. In Foucault's terms, both forms of the UDC's struggle were 'not for or against the "individual"' but rather a 'struggle against the "government of individualization"' *from within*.[33]

The coexistence of these two seemingly contrasting subject positions (the unemployed as both passive victims and active protesters) was often found in the UDC's counter-securitising practices. A remarkable rhetorical device that sustained both subject positions was the differentiation of the subject nouns articulated. While the victim subject position was promoted through the use of pronominal subjects, such as 'a lot of youth' or a hypothetical 'he' and 'others', the active subject position of the unemployed often was promoted through the use of first-person perspective or nominal subjects. The following excerpt from my interview with Yassine Jawedi, UDC activist in Sidi Bouzid, shows how the active subject position was drawn upon to subjectify UDC members as progressive revolutionaries and a self-critical force against terrorism:

> Terrorists benefitted from the Arab revolution and used it as a backup for their appearance later. President Beji did not stand in the streets to [counter] the Salafists; it was rather us, the youth who organised for that and stopped them from creating their own Islamic structure. Neither Beji, nor his supporters, nor his activists, but the progressive youth were the ones that clearly intervened in this, when those groups were close to having control over universities and popular cities. [Also], the one benefitting from this resistance is the state because this resistance was not political, meaning that it was the people's resistance, but without a political agenda. For that, I am thinking today that, before we enter resistance, before we continue our activism, before we confront the state and corruption, we must find an answer to the question of how we can organise […] what the best format of organising can be. When we agree on this and have social, political and economic plans, then we will find a way for the democratic revolutionary path in Tunisia. This requires work.[34]

When asked about the outcomes of the political upheaval in January 2011, Yassine presents 'terrorists' as those who benefitted from the Arab revolution. His description of terrorists as Salafists who attempt to create their own Islamic structure echoes the elites' narrative that Islamist terrorists exploited the instability caused by the Tunisian revolution in order to Islamise the country. Yet, as narrated in this interview, Yassine is re-appropriating the discursive terrain of Islamist terrorism in order to tie himself to the unemployed as a progressive force that stopped those terrorists on the ground. This progressive unemployed subject position is constituted with the use of the first-person perspective – that is, 'we' and 'us'. The projection of the unemployed 'we' subject as progressive and as defender of the revolution is also enhanced by contrasting it with the ruling elites, as marked by President Beji (Essebsi's first name) and his supporters, whom he considered to be not only unwilling to counter terrorism but even benefitting from it.

More interestingly, by describing the UDC's resistance during and after the revolution as lacking a political agenda and concrete social, political and economic plans, Yassine attributes the responsibility for the revolution and for terrorism being manipulated by the state to the unemployed 'we' subject. His subjectification of the unemployed as a self-reflexive force that has the capacity to learn from its previous mistakes and has the potential to work better is indicative of the ethical dimension of the UDC's struggle for the right to work and social justice – that is, 'an exercise of the self on the self' by which to 'develop and transform oneself'.[35] While the elites' securitisation of the unemployed involved the empowerment of the unemployed subject so that they can govern themselves as free and independent citizens in conformity with the marketisation of Tunisia, the UDC activists' counter-securitising practices defined and practised their freedom in an alternative way, by thinking *critically* about what a successful revolution should look like and by asking what they and their fellow activists should do if they were to remain revolutionaries.

We are the Victim of and Revolutionaries against State Terrorism

The UDC also intervened in and strategically made use of the elites' construction of the unemployed as free and self-responsible citizens and, in doing so, they sought to re-define the ways in which they were securitised. The (ab)use of terrorism and counter-terrorism in the process of securitising the unemployed was 'never complete or irreversible'.[36] Rather, it entailed 'unintended consequences and inadequacies of conduct' which, in turn, intensified the 'fragility and reversibility of conducting processes'.[37] This was particularly evident in the ways in which the UDC re-appropriated the negative connotations of terrorism in order to delegitimise and criminalise sovereign violence. While the previous section has shown how the UDC constituted the unemployed as a victim of terrorism characterised by 'radical Islamism', the example below illustrates how it also created a category of 'state terrorism' that signifies state violence against protesters by which to subjectify the unemployed as a victim of state terrorism:

> In one week, two young men committed suicide, one in Sfax and the other in Monastir [...] In the same month, a young woman suffered and died from a heart attack after a long struggle in the union of unemployed degree holders (UDC) in defense of youth issues. And yesterday, there was news about the death of a young man who was shot by the legitimate terrorist group of the state, represented by its terrorist ministry following the recent protests in Kasserine [...].[38]

This statement came after the death of an unemployed youth during a violent confrontation between the security force and unemployed protesters in Kasserine in January 2014. Instead of mentioning specific names, the UDC uses the pronominal subjects 'two young men', 'a young woman' and 'a young man' to describe several deaths that occurred in January. As with the case of the discursive construction of the unemployed as a victim of

Islamist terrorism, the use of these pronominal subjects impersonalises the four youths, rendering them passive victim subjects. Also, by placing these otherwise individual and separate events in parallel with each other, the deaths of these youths are projected as representing the reality of the unemployed. Notably, the UDC describes the death of the unemployed protester in Kasserine as a terrorist event committed by the 'legitimate terrorist group of the state represented by its terrorist ministry'. In the Tunisian context, it should not be too difficult to identify the 'terrorist ministry', given the famous slogan *Uzarah al-dakhaliyah, uzarah al-irhabiyah* ('the Interior Ministry, the Terrorist Ministry') raised by protesters in 2011, as well as during the 2021 protests against police violence. The portrayal of the police force and the Interior Ministry as terrorists discursively emphasises both the brutality of police repression and the victimhood of the unemployed protesters. Also, importantly, the use of the paradoxical combination of the two evidently contradictory terms 'legitimate' and 'terrorist' can be interpreted as a satire to underline the role of the state behind the police violence. With the use of satire, the statement not only criticises individual police officers, but also presents their brutality as systematic violence committed by state institutions in the name of the rule of law.

The UDC's construction of the unemployed as a victim of state terrorism also serves as a care of the self, in the sense that it is used to directly confront and criticise the elites' truth claims and, in doing so, seeks to escape the subjectivity of the unemployed as deviant and/or terrorist. The following interview with Hassan, an UDC activist based in Tunis, illustrates how the UDC constituted the notion of state terrorism to expose and question the elites' abuse of the terrorism discourse and their association of terrorism with unemployed protesters as a whole. When asked to elaborate why he views the state as taking advantage of terrorism to control social movements, he provides the example of the unemployed protests organised on the Kerkennah islands in 2016:

> In Kerkennah, we, the union of unemployed degree holders [UDC], were convicted of terrorism because of the dilemma of the petrol company in Kerkennah. However, whoever visited Kerkennah and analysed the protests and movements will say that the state was exercising terrorism. The citizens on Kekennah asked to drop the agreements of Petrofac, and the media worked to worsen the case and criminalised the social movement. When they [the state and media] could not stop it, they condemned it as terrorism. The state suppressed the peaceful protests with tear gas against them, arrested and imprisoned them, and so forth.[39]

Through his description of the Kerkennah unemployed mobilisation, Hassan rejects and criticises the terrorism charge against the unemployed protesters, by performing a kind of 'game of truth'.[40] To reveal the false-ness of the terrorism charge, he produces a hypothetical individual who has the capacity of thoroughly and objectively investigating what hap-pened in Kekennah and providing the 'truth' that the state and media fabricated the charge in order to stop the protests. Further, the exculpation of the protesters is supported by his re-signification of the term 'terrorism', from being a charge commonly imposed on non-state actors to that of state repression of unemployed protesters, as represented by the state's use of tear gas and arbitrary arrests. Consider that claiming 'truths' is one of the key discursive techniques deployed in the elites' securitising practices. The UDC's presentation of an alternative 'truth' that victimises the unem-ployed and criminalises the state escapes from the 'truth' produced by the elites, 'not by playing a game that was totally different from the game of truth but by playing the same game differently'.[41]

Constructing state violence against the unemployed protesters as terror-ism not only promotes them as a victim of state terrorism, but also serves to legitimise and even necessitate their 'fight back' against state violence. In particular, the notion of state terrorism was often deployed by the UDC to subjectify the self as 'revolutionary' whose aim, by definition, was to create systematic changes. The below excerpt reflects how the notions of state terrorism and revolutionary were mobilised in such a way as to resist the elites' view of Tunisia's post-2011 trajectory as a post-revolution and to render it as a revolutionary *path* towards the right to work and towards dignity:

> No to state terrorism against the revolutionaries: The state is now practicing real terrorism against the people, especially the revolutionaries, activists and unemployed. Today, the secretary-general of the UDC, Salim Al Ayari, was violently assaulted against the background of the protest movement in front of the ministry. [...] We do not fear the stick of the executioner and deten-tions, and investigations do not frighten us. Your crime will only increase our determination to continue the path of our revolution, until the hordes of the unemployed get their right to work and dignity and take revenge against all their enemies without exception.[42]

In this text, the UDC frames the police repression against Salim Al Ayari, a leader of the organisation, during a protest in front of the Ministry of Interior as 'real terrorism' while presenting the UDC as revolutionaries. This revolutionary subjectivity might seem at odds with the UDC's posi-tion, not least because it partially contributed to the context of the War on Terror in which any manoeuver for political change is deemed to be a 'misconduct'. Its invocation of liberal democratic values and a perceivably reformist approach to the problem of unemployment were, from the view of many inside and outside its organisation, *not* revolutionary inasmuch as revolutionary is understood as a form of radicalism demanding a 'fundamental break from the old order'.[43] From the governmentality approach, however, the significance of its claim to be a revolutionary lies not so much in whether the UDC was indeed revolutionary, but in how it worked on this subjectivity to escape the relations of power within which it was placed and to define the way in which it conducts the self.[44]

The UDC's revolutionary subject position, first and foremost, rested on its understanding of revolution as a *process* rather than an outcome resulting from a dramatic political upheaval. This statement indicates that, for the UDC, the current trajectory of Tunisia was not a post-revolutionary phase that required the stabilisation of society, but a revolutionary path on which the most fundamental demands of the 2011 Uprising – work, freedom and dignity – would be accomplished only when the revolutionaries kept united and continued their struggle. In this sense, the organisation's invocation of state terrorism and revolutionaries contested the elites' understanding of the revolution as having been completed and of the way in which they justify sovereign violence as legitimate rule for the stabilisation and consolidation of the new democracy in Tunisia. As the second half of the text indicates, the UDC's refusal to consider sovereign violence as a legitimate way of governing democracy and its notion of state terrorism against the revolutionaries operated for the formation of its self – as the 'not so governable'[45] subject who 'does not fear the stick' and works to 'continue the path of our revolution, until the hordes of the unemployed take their right to work and dignity'.

Concluding Remarks

This chapter has provided a detailed analysis of the UDC's responses to the dominant securitising practices performed by the ruling elites. Here, I have sought to elucidate how the UDC's counter-narratives and subjectivities unsettled and undermined the elites' securitising practices, while partly approving and reifying them. In the process of building its alternative meta-narrative of 'the elimination of unemployment as the best method of countering terrorism', the UDC reproduced the securitisation of the unemployed, by endorsing and performing notions of the increasing threat of Islamist terrorism, deviant/violent unemployed protests and civil police. Yet, at the same time, the UDC strategically re-appropriated them in such a way as to responsibilise the state, escape the unemployed subjectivities imposed by the elites and, more importantly, push forward its key demand of 'the right to work' as the most fundamental and urgent task that Tunisia had to address.

These findings complicate binary understandings of the unemployed struggle represented by the UDC in Tunisia as either successful, autonomous and revolutionary, or as failing, subordinated and non-revolutionary. The governmentality approach provides a more nuanced way of understanding the UDC's resistance, in that it elucidates a mutually constitutive aspect of the relationship between the ruling elites and the unemployed in the field of security, the implications of which reach far beyond the narrowly defined field of 'security'. Also, an analysis of the UDC offers an important empirical case to illuminate the Foucauldian understanding of resistance in critical security studies, in that it captures a subtle form of resistance that is neither for de-securitisation nor for re-securitisation. As will be further supported by another case-study in Chapter 6, the Tunisian unemployed struggle involved a form of *counter*-securitisation in which the unemployed protesters both reproduced and challenged the process of being securitised.

Notes

1. Interview with Chahed Mohamed, UDC activist, Tunis, 27 March 2017.
2. Interview with Ghassen Harim, UDC activist, Sidi Bouzid, 23 March 2017.
3. This observation is based on the researcher's informal conversations with unemployed youths, mostly held in street cafés in Tunis, Gasfa, Sidi Bouzid, Kasserine, Gabis and Tatawin between November 2016 and April 2017.
4. The ambivalent position of the Mafrouzeen Movement in the broader unemployed movement is indicated in that, while the movement framed itself as part of the struggle over the right to work, at the same time it promoted the individualised notion of human rights and justice in the process of engaging with formal transitional justice mechanisms. For more information on the relationship between the Mafrouzeen Movement and the UDC, see Han, 'Transitional justice for whom?'
5. Ibid.
6. Interview with Ahmed Murad, member of the UDC executive board, Tunis, 3 April 2017.
7. Chahed Mohamed, author interview.
8. Interview with Jamel Ghafr, UDC coordinator in Sidi Bouzid, Sidi Bouzid, 20 December 2016.
9. Interview with Mohamed Salmi, UDC coordinator in Gafsa, Gafsa, 14 November 2016.
10. Foucault, *Security, territory, population*, p. 28.
11. Ahmed Murad, author interview.
12. Malmvig, 'Governing Arab reform', p. 7.

13. Foucault, 'The subject and power', p. 790.
14. UDC Bureau National, 28 November 2013.
15. Interview with Yousef Hamdi, UDC activist, Gafsa, 11 January 2017.
16. See, for example, Ahmed, 'Designate the Muslim Brotherhood a foreign terrorist organization'.
17. Odysseos, 'Governing dissent in the Central Kalahari Game Reserve', p. 440.
18. Howarth, 'Power, discourse, and policy', p. 321.
19. U.D.C Page Officiel, 25 January 2016.
20. Death, 'Counter-conducts', p. 240.
21. Ghassen Harim, author interview.
22. Foucault, *Security, territory, population*, p. 201, emphasis added.
23. U.D.C Page Officiel, 17 December 2015.
24. Pottage, *Power as an art of contingency*, p. 17, emphasis added.
25. Ahmed Murad, author interview.
26. UDC Bureau National, 17 March 2015.
27. Rear and Jones, 'Discursive struggle and contested signifiers in the arenas of education policy and work skills in Japan', p. 379.
28. U.D.C Page Officiel, 22 April 2015.
29. Death, 'Counter-conducts', p. 244.
30. Foucault, *Security, territory, population*, p. 195.
31. Mohamed Salmi, author interview.
32. U.D.C Page Officiel, 1 May 2014.
33. Foucault, 'The subject and power', p. 781.
34. Interview with Yassine Jawedi, UDC activist, Sidi Bouzid, 17 February 2017.
35. Foucault, *The essential works, 1954–1984*, vol. 1, p. 282.
36. Odysseos, 'Human rights, self-formation and resistance in struggles against disposability', p. 194.
37. Ibid.
38. U.D.C Page Officiel, 27 January 2014.
39. Hassan Sharfi, UDC activist and Mafrouzen, Tunis, 15 February 2017.
40. Foucault, *The essential works, 1954–1984*, vol. 1, p. 295.
41. Ibid.
42. UDC Bureau National, 25 February 2014.
43. Bayat, *Revolution without revolutionaries*, p. 11.
44. Foucault, *Security, territory, population*.
45. Odysseos, 'Human rights, self-formation and resistance in struggles against disposability', p. 182.

6

The Maknassy Protesters' Counter-securitising Practices

The unemployed were discursively associated with terrorism not only by the state, security experts and political and economic elites, but also by some unemployed protesters themselves, as the UDC's case has illustrated in the previous chapter. Countering the top–down securitising practices that subjectified the unemployed as neoliberal citizens, the UDC resisted, not by rejecting its status of being securitised, but by securitising the self with the counter-narrative positing that 'the elimination of unemployment is the most efficient way to win the war against terrorism'. Thus, the protesters sought to govern themselves as not-so-governable subjects, while at the same time sustaining some of the governing techniques that they in principle opposed. These findings, however, raise the question of whether this is also the case for unemployed movements that do not belong to the UDC. This question is relevant not only because many young unemployed youths do not necessarily recognise the organisation as representing their voice, but also because of its decreasing popularity and reputation of being closely connected to party politics.

This chapter turns to a locally organised unemployed movement in the small town of Maknassy in order to compare its reaction to the securitisation of the unemployed subject to that of the UDC. I begin by outlining the emergence of the Maknassy unemployed struggle and the role that the War on Terror played in its development. The dominant securitising practices partly but significantly affected the protesters' ways of protesting socio-economic marginalisation, leading them to intervene in the production of the counter-terrorism discourse. The following sections will then show that, while also presenting some significant variations from the UDC case, the Maknassy protesters' responses to the elites' securitisation entailed similar ambiguities, as observed in the previous chapter. The protesters resisted not by rejecting but by re-appropriating the dominant security rationalities and techniques; in doing so, they both reiterated and destabilised them. The Maknassy protests in the name of civil disobedience show that they were implicated in and at the same time posed a challenge to the ways in which liberal democracy operates for neoliberal governing.

'Civil Disobedience' and the War on Terror

> The Maknassy model was supported because, if it fails, the social movement as a whole will shrink. That is because of the fact that our movement has been the most mature and successful social movement model since 2011. I shall say that civil disobedience had been practiced since 1978, and more specifically within the UGTT. Since then, our civil disobedience has been the first to follow the standards of disobedience with a clear message and purpose and without any vandalism.[1]

In January 2017, the small municipality town of Maknassy in the governorate of Sidi Bouzid emerged as the centre of yet another wave of protests for work, freedom and national dignity. Having no more than 25,000 inhabitants, Maknassy successfully attracted public attention with what the local protesters considered to be an experimental mode of resistance – namely, 'civil disobedience'. Blocking roads with burning tires and initiating general strikes at a local level were not at all new in the post-uprising landscape in Tunisia. Yet, the coordinator of the Maknassy civil disobedience, Abdelhak Jaouadi, claimed, as narrated above, that the Maknassy resistance was recognised as a first attempt to initiate a well-structured civil disobedience movement at a local community level[2] and that it also inspired and facilitated socio-economic struggles in other regions.[3] The protesters' emphasis on the imperative nature of resistance in creative ways was also indicated in one of their slogans, '*Hekaya akhrah*' ('another story'), characterising their desire and efforts to make their local movement different from others, which they considered easily ignored and domesticated by the authorities. In this sense, the Maknassy resistance witnessed in January 2017 was reflective of the post-uprising context in which political freedom needed to be more actively and innovatively exercised, if people were to effectively protest the unchanging socio-economic structure. Equally important, however, it was also a continuation of their everyday struggles that took place before and after the Ben Ali regime.

Located at the centre of Tunisia, Maknassy had been one of the poorest towns in the interior regions since the independence of Tunisia. The local economy predominantly depended on farming, and the lack of infrastructure (such as irrigation systems and factories to process olives) made it hard for the local populations to enjoy a stable income derived from their labour.[4] In fact, Maknassy had other sources of income. For example, approximately 18 kilometres from the town, there is a phosphate mine that had operated during the French colonial period and stopped its operation after World War II. Despite its strategic location bridging Gafsa, the centre of the phosphate industry, and Sfax, the second-richest coastal city in Tunisia, Maknassy had been largely excluded from the state's development plans. This led to high unemployment rates and a sense of grievance among the local population, especially the unemployed youth. Like many other marginalised towns in Tunisia, Maknassy had witnessed mundane resistance through hunger strikes, suicide attempts and marches, long before the Uprising. The political upheaval between December 2010 and January 2011 was not the result of Mohamed Bouazizi's self-immolation, according to the view of many local inhabitants. Rather, it was the outcome of their everyday struggle, fed by the grievances accumulated over the past five decades.[5]

The Maknassy resistance to the socio-economic marginalisation continued after the fall of the Ben Ali regime. On 28 January 2011, a number of local youths initiated a sit-in demanding regional development and employment in public and private institutions.[6] In particular, the unemployed youths demanded the re-opening of the phosphate mine located to the northeast of Maknassy which, so they argued, was capable of creating more than 400 jobs. Throughout sporadic protests, marches and sit-ins, they succeeded in pushing the authorities to announce several plans for regional development. On 26 April of the same year, for instance, then governor of Sidi Bouzid, Nabil An-Nusairi, visited Maknassy, promising the improvement of the quality of drinking water, regional roads and schools, as well as a study for the establishment of industrial zones in order to boost job creation.[7] In the following year, the state-run phosphate company of Gafsa also announced that they would be setting up a branch in Maknassy, as an initial stage of the operation of the phosphate mine. The company promised to hire immediately 150 local residents, with the aim of achieving the full operation of the mine in 2014 and the creation of around 450 more jobs.[8]

However, such promises of employment and regional development have not yet been realised at the time of writing this book. The authorities' relatively prompt responses to the unemployed mobilisations in Maknassy in the first three years after the Uprising were no more than gestures to prevent a further escalation of the protests. In particular, the authorities were keen to tame the protesters' 'revolutionary spirit' during the period of the anniversary of the 2011 revolution. For instance, when local youths were preparing a large-scale mobilisation against socio-economic marginalisation to mark the third anniversary of the revolution in January 2013, a sudden press conference to initiate an automobile factory project was held in the town, announcing that this project – valued at 1,500 million dinars (nearly $522 million) – would provide more than 8,000 jobs.[9] The local population patiently waited, expecting that the authorities' promises would be addressed once Tunisia's political institutions stabilised. But soon they realised that 'these promises were no more than a painkiller'.[10]

Facing the regional and central authorities' policy of procrastination in dealing with the socio-economic problems in Maknassy, four local movements – including the *'Harmna'* ('Old men', in Tunisian Dialect), candidates for phosphate mine employment, casual workers and farmers – established a coalition movement in the name of civil disobedience. The leading movement was the 'Sit-In Harmna' organised by twenty-four unemployed graduates, the majority of whom had been unemployed for more than ten years. They launched an open-ended sit-in in front of the municipality headquarters on 3 February 2016, claiming that they would continue their peaceful movement guaranteed by the constitution until the authorities provided them with jobs based on their seniority.[11] With the support of other unemployed activists, the UGTT and civil society organisations in the region, the Harmna Sit-In succeeded in forcing the regional authority to promise to launch the Maknassy phosphate mine within three weeks and to create more than 400 jobs immediately.[12]

Yet, the phosphate project announced in March caused new tensions, as many local unemployed people perceived that, as had been the case with the Gafsa phosphate company in 2008, the hiring process lacked transparency and favoured those who had connections with the regional authority and the local elites. The project's announcement of the list of 100 successful candidates who would be hired in the initial stage also created a divide between those hired and those not hired. In July of the same year, a separate protest movement was organised by the successful candidates on the list and their families, accusing the authorities of delaying the opening of the phosphate mine.[13] The authorities blamed the continued delay on land disputes between landowners and the Gafsa phosphate company. For many local residents, however, it was rather the authorities' unwillingness and corruption that impeded the new phosphate project, which they considered to be a key to regional development and employment.

When nearly half a year of struggles did not result in any concrete changes, the Harmna movement approached other local groups, including farmers and casual workers, who had been struggling for their own causes and persuaded them to be incorporated into a collective local movement. The spokesman of the Harmna movement, Jaouadi, noted that bringing different groups to work together was not an easy task. Facing the authorities' repeated neglect of their demands, however, the hetero-geneous movements began to build a common ground on which they could establish a unified local movement under the broad slogan '*Haq fi al-'amal wa al-tanmiyah*' ('The right to work and development'). On 30 December 2016, the coalition movement initiated civil disobedience by shutting down public institutions and stopping all vehicles for administra-tive and business purposes on the National Highway 14. which bridges Gafsa and Sfax.

> There were many social movements with many demands. [...] It was quite difficult to convince those people in the beginning. But when they couldn't achieve what they targeted with their limited capacities and lost hope, we asked for coordination. Then they responded promptly because [they realised that] unity was the source of strength. [...] We've been able to work together for a common purpose. The danger coming from the authorities was to strip us of our lands, our jobs, our lives and our art.[14]

According to the unemployed protesters in Maknassy, the imperative of an alternative form of resistance was discussed, not only due to the authori-ties' policy of procrastination, but also due to the fear of terrorism and religious extremism. The below quote from an interview with Mourad Badraoui, an unemployed protester who participated in civil disobedi-ence, indicates that the issue of terrorism was connected to the Maknassy unemployed resistance. While describing various constraints that the unemployed protesters encountered, he noted:

> Something new appeared in Tunisia after 2013, which is called terrorism. [...] There is fear in Tunisian society that this phenomenon will spread across the country, causing security problems. [...] I will give you an example of Maknassy. Maknassy had six days of clashes with the police on this street near the police station over there. But over time, people started worrying that this would lead to a security vacuum that can affect society. When we were working to fix our economic political and social institutions, we found ourselves stuck in the same cycle – that is, security. This is being taken into consideration by the activists. This is why they escalate confrontation with the government at some specific times and, at other times, they sit back and keep things calm. They then take the time to get organised again and go back to conflicts with the government.[15]

Badraoui's narrative reflects that the fear of terrorism among the Tunisian population affected the resistance tactics deployed by the unemployed protesters in the town. While the confrontation between protesters and police occurred mostly when the latter attempted to thwart the protests through violent means, the escalation of tension between the two parties was also often used as a protest tactic in order to attract the attention of the authorities and the media, as well as to justify their more disruptive actions. Local UGTT activist Mohsen Ghafr noted that the authorities' conflation of vandalism and terrorism led various local social movements to rely more on non-disruptive actions so that they could escape these actions' association with terrorism.[16] As the next sections will elaborate in detail, the Maknassy unemployed protesters' rationale behind initiating civil disobedience and their tactics cannot be understood in isolation from how they responded to the perceived increasing threat of terrorism and the authorities' abuse of this threat.

The State is Behind the Rise of Terrorism in Tunisia

An important similarity between the Maknassy and the UDC unemployed protesters consists of the fact that they actively utilised the discursive terrain of global Islamist terrorism in the process of criticising the ruling elites. The protesters presented Islamist terrorism as an objective fact that had emerged in Tunisia since 2011, and their notion of terrorism revolved around two categories of terrorists, those coming from outside and those going abroad, thereby rendering Tunisia both a target and an exporting country of terrorism. In doing so, they did 'adopt and invoke the tactics of government'[17] in a strategic way in order to blame those who ruled the country for the worsening social and economic conditions. The below quote from an interview with Badraoui illustrates how the protesters categorised Tunisian youths who travelled to the 'conflict zones' as terrorists and used this category to amplify the perceived responsibility of the state for the absence of democracy and security. When asked about his opinion on Tunisian democracy, he answered:

> The whole thing is media marketing, marketing Tunisia's image abroad as an emerging democracy that is currently building its institutions and completing its democratic process. It's also internal marketing to neutralise the majority of the population in these conflicts. […] It is still not the case in Tunisia, the government is still centralised, it controls everything. There exist dialogues in the media, it [the government) works, but it does not work to solve problems. The opposite is the case. It wants to deepen the crisis. The subject of bringing the Tunisian terrorists in the conflict zones back to Tunisia… that was proposed by the government, on its insistence. We have thousands of our youth, we do not know who was supporting the course of their travel to conflict zones. […] After the revolution you hear about thousands of Tunisian terrorists. Who is responsible for recruiting them? What are the mechanisms that were provided for them to ensure their

travel and logistics? We need to find answers to all of that. [...] The regime is working to maintain stability in the country, no more and no less, with all means, oppression, dictatorship, bribery, corruption and terrorism.[18]

Badraoui explicitly challenges the idea that Tunisia is a democratic country, by framing this view as the outcome of 'media marketing', the intended effect of which was to make invisible the struggle for the right to work and regional development in the interior regions. While being against what he considered to be media propaganda, he criticises the government as controlling the media and working to deepen the crisis rather than solving problems. He then links his criticism of the lack of democracy and the government's attempts to neutralise the socio-economic struggles in the interior regions to terrorists coming back to Tunisia. Through his narrative, Tunisian youths who travelled to 'conflict zones' are described as terrorists, rendering Tunisia a country vulnerable to the threat of terrorism. His emphasis, however, is on 'the state' that he considers to be directly involved in the increasing number of Tunisian terrorists. By depicting those travelling to conflict zones as being recruited and supported with logistics, he constructs terrorists as passive subjects and the state as an active agent in producing terrorists. His negative portrayal of the state is also amplified by placing terrorism as one of its authoritarian means to maintain the *status quo*.

The Maknassy protesters' framing of terrorism also indicates that their association of those ruling the country with terrorists was constituted by and re-constitutive of the discursive terrain of terrorism, where Islam is understood as providing symbolic and material sources for extreme violence. The below texts posted on the public Facebook page of the Maknassy movement in May and July 2014 illustrate how the protesters perceived and reproduced terrorism as being closely related to Islam, and how their notion of Islamist terrorism was in turn used to render it as being created and manipulated by those in power:

> The truth of what is happening in Tunisia:
>
> The exploiters tried to make a coup before 14 January 2011, using popular pressure... The revolution ruined their plan to calm down the street and to take over power... Then they ran the election to return to power, [...] it didn't work... Then they changed their tactics... They created crises... They created terrorism by investing in the enthusiasm of some takfiri groups and in the infiltration of their ranks, so that they can be used as a façade... External parties intervened to help them... They will continue their attempts to take the power...[19]
>
> Why do not the terrorists record their operations in video, if they have all these capabilities to penetrate the Chaambi area and if they believe in their

false faith? […] How can they have the wonderful abilities to get to know the movements of the army and their sites? Everyone is convinced that some of those who fall into religion are at the forefront [of terrorism], but who is behind them and who is playing the game? We sacrifice ourselves for you, Tunisia, the victory of our National Army.[20]

As the texts indicate, the speakers' acts of claiming 'truth' and casting doubt on terrorist operations in Tunisia were performed to criticise part of the ruling elites. These posts did not specify who was deemed to be behind terrorism. Yet, their identity can be inferred from the description of the exploiters: in the first text, it is those who tried to stage a coup and ran the election; in the second text, the speaker targets particular individuals or groups of the domestic elites that (re)emerged after January 2011, based on the portrayal of those supporting terrorists as having access to sensitive information about the Tunisian military. From the governmentality perspective, the significance of these posts lies in the following: in an attempt to amplify the elites' negative image, the speaker reproduces and at the same time tactically makes use of Islamist terrorism, which operates as an important discursive element of the securitisation of the unemployed. In the texts, terrorism is constructed as committed by global jihadi organisations, as marked by the use of language such as '*takfiri*',[21] the 'infiltration of their ranks', 'external parties', 'those who fall into religion' and the 'Chaambi area', which is known as a stronghold of jihadi militant groups, especially Al-Qaeda in the Islamic Maghrib (AQIM), the IS and their local affiliations, such as Katibah Uqbah bn Nafa'a and Jund al-Khalifah (KUNJK).

The above Facebook posts and Badraoui's narrative criticising the state and political elites with his reference to Islamist terrorism show that, similar to the UDC case, the Maknassy unemployed movement and the ruling elites were antagonistic to each other – in Laclau and Mouffe's sense – but this antagonistic frontier between the two parties was not totally 'sutured'. Their relationship was antagonistic yet not fully sutured in the sense that – while competing with each other for starkly different approaches to what a post-uprising Tunisia should look like – they operated within and upon the same 'field of actions'[22] represented by global Islamist terrorism in the process of delegitimising each other. From the governmentality approach, the porousness of the antagonistic frontier between the elites and the protesters reflects a mutually constitutive relationship between the two parties. Inasmuch as the inevitable threat of terrorism served as an essential discursive element of the elites' neoliberal governing of the unemployed subject, the protesters' invocation of the danger of Islamist terrorism had an effect of justifying and reifying the exercise of domination that they intended to resist. At the same time, however, it also points to the limitations inherent in the elites' securitisation of the Maknassy unemployed movement. The protesters' re-signification of terrorism as being created and supported by the ruling elite shows how the dominant logic of security operated against the will to govern the unemployed protests and destabilised their attempts to stabilise the *status quo*.

They Deceive the People in the Name of the War on Terror

While the UDC emphasised the War on Terror as necessary but failing due to the authorities' use of violence against civil society, the Maknassy protesters focused more on revealing the abusive aspect of the elites' counter-terrorism practices. One such example is the Maknassy protesters' narrative that the elites' counter-terrorism 'deceives' the people. This disparity between the UDC and the Maknassy movement can be interpreted partly as a result of the Maknassy protesters' experience of living in one of the interior regions that have been historically labelled and securitised as 'dangerous zones', where foreign and domestic terrorists reportedly reside and constantly attempt to manipulate the grievances of the local people. As illustrated earlier, not only the ruling elites but also Maknassy's local inhabitants claimed that terrorists were present in Sidi Bouzid. Having occasionally witnessed violent confrontations between the security forces and armed individuals or groups in their region, the Maknassy protesters also identified these militant groups as terrorists. Yet, at the same time, their prolonged experience of being discriminated against and policed by the coastal elites in the name of national security intensified their hostile attitude towards the newly declared War on Terror.

'Living in Sidi Bouzid' was the very condition that partially structured the protesters' ways of thinking and behaving, making their resistance to the elites' securitising practices paradoxical and, in the Foucauldian understanding, counter-conductive. As the below excerpt from an interview with Maknassy unemployed protester Abou Nabil shows, the protesters' ambivalent attitude towards terrorism and counter-terrorism is reflected in the way in which they accepted terrorism as a real threat, while destabilising and working not to be deceived by the counter-terrorism agenda that the authorities deployed as a technique of domination:

> We inform the activists not to obtain papers, CDs [compact discs] and so forth [and not to keep them] in the house, as they may have recordings about terrorist attacks. For example, I give you a CD or go to your house and find your mother

and tell her to give this CD to you. Then, the police will come and search the house and find the CD containing recordings related to terrorist attacks so that you can be accused. [I: Did this actually happen?] I predict this because, in my opinion, the public institutions can do this. This is what actually happened lately with an activist among the so-called site workers. They wanted to fake an accusation against him as a terrorist without evidence. What if there was evidence? He would have disappeared. He was released [and the police said that] it was because his name was similar to a name they had. […] They [worked] to make us believe that it was a terrorism accusation, so that we didn't support him. But we said that we trusted our friend and that he's far from this ideology and the extremist movements. We did stand up for him.[23]

Explaining how the unemployed protesters became subject to the charge of terrorism, Nabil identifies terrorism as a label fabricated by the authorities ('public institutions') to criminalise certain individuals and to deceive other protesters so that they will not support those criminalised. Importantly, although this narrative began with his imagined scenario, his perception that the authorities can easily fabricate a terrorism charge is based on an actual case that his fellow activist experienced. It is notable that his portrayal of a terrorism charge as created by the authorities parallels his projection of terrorism as a 'real thing'. The idea of terrorism as an object is constructed by his portrayal of the CD's content as related to 'terrorist attacks', as well as his attempts to defend his fellow protester as being far removed from 'terrorists' marked by 'this ideology and extremist movements'. Having acknowledged the presence of terrorists, the protesters rejected the authorities' terrorism charge by standing up for the activist accused of terrorism.

The Maknassy protesters' efforts to avoid any accusations while defending their fellow activists associated with terrorism may appear to be an insignificant distraction or irrelevant to the unemployed resistance in general, if resistance is construed as a 'coherent and progressive counter-hegemonic challenge'.[24] Yet, from the governmentality perspective, these acts are a manifestation of the counter-conduct entailed in the Maknassy unemployed movement. Unpacking this seemingly insignificant counter-securitising practice helps us understand the relationship between the authorities and the socio-economic protests, beyond the simplistic notion that the former governs and that the latter are either in compliance with or opposition to the regime. What we can read from Nabil's narrative regarding the notion of counter-conduct is that the protesters both reified and challenged the elites' securitisation of the unemployed by wanting to be governed differently. They reified the responsible and vigilant unemployed subject who can exercise a disciplined freedom by distancing themselves (and encouraging others to distance themselves) from 'terrorism-related materials' and 'extreme movements'. In doing so, the protesters unwittingly validated the authorities' 'right to enunciate and enforce'[25] the controversial anti-terrorism measures, which they intended to criticise. As the last two sentences of his narrative indicates, however, the protesters also worked to escape the way in which the state attempted to divide and rule the unemployed protesters, by not believing in what the authorities intended to make them believe.

The Maknassy protesters also actively used satire and humour to disrupt the ways in which they became subject to securitisation. As Malmvig has pointed out in his analysis of counter-conductive resistance to the authoritarian regime in Syria, although the use of ridicule and satire does not aim at a direct challenge, they often operate in novel ways, thereby opening up possibilities for resistance against 'relations of power that seek to steer and guide behavior towards specific goals'.[26] The below Facebook post provides an example of how the Maknassy movement used satire as a way of resisting the media's invocation of the War on Terror in criminalising the unemployed protests:

> One of the law students in Sfax assaulted the 'Batons' [police] with his head while supporting the protesters in Sfax. So, those who had sympathy for the innocent victim initiated the campaign 'I am Batons' and called for ruling the aggressor under the law of terrorism... !!!!!!! This is the reality of our media. Don't be surprised.[27]

This text was posted in April 2017, with the image of a young man's head injured by police batons. While illustrating the police brutality against the unemployed protesters with this image, the speaker provided a version of what is considered a typical media narrative of police violence against protesters. By describing the actual victim of police brutality as the 'aggressor' and the police (marked by the metaphorical term 'batons') as the 'innocent victim' in a sarcastic manner, the speaker criticises the media's responsibilisation of the protesters for violent confrontations between them and the security forces. In doing so, the speaker particularly problematises the ways in which the anti-terrorism laws are invoked in the media in order to associate the protests with terrorism, by presenting the imagined 'I am Batons' campaign as a parody of media performance. The speaker uses what Malmvig has called a 'strategy of Othering',[28] by inverting the relationship between the security forces and the protesters and using humour as counter-conduct so as to expose and reject the ways in which anti-terrorism measures operated against the protesters.

Not only did the Maknassy movement use humour, but it also took genealogical critique as a counter-securitising strategy to make counter-terrorism into the ruling elites' political tool, as the following Facebook post shows:

> Terrorism is not a new story in Tunisia, and this subject played out when they [political leaders] wanted to take power. If we look at the history, Bourguiba took power over the corpse of many freedom fighters who were called 'Falaga', because at that time the word 'terrorism' did not exist, and then he made many agreements with the coloniser, and a number of assassinations happened, like Hachad. […] Later, Ben Ali came and used fighting terrorism to get close to Bourguiba and removed him through a coup. Now we are witnessing Essebsi who reached Carthage to eliminate terrorism.[29]

This text can be interpreted as a criticism of the return of the old political figures, represented by former President Essebsi who took control of the government, by positioning themselves as the only force that could eliminate terrorism in Tunisia. It is a genealogical critique in the sense that, rather than relying on abstract values as a method of criticism, it offers a 'historical investigation' into specific events in Tunisia's contemporary history – events that have constituted Tunisians as subjects of what they are 'doing, thinking, saying'.[30] Negating the elites' narrative that 'terrorism is a new phenomenon in Tunisia', the speaker investigates how fighting terrorism was constructed and 'played with' by the political leaders 'to take power', by revealing that the term 'terrorism' did not exist during the era of Bourguiba, the first President of Tunisia after independence. In doing so, the elites' notion of counter-terrorism is historicised with the term *'falaga'* ('Bandit'), which Bourguiba used to criminalise and repress the armed resistance groups against the French domination in the process of consolidating his rule and which was then re-used with Ben Ali's War on Terror. What should be noted is that the speaker's equation of *falaga* with 'freedom fighters' is closely connected to the perception of many Maknassy protesters; according to them, their region has historically been marginalised and securitised in favour of the coastal regions, due to their parents and grand-parents' continued resistance against the French domination and the domestic authoritarian regime. As such, the speaker's positive connotation of *falaga* and critique of counter-terrorism lie in the particularity of the protesters' experience of living in the interior region as 'sons of fighters'.

The above narrative provides an example of how the UDC and the Maknassy movement took different forms of resistance when it came to their counter-securitising practices. As Chapter 5 has illustrated, the UDC criticised the elites' use of anti-terrorism to police the unemployed by uti-lising a liberal notion of human rights, rule of law and democracy, which, in Foucault's understanding, is not genealogical as such, as it sought to 'make possible a metaphysics' to counter a metaphysics.[31] Compared to the UDC, the Maknassy movement's criticism took a more genealogical form of criticism, in the sense that its problematisation of the notion of terrorism and counter-terrorism deconstructed the way in which a set of specific and contingent historical events came to structure the discourse of security.[32] Both forms of critique exercised their 'right to question', but the Maknassy protesters' unique experience – resulting from the political, economic and social marginalisation of the interior regions – rendered their narratives more subversive than those of the UDC.

No Trade-off between Counter-terrorism and the Right to Work

> When it comes to terrorism, most lawyers would find it very difficult to defend [the protesters charged with terrorism]. Here in Maknassy, the situation is different, because we initiated our civil disobedience on 30 December and included slogans such as 'in the name of hunger, the law [that criminalises social movements] should be abolished'. The message we tried to convey through this slogan was that a man-made-cultural law cannot stand against our national rights. Civil disobedience in its essence is a message to the authorities, telling them that we are going to disobey the law deliberately, because they violated the constitution, and that violating the constitution is a much more serious crime than breaking a law.[33]

As the coordinator and spokesperson of the Maknassy civil disobedi-ence, Jaouadi was keen to highlight the novelty and uniqueness of the Maknassy unemployed movement. Explaining how other interior regions became subject to both 'actual' and 'fabricated' terrorism, he emphasises that, 'here in Maknassy, the situation is different'. The above narrative produced by Jaouadi illustrates that the Maknassy movement's uniqueness lay in the protesters' counter-conduct – that is, the *will* not to be dominated in the name of counter-terrorism. This will was expressed through their counter-narrative – namely, that fighting terrorism cannot be an excuse for the state to ignore their right to work and regional development. Similar to the UDC's case, the Maknassy protesters' counter-narrative reflects 'the connections that were immediately established'[34] between their counter-securitising practices and economic problems embedded in Maknassy. Notably, however, while the UDC attempted to weave together the two subjects, counter-terrorism and unemployment, in such a way as to render employment the right way to counter terrorism, the Maknassy protesters focused more on the disentanglement of the link between the two. As marked by Jaouadi's claim 'in the name of hunger, the law should be abolished', the protesters sought to destabilise the dominant narrative of counter-terrorism not through practices of re-articulation, but mainly through practices of disarticulating and rejecting such articulation.

When asked about the authorities' responses to their civil disobedience, Jaouadi answered that their attempt to distort and oppress the Maknassy movement failed, given the protesters' clear message and tactics. Yet, he went on to warn the government of what might come after civil disobedience, if the government did not meet the protesters' demands; he noted:

> When I am asked the question of 'civil disobedience, and what's next?' by the press, I respond by raising the following question to the government. 'Civil disobedience, and what's next? Are you pushing it towards chaos or towards a new revolution without horizon?' All that happens at a time when the regional circumstances are critical. People know that terrorism is waiting for the right moment, and that it is nourished by social chaos. We have a profound battle for survival, and we don't fear the mess. We warn the government that we don't fear the chaos when we feel hungry. We are concerned for our country, but we hold you [the government] accountable, and we will keep doing so by hook or crook.[35]

This excerpt provides an elaboration of how the Maknassy protesters' act of rejecting the elites' association of the unemployed protests with terrorism was rationalised based on their sense of poverty and deprivation. In Jaouadi's narrative, terrorism is constructed as an objective and impending threat, as marked by the sentence 'people know that terrorism is waiting for the right moment'. He also associates terrorism with social movements, by framing the latter as linked to the 'social mess' that feeds terrorism and allows it to flourish. This social mess, however, is constructed as result of what would happen if the government ignored civil disobedience, thus rendering the government responsible for any potential disorder. More importantly, he presents the social instability and the potential threat of terrorism as dismissible in that he frames the Maknassy struggle for the right to work as a 'battle for survival', and there is nothing to fear of the latter. As clearly indicated in the last two sentences, Jaouadi's association of social movements with terrorism was not meant to integrate the struggle for employment with the War on Terror, which was the case with the UDC; rather, his articulation is meant to reject the ways in which the elites' counter-terrorism operates against the protesters' claim to the right to work.

The protesters' problematisation of the elites' neglect of the interior regions based on the excuse of combatting terrorism had already existed prior to their civil disobedience in 2017. The below Facebook post was written after two speeches by former President Essebsi and Prime Minister Youssef Chahed. In his speech during the Labour Day celebrations on 1 May 2015, Essebsi had highlighted the importance of security, stability and a favourable environment for attracting foreign investment in the face of terrorism, while also calling for the suspension of protests until Tunisia would become stabilised.[36] Ten days after this speech, Chahed also announced his government's determination to fight terrorism, at a press meeting where he discursively linked the protests in the interior regions to terrorism, noting that they 'allowed for the passage of terrorists'.[37] Countering these speeches, the Maknassy movement claimed:

> We told the government, give us our right to work and development. The government said that the priority is the War on Terror. No, we do not accept the trade-off [between the two]. Give us our right, and the terrorists, if they exist now, we will eat them with our teeth.[38]

The sentence 'no, we do not accept the trade-off' clearly indicates that the speaker directly challenges the state's association of the unemployed struggle with impeding the War on Terror, through the practice of unmasking and exposing the government's intention to construct counter-terrorism and the protesters' demands as two competing objectives and to place the former as superior to the latter. Also, the state's attempt to 'trade off' counter-terrorism against the protesters' right to work is rejected, by doubting and invalidating its claim about the War on Terror. Interpreted in relation to the protesters' narrative of terrorism as a real object and of counter-terrorism measures as a fabrication of the regime, the hypothetical conditional sentence 'if they exist now, we will eat them with our teeth' can be understood not as a refusal of the necessity to fight terrorism as such, but as a sarcastic refusal of the ways in which the protesters were securitised in the name of the War on Terror.

The Maknassy protesters' first narrative (Islamist terrorism as a real object supported by the elites) and second narrative (the existing counter-terrorism measures as the regime's political tool) are chained together in a hierarchical way, under the meta-narrative of 'no trade-off between counter-terrorism and the right to work'. While the Maknassy protesters produced counter-narratives more radical than those of the UDC, the protesters' (re)production of the dominant notion of terrorism indicates that their resistance was also partially implicated in the elites' securitisation of the unemployed. The next section will elaborate on how their resistance to the dominant securitising practices *from within* was performed through their efforts to escape the given subjectivities and to redefine ways of conducting the self.

Fighters against Terrorism and Victims of State Terrorism

> Traditional terrorism does not frighten us; we are the grandsons of the freedom fighters. The ownership of this homeland has been achieved through the blood of our parents and grandparents, so we will not allow our land to be defiled by the instigators of sedition.[39]

While the UDC identified itself as the national union representing the Tunisian unemployed population in its entirety, the Maknassy unemployed protesters emphasised their locally constructed collective identity, as marked by one of their slogans: 'I am Maknassy'. Having identified themselves as different from the UDC, the Maknassy unemployed protesters' counter-securitising practices also entailed a struggle for 'the care of the self'. They performed alternative subjectivities partly beyond what the Maknassy unemployed youth ought to be from the perspective of the ruling elites and by reconstituting what they should be and do from their own perspectives. Firstly, similar to the UDC, the Maknassy protesters' perception of terrorism as a real object and threat was reflected in the way in which they subjectified the self as being immune to and against terrorism. As the above Facebook post illustrates, the protesters often invoked their locally constructed subjectivity as 'grandsons of the freedom fighters' who fought to protect Tunisia from French colonialism, in an attempt to distance themselves from the stigmatising term 'terrorism'.

The Maknassy protesters' active denial of the terrorist label was also performed during their acts of civil disobedience. Civil disobedience, by definition, is meant to be disruptive and to involve actions of violating certain laws, with the aim to bring about social, economic or political changes. Indeed, the protesters deliberately chose what the elites considered to be violent and illegal means – that is, blocking off a national highway with burning tires. The purpose of their law-breaking was partly (but significantly) to convey the message that the elites' implementation of anti-terrorism laws cannot be used against the protesters' right to work. In the language of one of the coordinators of the Maknassy civil disobedience, 'civil disobedience in its essence is a message to the authorities, telling them that we are going to violate the law deliberately, because they violate the constitution'. However, when it comes to the ways in which their message was performed on the ground, the protesters were concerned with not being seen as violent bandits and terrorists as much as with maximising the effects of law-breaking:

> We are going to violate the law deliberately, because they violate the constitution. That is our overall message, but in terms of the way in which we practice it, we have certain rules that we follow. Indeed, the rallies are held only until 5 pm. We asked the security forces to protect the public facilities and sent invitations to activists and journalists to come to Sidi Bouzid, [making them] see what was really happening. Luckily, a few days thereafter, the truth was revealed. It was proven that Maknassy had peaceful strikes, and that it was a model of discipline and absence of vandalism. Concerning terrorism, the youth went out playing music day and night in front of the police stations to show that they call for culture, art and painting. […] We all know that terrorism breaks with art, painting and music. In this way, we showed that we weren't terrorists.[40]

While performing civil disobedience, the protesters sought to act peacefully at the site of their protests, the aim of which, according to Jaouadi, was to prove the truth that the Maknassy civil disobedience did not consist of vandalism or terrorism, but of a peaceful and disciplined civic movement. This intent was demonstrated by limiting their acts of resistance to daytime, cooperating with the police and, interestingly, performing arts, since, according to him, terrorism is incompatible with art. The protest tactics deployed by the Maknassy protesters show how their acts to 'refuse to be conducted *like that* and to experiment with *other* forms of conduct and self-conduct'[41] simultaneously reified the subjectivities promoted by the elites. By performing the civil, peaceful and artistic characteristics of their resistance, the protesters attempted to challenge and reject deviant, violent and terrorist-like subjectivities. As Chapter 4 has illustrated, however, these categories of action are not external to the 'technologies of the self' promoted by the elites to encourage the protesters to be able to govern themselves as patriotic and vigilant citizens. The notions of 'civil, peaceful and disciplined' constitute the key discursive elements mobilised to tame the unemployed protesters, not through force or violence, but through the management of the protesters' exercise of free will.

The immediate effects of this 'non-violent-but-disruptive' protest were ambivalent. The protesters were successful in terms of presenting their struggle as a novel mode of civil disobedience, and by doing so they attracted the attention and support of several influential civil society actors. Yet, as the Maknassy civil disobedience operated within the limits set by the authorities, it ended up being quite easily manageable and governable, and therefore could be ignored. The ambivalence of the 'civil' subject position constructed through the protesters' non-violent disruption in a way points to the limitations of the liberal notion of civil disobedience.[42] According to several critiques, a key limitation of modern civil disobedience has to do with its commitment to non-violence and respect towards the rule of law, in the sense that it can operate only as, not a rejection, but an acceptance and legitimisation of the established authorities.[43] As Roland Bleiker has argued in his critique of civil disobedience, while civil disobedience may challenge certain laws or bring down a government, it inevitably 'incarnates the modern obsession with control, the desire for order, for certainty, and for essences',[44] which are the very techniques to nurture docile citizens. The Maknassy protesters' decision to initiate civil disobedience was a tactical choice, partly but importantly to escape the label of terrorism. This indicates that the discourse of the War on Terror shared by both the elites and the unemployed protesters served as an important facilitator in encouraging the protesters to exercise order, control and self-surveillance, while they resisted the ways in which the authorities securitised the protesters.

It should be emphasised, however, that the protesters not only reproduced the hegemonic discourse of terrorism through their performance of the docile and vigilant citizen subjectivity, but they also re-appropriated the stigmatising term 'terrorism' to denounce the state. Whereas the UDC protesters used the term 'state terrorism' to emphasise the illegitimacy and brutality of sovereign violence, the Maknassy protesters deployed the same term to responsibilise the state for the socio-economic marginalisation and its negative impact on their life. The protesters' identification of poverty as state terrorism then served to subjectify them as victims of terrorism. The following Facebook post illustrates how the Maknassy movement strategically exploited the hegemonic notion of terrorism so as to emphasise their own notion of state terrorism:

> Traditional terrorism does not frighten us; we are the grandsons of the freedom fighters. The ownership of this homeland has been achieved through the blood of parents and grandparents, so we will not allow our land to be defiled by the instigators of the sedition. But there is another terrorism that we have no ability [to control], and this is state terrorism. The project of marginalisation has tired us, the impoverishment has destroyed us.[45]

The speaker first describes terrorism as a type of invasion of Tunisia, carried out by instigators. Yet, it soon becomes clear, based on the use of the contrastive conjunction 'but', that the emphasis of this post is placed on 'another terrorism', which the speaker considers to be committed by the state. It is notable that, whereas 'we' is framed as an active subject in relation to 'traditional terrorism', the same 'we' is presented as a passive subject, lacking the 'ability' to confront state terrorism. The protesters' passive subject position is further solidified with the elaboration of 'we' as being destroyed, due to impoverishment. Subjectifying the state as terrorist based on the use of parallelisms shows how the protesters' reproduction of the 'established orders of subjection'[46] served as a resource with which they not only sustained some of these orders, but also subverted them. While the protesters' fighter subject position escapes a naïve and/or deviant subjectivity but reifies a self-disciplined and vigilant subjectivity, the construction of the victim subject position and state terrorism destabilises both subject positions. They do so by challenging the dominant meaning of terrorism with an alternative notion of terrorism – that is, 'poverty caused by the state'. Also, the fighter subjectivity was re-utilised by the protesters for constructing another category of terrorism that discursively subverts the subject position of the state as the one authoritative and credible institution having knowledge on terrorism.

We are Revolutionaries

Lastly, the Maknassy protesters sought to escape the subjectification of the unemployed as self-helping entrepreneurial citizens by redefining themselves as (potential) revolutionaries. Considering the protesters' liberal form of civil disobedience, one may see the claim to revolution as contradictory to their actual practices. As I have discussed in the context of the UDC's case, however, what makes this revolutionary subjectivity interesting for the governmentality approach has not so much to do with evaluating what such a contradiction means from one's own normative perspective, but with the question of how the protesters (re)appropriated and 'normatised' revolution differently, and for what purposes. The practice of protest itself is a 'powerful site' through which new subjectivities are constituted.[47] In the context of the Maknassy unemployed movement, this *being otherwise* was clearly connected to the protesters' previous experience of the revolutionary moments and their continued street protests afterwards. Also, similar to the UDC, the protesters' identification of their revolution as a process which had not yet been completed was constitutive of their revolutionary subjectivity (and *vice versa*).

The following excerpt of an interview with Nabil illustrates how his revolutionary experience during the 2010–11 political upheaval and his notion of revolution as a process are outlined to constitute the Maknassy protesters as potential revolutionaries. When asked about the protesters' future plan of action, he noted:

Similar to now, at the time of Ben Ali we were associated with terrorism and vandalism. As we haven't been able to achieve our goals, we decided to go back to the way in which we protested on 17 December. We're ready to be criminals, and we will face bullets if necessary. [...] In my point of view, the revolution is not complete yet. The revolution won't succeed unless it achieves its goals: social, cultural and economic improvement. We're still at the level of demands, and we fear for our country because the costs of the revolution were so high at all levels. But we're willing to sacrifice more if that's necessary. This means that we'll move from the level of demands to the revolutionary level, like in the time of Ben Ali.[48]

According to Nabil, the Maknassy unemployed movement until then had maintained its moderate and peaceful forms of action, but it could shift to a more radical and revolutionary movement. Interestingly, in the last sentence he describes the shift from non-violent to revolutionary level not as an unpredicted and sudden change, which had been the case of the 2011 Uprising from the perspective of many Tunisian people as well as observers outside, but as a change that the protesters could consciously bring about. As indicated in the clauses 'like in the time of Ben Ali', 'decided to go back to the way' and his description of the revolution as 'not complete yet', his self-formation as a potential revolutionary is achieved through his memory of confronting state violence and leading radical change, as well as through his understanding of revolution as a path towards solving social, cultural and economic problems. The revolutionary subjectivity operates to subjectify the protesters as a not-so-governable subject in the name of the War on Terror, as marked in his claim that 'we're ready to be criminals, and we will face bullets if necessary'.

Not only did the revolutionary subjectivity signify a more radical mode of actions, but some Maknassy protesters also connected 'being revolutionary' to a new way of thinking about and approaching the revolution. Badraoui's narrative can serve as a representative example:

Now, after, let's say, six years [after the Uprising], social activism is improving its structures and mechanisms. Civil disobedience is the last step of protesting; we did simple protests, strikes, etc. for one year, then evolved into civil obedience. [...] We have not surrendered for the past six years. At least the youth in the community who were in conflict with the authority knew that the state was neither able to find solutions nor looking for solutions. It wants to keep this reality by all means, such as dictatorship and terrorism. How to escape this reality? With organisation. Today people are getting closer to each other. [...] Finding a local popular authority capable of making changes, away from the ideological speeches of Marxists, Nasserism, or Ba'athism, would lead to an alternative [to them] in the revolutionary path.[49]

While Nabil promotes the revolutionary subject position through his emphasis on the Maknassy protesters' role during the revolutionary moments in 2010–11, Badraoui's focus is on the protesters' ability to be self-reflexive and progressive. By describing the Maknassy unemployed movement as having evolved over the past six years in terms of its organisational structure and protest repertoire, he subjectifies the protesters not only as resilient, but also as capable of learning from their previous experience and of searching alternative ways of resisting. In his view, the protesters' progressiveness is an outcome of the practice of *knowing* from their interaction with the authorities that 'the regime was neither able to find solutions nor looking for solutions'. This knowing is an active and progressive 'exercise of the self on the self'[50] to develop and transform the self, in that it is translated into the self-reflexive question 'how to escape this reality?' He notes that organising a 'popular local authority' should be their alternative to Marxism, Nasserism or Ba'athism, if they are to accomplish the revolutionary path. According to him, while Tunisian leftist movements with these political ideologies positioned themselves as alternative to Ben Ali's authoritarian neoliberal regime, they failed to live up to the expectations of the grassroots revolutionaries and ended up serving the *status quo* due to their 'elitist approach' – that is, their obsession with electoral competition, without any concrete strategies and actions for socio-economic change for the marginalised segments of Tunisian society.[51]

Although Nabil's and Badraoui's emphases vary, both narratives involve a struggle of 'not being like that'. The revolutionary subjectivity is implicitly constituted by their notion of revolution as a path towards socio-economic justice, a path that requires alternative modes of being and thinking and, if necessary, a more radical mode of action. This indicates that the revolutionary subjectivity produced by the Maknassy protesters was not merely a rejection of the ways in which the ruling elites policed them. Rather, they sought to escape or, at any rate, to subvert the given securitised subjectivities that rendered them free subjects able to exercise their political liberties, but only to the extent that they do not dare to threaten the neoliberalisation of Tunisian democracy. In this sense, the will to live as revolutionaries as performed in Maknassy was a struggle to govern the self beyond that 'artificially arranged liberty'[52] and a refusal to live as *homo oeconomicus*.

Concluding Remarks

The Maknassy protesters' counter-securitising practices presented both similarities and dissimilarities with the UDC case. Compared to the UDC protesters, the protesters in Maknassy produced more critical and subversive narratives focusing on separating the self from terrorism and on discursively associating the ruling elites with terrorists. That being said, the Maknassy protesters' resistance was neither totally subversive nor entirely antagonistic against, but rather implicated in, the dominant securitising practices. Above all, the protesters' invocation of Islamist terrorism and a liberal mode of civil disobedience were not external to the security logic of Tunisian neoliberal governing, to the extent that they were governed to think and behave rationally, so as to be vigilant about the threat of terrorism and be self-disciplined while performing their political rights. Yet, the protesters' responsibilisation of the ruling elites for terrorism and poverty, their deconstruction of the elites' notion of counter-terrorism through a genealogical approach and, particularly, their subjectification of the self as (potential) revolutionaries indicates that, similar to the UDC protests, the Maknassy protests needed to be conducted differently and had to re-define ways to govern the self.

The two unemployed movements suggest that the process of securitisation of the unemployed was not so much what the state imposed and what the unemployed were passively subordinated to. Rather, it was a convoluted process that involved multiple actors, including those governing, those governed and, most importantly, those resisting. The unemployed protesters' location in the securitisation process was ambivalent. They resisted the elites' association of the unemployed with terrorists, not by entirely refusing such articulation, but instead by re-appropriating, distorting and deconstructing the elites' narratives as well as by producing alternative subjectivities.

Notes

1. Interview with Abdelhak Jaouadi, aged forty-three, spokesman of the Harmna movement and coordinator of the civil disobedience, Maknassy, 3 February 2017.
2. Interview with Abdul Ahman, aged forty-three, head of the Forum Tunisien pour les Droits Economiques et Sociaux (FTDES), Tunis, 6 February 2017.
3. Interview with Rached Ghassen, aged thirty-two, independent unemployed activist, Kasserine, 3 February 2017.
4. Yehia, 'Tahqiq: al-Maknassy al-Ghadbah al-Maghniyah ... 'Alam Ahly wa Nasi'.
5. Interview with Mohsen Ghafr, aged forty, local UGTT activist, Maknassy, 31 January 2017.
6. TAP, 'Mutalib bi Tamiyah al 'Adlah fi Mu'tamdiyah al-Maknassy min Wulayah Sidi Bouzid'.

7. TAP, 'Mashari'a Tanmawiyah li Fa'idah Mu'tamditi al-Maknassy wa Manzil Bouzayn min Wulayah Sidi Bouizid'.

8. Assabahnews, 'al-Maknassy: Tauaquf Ishghal al-Mashari' Utheer al-Shik wa al-Ihtaj'.

9. Kalima Tounes, 'Sidi Bouzid: Ba'th Mashrou'a "Masna'a al-Sayarat" Qariban fi al-Maknassy'.

10. Interview with Rached Yousef, a young unemployed protester, Maknassy, 2 February 2017.

11. Hakaek, 'al-Maknassy: I'tisam 'Harimna' lil Mu'tlin 'an al-'Amal bi Maqr al-Mu'tamdiyah'.

12. Attounissia, 'Sidi Bouzid: I'ta' Isharah al-Intlaq li Munjim al-Phosphat bil-Maknassy'.

13. Hakaek, 'Najihoun fi Munadhrah Intidab 'Umal bi Manjim al-Phosphat bil Maknassy Yaqta'un al-Tariq baina Sfax wa Gafsa'.

14. Abdelhak Jaouadi, author interview.

15. Interview with Mourad Badraoui, aged twenty-seven, independent unemployed activist, Maknassy, 2 February 2017.

16. Interview with Mohsen Ghafr.

17. Death, 'Counter-conducts as a mode of resistance', p. 244.

18. Interview with Mourad Badraoui.

19. Maknassy Révolutionnaire, 30 May 2014.

20. Maknassy Révolutionnaire, 17 July 2014.

21. While *takfir* in Arabic refers to excommunication by designating someone as an infidel, the term *takfiri* is predominantly used to denote an extreme and violent Salafist.

22. Foucault, 'The subject and power', p. 790.

23. Interview with Abou Nabil, aged twenty-nine, independent unemployed activist, Maknassy, 31 March 2017.

24. Death, 'Counter-conducts as a mode of resistance', pp. 201–7.

25. Pottage, 'Power as an art of contingency', p. 16.

26. Malmvig, 'Eyes wide shut', pp. 264–68.

27. Maknassy Révolutionnaire, 18 April 2017.

28. Malmvig, 'Eyes wide shut', p. 269.

29. Maknassy Révolutionnaire, 1 April 2015.

30. Foucault, *The politics of truth*, p. 125.

31. Ibid. p. 126.

32. Ibid. pp. 124–25.

33. Interview with Abdelhak Jaouadi.

34. Foucault, *Security, territory, population*, p. 261.

35. Ibid.

36. Tuniscope, 'Qai'd Essebsi Yatrah al-Sabil lil Khuruj min al-Wada' al-Iqttisadi al-Sa'b wa Muwajihah al-Irhab'.

37. Hakaek, 'Fi Liqa' Jam'ah bihim S'aten: Essid Yunaqsh ma' al-Sahafeen 'Adeed al-Mlafat ... wa Yakshf 'an B'ad "al-Israr"'.

38. Maknassy Révolutionnaire, 17 May 2015.
39. Maknassy Révolutionnaire, 31 August 2016.
40. Interview with Abdelhak Jaouadi.
41. Lorenzini, 'From counter-conduct to critical attitude', p. 13, emphasis original.
42. One of the most widely accepted liberal definitions of civil disobedience is that of John Rawls who described it as 'a public, nonviolent, conscientious yet political act contrary to law usually done with the aim of bringing about a change in the law or policies of the government'; see Rawls, *A theory of justice*, p. 320.
43. Carl Cohen, cited in Arendt, *Crises of the republic*, p. 77.
44. Bleiker, 'Rawls and the limits of nonviolent civil disobedience', p. 39.
45. Maknassy Révolutionnaire, 31 August 2016.
46. Butler and Athanasiou, *Dispossession*, p. 15.
47. Death, 'Counter-conducts as a mode of resistance', p. 246.
48. Interview with Abou Nabil.
49. Interview with Mourad Badraoui.
50. Foucault, *The essential works, 1954–1984*, vol. 1, p. 282.
51. Follow-up interview with Mourad Badraoui, Tunis, 26 February 2017.
52. Lemke, 'The birth of bio-politics', p. 200.

7

Conclusion

This book began by asking how we can make sense of the control of the unemployed subject in the name of the 'War on Terror' in the context of democratising Tunisia. This question has been addressed by exploring the ways in which unemployed protesters were discursively linked to terrorists, as well as how they experienced and navigated through such an articulation. In doing so, I did not aim to provide a 'better' taxonomy or analytical model that can replace the existing approaches which have defined, categorised and evaluated post-uprising Tunisia in one way or another. Nor has this study attempted to provide definitive answers or solutions regarding commonly raised concerns related to terrorism, unemployment and democratisation in Tunisia. Rather, its main purpose is to offer a different way of interpreting these issues, by exploring their interlocking relationship in Tunisia.

Deploying a Foucauldian approach to democracy, security and resistance, I have shown that the War on Terror in post-2011 Tunisia has operated as a governing technique to facilitate democratisation in a neoliberal direction, by managing and regulating the 'deviant' unemployed protesters and by encouraging unemployed populations at large to govern themselves as self-responsible and entrepreneurial citizens. Importantly, the process of securitisation of the unemployed was not what the state imposed and what the unemployed were passively subordinated to. Rather, it was a convoluted process that involved multiple actors, including those governing, those governed and, most importantly, those resisting. In particular, the unemployed protesters' location in the securitisation process was ambivalent. They resisted the discursive association of the unemployed with terrorists, not by entirely refusing such association, but instead by re-appropriating, distorting and deconstructing the dominant narratives on the unemployed subject, as well as by

154

154

producing alternative subjectivities. This conclusion will summarise the key findings and explain what the Tunisian case adds to current debates on the democracy–security nexus and resistance in neoliberal times. It will also discuss what the democratisation process studied here tells us about the 'crisis' of democracy that Tunisia is reportedly experiencing with the emergence of President Kais Saied's rule.

The Democracy–Security Nexus

Although the transition paradigm has long been criticised as having 'outlived its usefulness',[1] its liberal assumptions and categories continue to be found in the ways in which democracy and democratisation are invoked and studied today. This is particularly the case in the MENA region where, for little more than a decade, there have occurred several bottom–up mobilisations and de-mobilisations, the rise and repression of civil society, consensus and splits among the elites, the moderation and radicalisation of Islamists, as well as the formation and de-formation of liberal democratic institutions. In many cases, discussions on democracy/autocracy and democratisation in the region have been anchored in the assumption that there exists a universally agreed upon and ideal form of democracy. Relatively little attention has been paid to the contested nature of democracy and the power relations within which it is embedded. One of the important exceptions is Larbi Sadiki's critical approach to the production of democratic knowledge(s) in the Arab context. He has articulated democracy as a set of knowledge productions and practices (in both Foucault and Bourdieu's terms), emphasising the discursively constructed and thereby highly contingent and political nature of democratic knowledge. As he has put it, '[d]emocratic knowledge, theoretical or practical, is not neutral. It is implicated in the web of power relations that is moulded by knowledge or, in turn, moulds it'.[2] The quest for democracy and democratisation in the region therefore must include analyses of knowledge production and its link to power dynamics.

This book underscores the importance of studying the production of democracy knowledge(s) in and about Arab societies and suggests that Foucault can offer a way of doing so, by critically assessing what political and economic ideals are envisaged and practised through democracy, as well as how they converge with or diverge from neoliberalism. It has unpacked the instrumentalisation of liberal democracy for the purposes of neoliberal governing in post-authoritarian Tunisia. Scholars have pointed out the lack of socio-economic reforms for marginalised segments of society and Tunisia's heavy reliance on IFIs and Western states, which makes its economy vulnerable to global market forces, as they challenge the country's nascent democracy.[3] Which democracy was challenged and in danger? The democratisation process studied here implies that there have existed tensions between the dominant model of democracy and the democracy demanded and practised by the unemployed populations, and it was the latter who became frustrated by the former's operation in favour of a neoliberal mode of governance. As will be discussed below, this, in turn, had repercussions on the elected democratic institutions in Tunisia.

I have discussed how liberal democracy has served Tunisia's neoliberal governance at the micro level, by exploring its intersection with the securitisation of the unemployed in the name of the War on Terror. Chapter 4 has shown that the unemployed subject was associated with terrorist, through liberal democratic norms and values having the effect of regulating 'unruly' unemployed protesters whose demands were incompatibale with the neoliberalisation of the economy and with responsibilising the unemployed as self-governable and entrepreneurial democratic citizens. This indicates that the continued marketisation of the Tunisian economy is not necessarily an unfortunate obstacle to an otherwise successful democratisation, but that it can be seen as a symptomatic instance of the instrumentalisation of liberal democracy for a neoliberal regime. The securitisation of the unemployed in this regard is but *one* important example of the operation of neoliberal democratisation in Tunisia, which deserves more attention in future research.

These findings also shed new light on the juxtaposition of securitisation and democratisation in the MENA region more broadly. The democracy–security nexus has become a recurring theme in debates on political reforms in the region, especially since democracy and security concerns have become increasingly interlinked in the United States' and the EU's foreign policy in the wake of 9/11. Therefore, the discussion has predominantly focused on the two external parties' policy shift towards security, as well as the shift's link to and implications for the promotion of democracy in the Arab world.[4] For instance, scholars have argued that, while the US and the EU methods of democracy promotion in Tunisia differed from each other, both were essentially 'a strategic goal' of their security interests.[5] The external actors' relationship to Tunisia so far has favoured stability over genuine political reforms, indicating that democracy was 'neither the end nor the only method of achieving other ends'.[6] However, Pietro Marzo has recently challenged the dichotomy of liberal (democracy) and realist (security) approaches for understanding the US foreign policy in the MENA region, noting that both interests may co-exist; which one prevails depends on local factors and their perceived implications for US interests.[7]

These studies help understand how democracy and security are inter-connected in global actors' narratives and practices. Yet, what is still largely missing in current research is attention to the local actors' role in the reconfiguration of the security–democracy nexus. Drawing on the EU's democracy promotion in Tunisia and Egypt as a case-study, Assem Dandashly has sought to emphasise the role of local actors in the actual implementation of the European Neighbourhood Policy.[8] Giulia Cimini and Ruth Hanau Santini have also highlighted the plurality of agency in explaining the evolving security assistance practices in Tunisia.[9] And yet, their notion of local actors is narrowly defined and limited to domestic elites and state apparatuses. This book has explored a different kind of such nexus, with emphasis on local dynamics, and offered a nuanced interpretation of the often-assumed negative relationship between securiti-sation and democratisation. It has done so by revisiting a dominant belief concerning terrorism and counter-terrorism in Tunisia, in which they are construed as undermining and destabilising democratisation. As I have explained in Chapter 1, the literature on the post-uprising Tunisian politi-cal landscape has tended to reify this belief, either by (re)using the term 'terrorism' in discussing various non-state groups and presenting them as a fundamental source of instability, or by describing the counter-terrorism projects in Tunisia as state-driven authoritarian measures that hamper democratic norms and values.

This study has called into question these taken-for-granted 'truths', by favouring a Foucauldian approach to securitisation and considering terrorism and counter-terrorism not as objective threats to democracy, but as a discourse that is historically shaped and reshaped through complex power relations. The analysis of the governing elites' discursive practices towards the unemployed has shown how the threat of terrorism can be constructed and operate as a political tool that temporarily facilitates the stabilisation of the liberal democratic system, by managing and regulating those deemed to think and behave inappropriately as well as those whose behaviours are considered incompatible with the liberal notion of democ-racy. The Tunisian case suggests that the democracy–security nexuses in the MENA region are not necessarily top–down processes. While the dominant role played by external actors and the state should not be under-estimated, neglecting local actors results in an only partial story of the dynamic process in which democracy and security become organically interconnected. The discursive construction of the democracy–security nexus is not built by the state or external actors only. Civil society as well as social movement actors actively intervene and perform productive roles in the reconfiguration of such a nexus. The UDC and Maknassy unemployed movements have demonstrated that unemployed protesters did not remain passive subjects that either accept or reject the elites' securitising practices. Instead, they actively intervened in and challenged the process of securitisation, rendering themselves not-so-governable subjects.

Conceptually, the Tunisian case contributes to a critical understanding of securitisation, by incorporating non-state actors into the analysis of the processes through which domination through securitisation is (re)constituted, as well as by elucidating how the realm of security is closely connected to social, economic and political dimensions of governing. There have been continued efforts, particularly within the critical security studies driven by the Copenhagen School, to reconsider security not as an objective reality that needs to be addressed by the state, but as a discursively and intersubjectively constructed reality. Yet, the Copenhagen School falls short of meeting its own promises, due to its failure to challenge the underlying assumptions of the traditional approach to security informed by the dominant liberal idea that the state/civil society distinction is mediated through consent and procedural mechanisms. This is well-reflected in the way in which the Copenhagen School conceptualises the state as the main securitising actor, while presenting non-state actors as audiences that express either their acceptance or rejection of the state's securitising performance, as well as in the way in which it reduces the notion of the political to procedural politics. Likewise, the Copenhagen School's securitisation theory does not pay sufficient attention to how the construction of a threat is closely linked to broader political, economic and social domination.

This book is in line with several critical security studies, especially those inspired by Foucault's notion of power relations, which call for greater attention to the political economy of securitisation – namely, processes by which political economic knowledges constitute and are (re)constituted by the securitisation of certain actors and objects. At the same time, it advances the Foucauldian account of security in that it incorporates the notion of counter-conduct into the analysis of security and takes into account the role of resisting actors in the process of securitisation. According to Foucault, resistance is central to the understanding of power relations. If we are to approach securitisation as an intersubjective process involving power relations, our analysis should not be limited to dominant actors in the field of security, but must include those governed as well as those resisting.

Conclusion

Mobilisations for Social and Economic Justice in Neoliberal Times

Much has been written on the serious nature of unemployment, uneven development and socio-economic mobilisations in post-authoritarian Tunisia. As these writings highlight, the demise of the dictatorial regime and the emergence of a democratic system did not automatically transform Tunisian society into a society upholding the value of social justice. Recent outbreaks of mobilisations organised by unemployed populations in 2016 and 2017 have shown how unexpectedly their frustration can boil over and how quickly spontaneous and unorganised local protests can develop and spread to other regions. It is said that tension and conflict may continue if the problems of socio-economic marginalisation and injustice remain unaddressed. While underscoring all these widely-known observations, I have sought to shed light on some of the neglected aspects of the unemployed resistance; these include its engagement with the securitisation of the unemployed and the relationship of the protesters' moral claims and subjectivities to their struggle for the right to work and social justice. In doing so, I have shown that the antagonistic line between the protesters and the Tunisian governing elite, the principles of which they opposed, was not as sharp as one may assume.

Drawing on the counter-conduct analytic, this book has discussed the unemployed protesters' ambiguous position vis-à-vis the dominant democracy–security nexus, with particular focus on the ways in which they resisted the elites' association of the unemployed subject with terrorist, so as to govern the protesters as self-disciplined and responsible democratic citizens. As Chapters 5 and 6 have demonstrated, although presenting some variation in terms of their narratives and modes of action, the UDC and Maknassy protesters' acts of securitising radical Islamists inevitably had a legitimising effect on the authorities' politics of marginalisation and emergency measures. The unemployed protesters unintentionally participated in the marginalisation and scrutinisation of Salafists, for instance, by distancing themselves from 'Salafist-looking' Muslims when organising their protests, suspecting that they would deliberately commit violence to defame their otherwise peaceful protests and/or exploit their protests for the purpose of terrorist acts. By associating Salafists with 'jihadi' and 'takfiri', the protesters also contributed to the elites' construction of the narrative on Salafism; according to this narrative, internal diversities of the Salafi movements[10] are denied and Salafis are reduced to persons who adopt violent extremism and terrorist acts.

The criminalisation of the Salafi population is by no means irrelevant to the unemployed struggle. The literature on Tunisian Salafis has shown that the prolonged marginalisation of certain populations, especially those living in the central and southern regions, has brought a sense of injustice to a number of unemployed Tunisian youths, leading many to join the Salafi movements.[11] More importantly, in most cases, being labelled as Salafi in Tunisian society has led to unemployment, due to the resulting police attention and frequent interrogations.[12] In this sense, the protesters' participation in the securitisation of the Salafi subject was the very reification of the marginalisation of the unemployed against which they fought. Also, although the protesters criticised the authorities' abuse of counter-terrorism measures to thwart their movements, their construction of Tunisia as being under the threat of terrorism unwittingly lent approval to the implementation of exceptional measures, which were by no means limited to religious groups and negatively affected the unemployed movements at large.

Having said that, the securitisation of the unemployed subject was inherently limited, in the sense that the protesters were able to intercept the elites' securitising practices for their own purposes, by intervening in the process of securitising Islamists and the unemployed. In other words, the elites' negative association of the unemployed with terrorists provided the very conditions of possibility for the protesters to continue their struggle in the context of the War on Terror. By re-appropriating the elites' narrative of the imminent threat of terrorism, the protesters questioned the fundamental reason behind the instability and the source of terrorism in Tunisia. The framework of the inevitable threat was not rejected by the protesters, but instead re-articulated by them, as allowed and deliberately planned by the political and economic elites. They did so by constructing Islamist terrorists as passive subjects who cannot perform freely without the elites helping them with material and ideological resources, thereby subjectifying the elites as being behind and responsible for the rise of Islamist terrorism. Likewise, the protesters also attempted to dismantle and deconstruct the elites' narratives. Chapter 6 has illustrated that this was particularly the case with the Maknassy unemployed protesters whose counter-securitising practices were more subversive than those of the UDC. In Maknassy, the protesters focused more on separating themselves from terrorism and on re-associating the elites with terrorists, through acts of questioning and genealogical critique.

The unemployed protesters' counter-securitising practices indicate a notable transformation in the relationship between domination and resistance after 2011. Compared to the dictatorial period, the antagonistic line between domination and resistance in democratising Tunisia became increasingly porous, partly but significantly because the elites have now attempted to manage and govern the unemployed based on the principle of freedom guaranteed by a narrowly defined liberal democracy, more so than based on a democracy 'rhetoric' and brute authoritarian means. The findings provide a plausible interpretation of what several unemployed protesters called 'the dilemma of democracy' in Tunisia. Liberal democracy was a dilemma for them because they now had the freedom to speak out for their rights, yet not only were they forced to exercise this freedom in 'procedural ways', but their resistance within the procedural boundaries also became easily ignorable and manageable. The UDC and Maknassy protesters' counter-securitising practices show how the protesters both lived within and attempted to challenge this dilemma. The UDC's construction of the divide between legitimate and illegitimate protest through its invocation of democratic norms as well as the Maknassy Civil Disobedience were not external to the neoliberal modality of democracy, in the sense that they were voluntarily governed and participated in governing themselves, as liberal citizens able to exercise their political rights within a certain boundary. However, their resistance also entailed the struggle to create a space within which to constitute new ways of life and new ways of conducting themselves.

The ambivalent effects of democratisation on the relationship between domination and resistance is not unique to unemployed mobilisations in Tunisia. In their recently edited volume on social and economic protests in MENA and Latin America, Weipert-Fenner and Wolff have explored why demands for change to socio-economic orders were side-lined in the processes of regime change in Tunisia and Egypt.[13] Various empirical cases in the volume – particularly those of the UGTT's contribution to political democratisation,[14] the decreasing influence of independent trade unions in Egypt[15] and localised unemployed mobilisations in Tunisia[16] – reflect on this issue. They do so by examining how the political opening after the uprisings was accompanied by the prioritisation of politico-institutional reforms over changing socio-economic orders, as well as by the fragmentation of mobilisations for material improvement and social justice. The contradictory impacts of democratisation on contentious actions of socio-economically marginalised groups are most explicitly discussed in Wolff's chapter on social movements in Latin America. In assessing workers' popular protests in the region since the late 1970s, Wolff has emphasised that, while the dual transformation (that is, the formation of democratic institutions and neoliberal restructuring) served to fragment and weaken bottom–up collective actions, it also offered political and discursive opportunities for 'the formation of broader protest alliances'.[17]

As Weipert-Fenner and Wolff have argued, the immediate effects of the dual transformation in Tunisia resembles Latin American experiences.[18] Grassroots movements for socio-economic justice continued, but they became increasingly fragmented and issue-specific. The Tunisian case studied in this book also indicates that, to some degree, unemployed protesters were implicated in the neoliberalisation of democracy that favoured narrowly defined political and civil rights over socio-economic rights. However, over-emphasising this macro-level observation risks neglecting the everyday struggles and strategies to overcome the workings of the power relations in which they are anchored. As I have pointed out, unemployed protesters both lived with and challenged the interlocking of political democratisation with neoliberal governing.

The revolutionary subjectivity promoted by the protesters in particular can be interpreted as a way of destabilising the relations of power within which they are placed. It was a struggle to subvert and transgress the docile citizen subjectivity as well as to constitute themselves as a moral subject that can redefine the meaning of democracy and the meaning of democratic citizen. The protesters' revolutionary claim may not mean that they possess a concrete vision and strategies for fundamental changes to Tunisia's political, economic and social orders.[19] Yet, insofar as this revolutionary expression itself is in a way deviant with respect to the norms and values of the currently dominant liberal democracy in Tunisia, it may constitute a *heterotopic* space – that is, a space that is connected to, yet disruptive of the conventional way of life, a space that enables unemployed protesters to remain not-so-governable subjects.[20]

From a Foucauldian perspective, the revolutionary subjectivity promoted by the protesters is not simply an emancipatory expression. Rather, it suggests that their resistance against socio-economic marginalisation involved 'the care of the self' – that is, the ethical dimension of a struggle to conduct the self and others differently. This is also the case with the victimhood of the unemployed. The protesters' acts of subjectifying unemployed youth as being vulnerable to terrorism does not simply disempower the unemployed subject, as this subjectivity is mobilised for shifting the responsibility for the radicalised youth from the youth themselves to the system that deprives them of hope and social protection. The counter-conduct analytic helps us capture this organic linkage between the socio-economic dimensions of resistance and the care of the self.

More broadly, I believe that the Foucauldian analytic developed in this book can offer insights into the relationship between domination and resistance in the neoliberal era. While there exists increasing interest in the relationship between neoliberal capitalism and mobilisations, the debate often revolves around the question of how the former determines or affects the latter.[21] The unemployed resistance in Tunisia suggests that neoliberalism is not a mere background factor that either facilitates or constrains collective actions. It instead speaks for the possibilities of a more intricate interplay between the two. Insofar as neoliberalism operates through the construction of hegemonic discourse(s) which require the voluntary and active participation of the object populations, protests for socio-economic justice and neoliberalism (if the latter can be understood as a form of social movement) may not operate in isolation from each other.

Bottom–up mobilisations can not only be mediated by capitalist relations, but they can also play a productive and disruptive role in such relations.[22] The forms of intervention and disruption may vary across different contexts. However, a key dimension of such mobilisations, as we have seen, involves care for the self, acts upon the self and acts upon others. As much as neoliberalism structures and governs through rational and economic relations of power and through individuals as the product of the exercise of power, resistance is likely to occur to deter such individualisation. The UDC and Maknassy cases have shown that this resistance can take a form of counter-securitisation of the self. The close tie between 'being otherwise' and struggles over social and economic marginalisation is also observed in other contexts. Partha Chatterjee has illustrated, for instance, how alternative ethical attributes and perspectives as well as 'imaginative possibilities of community' played a central role in the struggle of the urban poor and precarious workers in India.[23]

The Tunisian case invites us to pay greater attention to the conditions for and dynamic of contemporary social movements, particularly those organised by unemployed and precarious worker segments of society, in their relationship to and interactions with 'capitalist transformations'.[24] Hence, we may better observe where and how the former and the latter converge and diverge in given contexts and understand why they do so.

Is Tunisia's Democracy in Danger Ten Years after Liberal Democratisation?

The narrative of a 'fragile' democracy and the possibility of setbacks have continued since the establishment of a new democratic system in Tunisia. However, the concern over democracy never reached the extent seen in the aftermath of President Kais Saied's decisions to put the brakes on elected democratic institutions and to re-write the constitution. On 25 July 2021,

Saied suspended the parliament for a period of thirty days, fired then Prime Minister Hichem Mechichi and lifted immunity for members of parliament. The president himself claimed these decisions to be in accordance with Article 80 of Tunisia's new constitution, which allows the president of the republic to declare a state of emergency and take the necessary measures in the event of an imminent danger threatening the country. Saied's radical measures were denounced as a coup by some, especially by Ennahda members and its supporters, in the absence of the constitutional court to rule whether it was indeed legitimate. Central to the debate on the July event were concerns over the potential rollback towards authoritarian rule.

What does the trajectory of democratisation discussed in this book tell us about the July 'coup'? The government's failure to handle the pandemic provided the immediate context for President Saied's intervention. However, the facts that the majority of Tunisians had voted for a law professor, a candidate without political party affiliation, as president of their country in 2019 and, then, two years later, hailed his decision to freeze the parliament are closely linked to their ever-growing distrust in and frustration with the current democratic system. Therefore, we need to pay attention to and understand, beyond the question of whether Saied's leadership is authoritarian or democratic, the wide gap and tensions between the political and economic system aspired to and demanded by the people, on the one hand, and the past decade's actual democratisation process, on the other hand.

Several surveys conducted after 2011 suggest that, for the majority of Tunisians, democracy first and foremost means a system that will work to reduce poverty and inequality by realising wealth redistribution and creating job opportunities. According to the Arab Barometer survey conducted in 2011, when people were asked to nominate the two most important features of democracy, 80 per cent of respondents chose socio-economic rights, while 55 percent chose civil and political rights.[25] The same survey conducted in 2013 also showed similar results. Over 48 per cent of the survey respondents chose providing basic necessities as one of the two most necessary elements of democracy, whereas 23.9 per cent of people chose the freedom to criticise the government.[26] Qualitative interviews also indicate that many Tunisian people, particularly those living under precarious conditions, perceive that democracy is more than freedom of speech and free and fair elections, and that socio-economic rights are essential to democracy.[27]

Achieving the type of democracy demanded by the majority of Tunisians would require the active and meaningful participation of previously marginalised segments of society in the new system-building process. As Chapters 3 and 4 have illustrated, the post-2011 governments instead promoted a type of democracy that facilitated a liberal notion of empowered civil society in its narrowest sense, while securitising those, including unemployed protesters, who did not comply with certain liberal procedural principles. More and more people became disillusioned with the top–down narratives and practices of democracy in which democratic norms were invoked in such a way as to not only avoid the responsibility for development, but also shift it to self-governing citizens. Parliament became a symbol of corrupt and incompetent politicians who care only about winning elections, while leaving political polarisation and the continued social and economic crises unresolved. It is in this context that President Saied appeared as an alternative to the existing democratic orders and institutions. He was and still is conceived by many Tunisians as a unique political leader, distinguished from his predecessors, from Habib Bourguiba to Essebsi. Borrowing Fadil Aliriza's phrase, he was the first president 'recognising the state and its authorities as agents of oppression'.[28] He described political parties as anti-revolutionary machines that operate for those interested in power-grabbing rather than serving the people.[29] His 'revolutionary' rhetoric against party politics and corrupt politicians and businessmen went hand in hand with his rhetorical support of victims of state violence and of those socio-economically marginalised in the interior regions, as marked by his meetings with the families of the 'martyrs' of the revolution and unemployed youth in Gafsa.

It should be emphasised that, while the majority of Tunisians associated democracy with social and economic rights and supported President Saied's measures to suspend democratic institutions, this does not mean that Tunisians rejected the idea of democracy as a whole.[30] Rather, many of them were against the way in which 'political freedom and democracy became the weapon against social movements of the poor',[31] as Tarek Aoun, a young Tunisian unemployed activist in Kasserine, put it. The dilemma of democracy experienced by the UDC and Maknassy protesters was also expressed by Aoun, who recognised political freedom as a key achievement of the Uprising but argued the following:

Why is political freedom important? To protect your rights, the rights of marginalised and poor people. They have had no voice for years. What did you [the government] do? You said, 'I am a democratic government. So, say what you want to say, and I will do what I want'. There is no programme and progress [for socio-economic problems]. There's freedom of expression. We have talked for the past six years. What do we have now?[32]

The democratisation process studied in this book, together with Aoun's conceptions of political freedom and democracy, informs us that, to many Tunisians, the elected democratic institutions were not only insufficient for, but also against what they conceive of as real democracy. The emergence of Saied's rule, then, is more than the outcome of the coexistence of two contradictory perceptions of democracy in the mind of the people. In Foucault's terms, it may be understood as a form of counter-conduct that seeks to imagine and live democracy differently. A significant number of Tunisians willingly supported a strong leader who, so they believed and hoped, could bring the process of revolution back on track and who could re-structure, rather than demolish, their democratic system in such a way that its priority becomes citizens' needs and well-being. With his revolutionary rhetoric, Saied has promised to make Tunisia's democracy truly democratic. Having been able to make key decisions with the domestic political oppositions much more weakened than ever before, his legitimacy and popularity now depend on his deeds rather than on his words. And there already appears a growing gap between the two.

Since President Saied's power-grab in July 2021, not much has changed, except for his radical transformation of the political system. In particular, the austerity agenda appears to continue to be the prescription for Tunisia's doomed economy. This was indicated, for instance, in a leaked proposal prepared by the new government for negotiations with the IMF, in which freezing public hiring and wages from 2022 to 2024 as well as a general reduction in subsidies were suggested as reforms to save the country from the current economic crisis.[33] It is important to note that the government's planned austerity measures targeting public-sector hiring is directly against what it has promised to unemployed graduates and precarious workers who were 'vocal supporters' of President Saied.[34] Four months after the July event, he officially reversed the law 38-2020 which had been enacted to open public-sector recruitment to university graduates who had been unemployed for more than ten years. If implemented, the freeze on public-sector employment may also reverse the previous government's decision of July 2020, according to which the state by 2025 must gradually incorporate into the public employment scheme site workers who had been working in public institutions under precarious conditions. The implementation of this law has already been delayed several times, under the excuse of political crises. Given this context, it is not difficult to predict that President Saied's rule will face a new wave of bottom–up mobilisations with socio-economic demands.

The new government, much like the previous ones, identified street mobilisations as an obstacle to the country's economic growth.[35]

This, together with the continuous police harassment of protesters and Saied's use of the security apparatus for quelling political opponents, raises concerns that the criminalisation and securitisation of protests organised by socio-economically marginalised groups may continue with very much the same discursive practices as deployed by previous governments. His hostile attitude and rhetoric towards Ennahda, which a large part of Tunisian civil society appears to like for the moment, can easily escalate the already existing Islamist-secular conflict, justifying repressive measures against either side and once again diverting attention away from the much-needed restructuring of the country's socio-economic system and towards fictious enemies against democracy.

That being said, one lesson to be drawn from this study is that it is the mobilised people who always open up new possibilities for change and, accordingly, new forms of power relations. However similar they may look, the new workings of domination will differ insofar as grassroots actors seek to learn from the past, to progress and to act differently. Therefore, we may have a better understanding of the reconfiguration of the post-July political economy, if we pay more attention to multiple sites and forms of resistance, as well as to their contentions and what might be a mutually constitutive relationship to the exercise of domination.

Notes

1. Carothers, 'The end of the transition paradigm', p. 168.
2. Sadiki, 'Towards a "democratic knowledge" turn?' p. 710.
3. See, for instance, Hanieh, 'Shifting priorities or business as usual?'; Singer, 'Development loans as a threat to young democracies'; Powers, 'Cartelization, neoliberalism, and the foreclosure of the Jasmine Revolution'.
4. See, for instance, Mouhib, 'EU democracy promotion in Tunisia and Morocco'; Dandashly, 'EU democracy promotion and the dominance of the security-stability nexus'.
5. Powel, 'The stability syndrome: US and EU democracy promotion in Tunisia', p. 63. See also Joffe, 'The European Union, democracy and counter-terrorism in the Maghreb'; Durac and Cavatorta, 'Strengthening authoritarian rule through democracy promotion?'
6. Powel, 'The stability syndrome: US and EU democracy promotion in Tunisia', p. 66.
7. Marzo, 'Solving the security-democracy dilemma'.
8. Dandashly, 'EU democracy promotion and the dominance of the security-stability nexus', p. 63.
9. Cimini and Santini, 'Applying principal-agent theory to security force assistance'.

10. While sharing certain religious beliefs, Salafi movements are characterised by their diverse positions concerning politics and violence. For instance, Wiktorowicz categorises them into three forms of Salafism: purist, political and jihadist. See Wiktorowicz, 'Anatomy of the Salafi movement'.
11. Wolf, 'An Islamist "renaissance"'.
12. Torelli, Merone and Cavatorta, 'Salafism in Tunisia'.
13. Weipert-Fenner and Wolff, *Socioeconomic protests in MENA and Latin America*.
14. Karray, 'Proposals, intermediation, and pressure'.
15. Abdalla, 'From the dream of change to the nightmare of structural weakness'.
16. Hamdi and Weipert-Fenner, 'Unemployed protests in Tunisia: Between grassroots activism and formal organization'.
17. Wolff, 'Contention by marginalized groups and political change in Latin America', p. 176.
18. Weipert-Fenner and Wolff, *Socioeconomic protests in MENA and Latin America*, pp. 257–58.
19. Bayat, *Revolution without revolutionaries*.
20. Beckett, Bagguley and Campbell, 'Foucault, social movements and heterotopic horizons', p. 171.
21. Hetland and Goodwin, 'The strange disappearance of capitalism from social movement studies'; Bayat, 'Workless revolutionaries'; Lahusen, 'The protests of the unemployed in France, Germany and Sweden (1994–2004)'; Badimon, 'From contestation to conciliation'.
22. Han, 'Transitional justice for whom?'
23. Chatterjee, *The politics of the governed*, p. 60. See also Hetherington, 'Identity formation, space and social centrality'; Death, 'Counter-conducts as a mode of resistance'.
24. Della Porta, 'Political economy and social movement studies', p. 468.
25. For further analysis of Arab Barometer survey data on democracy in Tunisia, see Teti, 'Beyond lies the wub', and Abbott and Cavatorta, 'Beyond elections'.
26. Ibid.
27. Teti, Pamela and Han, 'Dancing around democracy'.
28. Aliriza, 'Tunisia's Kais Saied becomes an ordinary politician'.
29. Hammami, 'Past as prologue: Kaïs Saïed's prior statements point to upcoming political moves'.
30. Grubman, 'Do Tunisians still want democracy?'
31. Interview with Tarek Aoun, independent unemployed activist, Kasserine, 3 February 2017.
32. Ibid.
33. IWATCH, 'Negotiations with the International Monetary Fund and the "secret" government program'. See also Aliriza, 'Tunisia's Kais Saied becomes an ordinary politician'.
34. Aliriza, 'Tunisia's Kais Saied becomes an ordinary politician'.
35. Ibid.

Bibliography

Primary Sources

INTERVIEWS CITED IN THIS BOOK

Abdelhak Jaouadi, Coordinator of the civil disobedience, Maknassy, 3 February 2017.

Abdul Ahman, Activist and researcher from Forum Tunisien pour les Droits Economiques et Sociaux, Tunis, 6 February 2017.

Abdul Ahmed, Casual worker and independent unemployed protester, Kasserine, 3 February 2017.

Abou Nabil, Independent unemployed activist, Maknassy, 31 March 2017.

Abou Salem, Human rights activist, Tunis, 28 December 2016.

Ahmed Murad, Member of the UDC executive board, Tunis, 3 April 2017.

Ben Mahmoud, Political activist, Tunis, 2 December 2020.

Chahed Mohamed, UDC activist, Tunis, 27 March 2017.

Ghassen Harim, UDC activist, Sidi Bouzid, 23 March 2017.

Habib Mahfoudh, Casual worker and activist, Medinine, 22 February 2017.

Jamel Ghafr, UDC coordinator in Sidi Bouzid, Sidi Bouzid, 20 December 2016.

Mohamed Salmi, UDC coordinator in Gafsa, Gafsa, 14 November 2016.

Mohsen Ghafr, Local UGTT activist, Maknassy, 31 January 2017.

Mourad Badraoui, Independent unemployed activist, Maknassy, 2 February 2017.

Tarek Aoun, Independent unemployed activist, Kasserine, 3 February 2017.

Rached Ghassen, Independent unemployed activist, Kasserine, 3 February 2017.

Rached Yousef, Unemployed protester, Maknassy, 2 February 2017.

Yousef Hamdi, UDC activist, Gafsa, 11 January 2017.

Yassine Jawedi, UDC activist, Sidi Bouzid, 17 February 2017.

NEWS ARTICLES

Alchourouk (2005a) 'Jam'yun I'lamiyun wa Muthaqafun Yaktabun: li-hadha Nantakhab Ben Ali [University students, media professionals and intellectuals write: This is why we vote for Ben Ali]', 18 June. Available at: https://www. turess.com/alchourouk/21936 (accessed 1 March 2019).

Alchourouk (2005b) 'Washington Times: Tunis Bilad Namudhaji Tataqadam fihi al-Dimoqratiah bi Najah [Washington Times: Tunisia is an exemplary country where democracy is advancing successfully]', 18 June. Available at: https:// www.turess.com/alchourouk/28172 (accessed 2 November 2017).

Alchourouk (2014) '81Taharoka iḥtijajiya shahr October al-maʻdi fi 16 Wilayah [81 protest movements in 16 governorates in the month of October]', 9 November. Available at: https://www.turess.com/alchourouk/1077703 (accessed 21 January 2022).

Alchourouk (2016) 'al-Mubaraki Yaḥmal al-Hukumah Masuw'liya al-auda' fi Gafsa [Al Mubarki holds the government responsible for the situation in Gafsa]', 8 May. Available at: https://www.turess.com/alchourouk/1176339 (accessed 21 January 2022).

Alfajrnews (2008) '400 Sujun Tounisi yadrabun 'an al-Taʻam [400 prisoners stage a hunger strike]', 23 August. Available at: https://www.turess.com/alfajrnews/7776 (accessed 14 November 2018).

Alfajrnews (2012) 'al-Beji Essebsi Yaʻaulan T'asis Harakat "Nidaa Tunis" lil-Tasdi li Haimanah "Ennahda" [Beji Essebsi announces the establishment of Nidaa Tunis movement to counter the hegemony of Ennahda]', 16 June. Available at: http://www.turess.com/alfajrnews/105857 (accessed 1 November 2017).

Alhiwar (2011) 'Essebsi: al-Amni Awalan [Essebsi: Security is the priority]', 31 March. Available at: https://www.turess.com/alhiwar/16387 (accessed 6 February 2019).

Alwasat (2008) 'al-Ra'is Ben Ali fi Hadith lil-Majlah "al-Hawadith" al-Lbnaniyah [President Ben Ali in the dialogue with the Lebanese magazine 'Incidents']', 24 August. Available at: https://www.turess.com/alwasat/7378 (accessed 21 January 2022).

Alwasat (2006) 'Nas Khitab al-Ra'is Ben Ali bil-Munasiba al-Dikri 19 lil-Sabaʻ min November [Part of President Ben Ali's speech on the 19th anniversary of the 7th of November]', 7 November. Available at: https://www.turess.com/alwasat/2754 (accessed 2 November 2017).

Alwasat (2012) 'Uzarah al-Dekhaliyah al-Tunisiyah Tamnaʻ Taẓaharah Daʻy al-Layha al-Sabt bi Sharaʻ al-Habib Bourguiba [The Tunisian Interior Ministry bans a demonstration called for Saturday on Habib Bourguiba street]', 1 June. Available at: http://www.turess.com/alwasat/23117 (accessed 3 October 2017).

Assabahnews (2014) 'Istaghalu Inshghal al-Amni wa al-Jeysh bil-Tasdi li Ahdath al-Shaghab ... Tasalul 450 "Murtazqah" ila Tunis.. li Tanfid Aʻmal Irhabiyah!? [The preoccupation of the security force and army to resist the riots was exploited ... the infiltration of 450 mercenaries into Tunisia ... for carrying out terrorist acts!?]', 17 January. Available at: https://www.assabahnews.tn/article/80134/ (accessed 26 June 2019).

Assabahnews (2015a) 'al Maknassy: Tauaquf Ishghal al-Mashari' Utheer al-Shik wa al-Ihtaj [Maknassy: Halting the projects causes doubt and protest]'. Available at: http://www.assabah.com.tn/article/101600 (accessed 6 November 2018).

Assabahnews (2015b) 'Taqrir li Lajnah al-Tahqiq fi Ahdath al-Dhahbah: al-Ihtijajat Silmiyah wa Mashroua'ah wa Tariqah al-Ta'ati Kanat 'Anifa wa Ghair Mutanasibah [Report from the investigating committee after the events of Al-Dehiba: The protests were peaceful and legitimate, and the method of handling them was violent and disproportionate]', 19 February. Available at: https://www.turess.com/assabahnews/99682 (accessed 26 June 2019).

Assabahnews (2016a) 'al Beji: Lan Aourath Ibni ... wa Mutamasak bil-Sayed Rai'sa lil-Hukumah [Beji: I will not bequeath power to my son ... and will keep Essid as Prime Minister]', 29 January. Available at: https://www.turess.com/assabahnews/117786 (accessed 18 July 2019).

Assabahnews (2016b) 'Mourou: Nakhsh Idkhal Tunis fi al-Fauda ... walla A'taqid an Hunalik Hilal Sahriyah Anye lil-Mashakil [Mourou: We fear that Tunisia will enter chaos ... I do not think that there is a temporary magic solution to the problems]', 24 January. Available at: https://www.turess.com/assabahnews/117405(accessed 8 June 2019).

Attounissia (2012) 'Kiliya al-Adaab bi Manoubah: Tawatur wa Mutaalib bi Rahil "al-Qajdughli" [Faculty of Arts in Manouba: Tension and demands for the resignation of "Al-Qazdaghli"]', 7 March. Available at: http://www.turess.com/attounissia/52161 (accessed 5 January 2017).

Attounissia (2014) 'al-Harakat al-Dimoqratiah lil-Israh wa Bina' Tahadhr min al-Inzlaq fi Muraba'a al-'unf [The Democratic Movement for Reform and Construction warns against slipping into violence], 11 January. Available at: https://www.turess.com/attounissia/110774 (accessed 9 September 2019).

Attounissia (2015) 'Khubra' Yajiboun: Hal anna al-Auen lil I'elan al-Tawari'? [Experts answer: Is it the time to declare an emergency?]', 2 July. Available at: https://www.turess.com/attounissia/155282 (accessed 27 May 2019).

Attounissia (2016a) 'Abd al-Hamid al-Jilasi (Nai'b al-Ghanouch) li "Attunissia": Ennahda D'd Taghir Essa'id wa al-Intikhabaat al-Mubakrah [Abdelhamid Jelassi (Ghannouchi's deputy) told Al-Tunisia: Ennahda is against changing Essid and early elections]', 30 January. Available at: https://www.turess.com/attounissia/165782 (accessed 29 May 2019).

Attounissia (2016b) 'Hal Tafadat Tunis "al-Fauda al-Khalaqah"? [Has Tunisia avoided "creative chaos"?]', 26 January. Available at: https://www.turess.com/attounissia/165508 (accessed 26 June 2019).

Attounissia (2016c) 'Mouz bil Haji Rouhmah "Ennahda" li "Attounissia": Barounat al-Tahrib Wara' al-Harq wa an Nahib [Moez Belhaj Rahouma ("Ennahda") for "Al-Tunisia": Smugglers are behind the burning and looting]',

25 January. Available at: https://www.turess.com/attounissia/165428 (accessed 23 August 2019).

Attounissia (2016d) 'Rai's al-Hukumah lil Nawab: al-Tashghil Masu'uliyah Jama'iyah [Prime Minister to the Representatives: Employment is a collective responsibility]', 28 January. Available at: https://www.turess.com/attounissia/165629 (accessed 7 June 2018).

Attounissia (2016e) 'Sidi Bouzid: I'ta' Isharah al-Intlaq li Munjim al-Phosphat bil-Maknassy [Sidi Bouzid: The sign of starting the phosphate mine in Maknassy]', 19 February. Available at: https://www.turess.com/attounissia/167181 (accessed 6 September 2018).

Babnet (2015) 'al-Aroui: Ist'amal al-Quah Kana li Himeyah Maqr al-Hars al-Hudoudi al-Mukalif bi Man'a Tasalul al-Irhabeen [Aroui: The use of force was to protect the security force for preventing terrorist infiltration]', 8 February. Available at: https://www.turess.com/babnet/99712 (accessed 15 August 2019).

Hakaek (2015a) 'al-Muhami Naman Mazid li Essesi: Sayedah al-Rai's, al-Harb 'ala al-Irhab Taftard Aidan Rijel Harb [Lawyer Naman Mazid to Essebsi: Dear President, the war on terror needs men for war]', 4 July. Available at: https://www.turess.com/hakaek/77644 (accessed 26 June 2019).

Hakaek (2015b) 'Fi Liqa' Jam'ah bihim S'aten: Essid Yunaqsh ma' al-Sahafeen 'Adeed al-Mlafat ... wa Yakshf 'an B'ad "al-Israr" [In two hours of meeting: Essid discusses a number of issues with Journalists ... and reveals some secrets]', 11 May. Available at: https://www.turess.com/hakaek/74978 (accessed 26 June 2019).

Hakaek (2015c) 'Hal Takun Ahdath Dhahbah Ghata' li Tahrib al-silahah ila Tunis?! [Are the Dhabha events to cover the smuggling of weapons to Tunisia?]', 9 February. Available at: https://www.turess.com/hakaek/70867 (accessed 20 July 2019).

Hakaek (2016a) 'al-Jama'iyah al-Tunisyah lil Hukumah: Min Sha'n Mubadrah al-Masarah al-Eqtisadiyah al-Dfe'a bil-Istithmar wa Tanmiyah.. wa Lekin ... [The Tunisian Association for Governance: The economic reconciliation bill will facilitate investment and development... but ...]', 12 July. Available at: https://www.turess.com/hakaek/94504 (accessed 26 June 2019).

Hakaek (2016b) 'al-Maknassy: I'tisam 'Harimna' lil Mu'tlin 'an al-'Amal bi Maqr al-Mu'tamdiyah [Maknassy: Old unemployed men's sit-in at the Municipality building]', 6 February. Available at: https://www.turess.com/hakaek/87726 (accessed 5 November 2018).

Hakaek (2016c) 'Najihoun fi Munadhrah Intidab 'Umal bi Manjim al-Phosphat bil Maknassy Yaqta'un al-Tariq baina Sfax wa Gafsa [Successful candidates for the Phosphate mine in Maknassy block the road between Gafsa and Sfax]', 14 July. Available at: https://www.turess.com/hakaek/94571 (accessed 6 September 2018).

Infosplus (2012) 'al-Nas al-Kamil lil Mubadrah Essebsi [The full text of Essebsi's initiative]', 21 April. Available at: http://www.turess.com/infosplus/10802 (accessed 1 November 2017).

Kalima Tounes (2013) 'Sidi Bouzid: Ba'th Mashrou'a "Masna'a al-Sayarat" Qariban fi al-Maknassy [Sidi Bouzid: The auto factory will be launched soon in Maknassy]', 15 January. Available at: https://www.turess.com/kalima/15351 (accessed 6 September 2018).

LTDH (2012) 'Bayan al-Rabitah al-Tunisiyah lil Difa'a 'an Huquq al-Insen' [LTDH's statement]', 28 May. Available at: https://www.tunisia-sat.com/forums/threads/2253928/ (accessed 1 November 2017).

Maknassy Révolutionnaire (2014a) 17 July. Available at: https://www.facebook.com/MAKNASSYREVOLUTIONNAIRE/photos/a.202298796472627/71622 0161747152/?type=3&__tn__=-R (accessed 15 March 2019).

Maknassy Révolutionnaire (2014b) 30 May. Available at: https://www.facebook.com/MAKNASSYREVOLUTIONNAIRE/photos/a.202298796472627/69217 5807484921/?type=3&__tn__=-R (accessed 15 March 2019).

Maknassy Révolutionnaire (2015) 1 April. Available at: https://www.facebook.com/MAKNASSYREVOLUTIONNAIRE/posts/8385985061759 83?__xts__[0]=68.ARArPFweZ8TnFTouIyqPzVCdGfiVqqsRmql AeLKmA6cFsVajxG1FlsljDRt3NVYJO5X9diM48OqfmhF9zAk3ojR AtW4qaJGiBZQeFIaA1vbiGFGFahQiy1u8VubM7lEA6TJCz36GiA7 af2b3EkV2FIwFiCHw7MfwjL1ZkFwjbzfSZPyXQUzq (accessed 8 July 2019).

Maknassy Révolutionnaire (2015) 17 May. Available at: https://www.facebook.com/MAKNASSYREVOLUTIONNAIRE/posts/857941384241695?__ tn__=-R (accessed 8 July 2019).

Maknassy Révolutionnaire (2016) 31 August. Available at: https://www.facebook.com/MAKNASSYREVOLUTIONNAIRE/photos/a.202298796472627/ 1100361329999698/?type=3&__tn__=-R (accessed 7 June 2019).

Maknassy Révolutionnaire (2017) 18 April. Available at: https://www.facebook.com/MAKNASSYREVOLUTIONNAIRE/photos/a.202298796472627/13210 50424597453/?type=3&__tn__=-R (accessed 3 June 2019).

Radiotunisienne, 2016 'Itihad Shogul Yada'u il-Hukumah ila Itkhadh Ijra'at 'Ajilah' [UGTT calls the government to take urgent and radical measures]', 21 January. Available at: http://www.radiotunisienne.tn/2016/01/21/-اتحاد-الشغل يدعو-الحكومة-الى-اتخاذ-اجر/ (accessed 17 January 2022).

TAP (2011a) 'Mashari'a Tanmawiyah li Fa'idah Mu'tamditi al-Maknassy wa Manzil Bouzayn min Wulayah Sidi Bouizid [Development projects for Maknassy and Manzil Bouzayn inhabitants in Sidi Bouzid]', 27 April. Available at: https://www.turess.com/tap/40843 (accessed 27 July 2018).

TAP (2011b) 'Mutalib bi Tamiyah al 'Adlah fi Mu'tamdiyah al-Maknassy min Wulayah Sidi Bouzid [Demanding equitable development in Maknassy in Sidi Bouzid]', 15 March. Available at: https://www.turess.com/tap/37795 (accessed 5 November 2018).

TAP (2012) 'Ahjab Siyesiya Ta'tabir Injaal al-'Alam al-Tunisi Ta'adiyan 'ala Ramj al-Siyedah al-Wataniyah [Political parties regard lowering the Tunisian flag as being in violation of national sovereignty]', 9 March. Available at: http://www.turess.com/tap/122106 (accessed 1 Nov 2017).

Tuniscope (2015a) 'al-Fadl Ben Omran: Ahdath Qibali Jas Nabd min Qibal al-Jama't [Fadl Ben Omran: The Qibali events were manipulated by terrorist groups]', 8 June. Available at: https://www.turess.com/tuniscope/71167 (accessed 14 July 2019).

Tuniscope (2015b) 'Qai'd Essebsi Yatrah al-Sabil lil Khuruj min al-Wada' al-Iqttisadi al-Sa'b wa Muwajihah al-Irhab [Essebsi suggests a way to get out of the difficult economic situation and to confront terrorism]', 1 May. Available at: https://www.turess.com/tuniscope/68246 (accessed 5 June 2019).

U.D.C Page Officiel (2014a) 1 May. Available at: https://www.face book.com/notes/العمل-عن-المعطلين-الشهادات-أصحاب-اتحاد-udc-page-officiel/811774462185979/اي-مـــــــرّة-غرّة-ان-بيـــــ (accessed 20 May 2018).

U.D.C Page Officiel (2014b) 17 July. Available at: https://www.facebook.com/697073200322773/photos/a.704955326201227/857096424320449/?type=3&theater (accessed 10 July 2019).

U.D.C Page Officiel (2014c) 27 January. Available at: https://www.facebook.com/permalink.php?story_fbid=759093484120744&id=697073200322773 (accessed 3 June 2018).

U.D.C Page Officiel (2015a) 17 December. Available at: https://www.facebook.com/permalink.php?story_fbid=1149852618378160&id=697073200322773 (accessed 15 June 2018).

U.D.C Page Officiel (2015b) 22 April. Available at: https://www.facebook.com/notes/العمل-عن-المعطلين-الشهادات-أصحاب-اتحاد-udc-page-officiel/-رسالة-خرايفي-شريف-1017481308281959/آخر-يخفي-إرهاب-حذارِ-الحكومة-إلى-العمل-عن-المعطّلين/ (accessed 3 July 2018).

U.D.C Page Officiel (2015c) 30 March. Available at: https://www.facebook.com/697073200322773/photos/a.704955326201227/1005325562830867/?type=3&theater (accessed 3 July 2018).

U.D.C Page Officiel (2016) 25 January. Available at: https://www.facebook.com/697073200322773/photos/a.704955326201227.1073741832.697073200322773/1174202275943194/?type=3&permPage=1 (accessed 1 July 2018).

UDC Bureau National (2013) 28 November. Available at: https://www.facebook.com/udc.org/posts/764870143530351:0 (accessed 23 June 2018).

UDC Bureau National (2014) 25 February. Available at: https://www.facebook.com/udc.org/posts/818696468147718:0 (accessed 20 June 2018).

UDC Bureau National (2015) 17 March. Available at: https://www.facebook.com/udc.org/posts/1062257047124991:0 (accessed 3 June 2018).

Secondary Sources

Abdalla, N. (2016) 'Neoliberal policies and the Egyptian trade union movement: Politics of containment and the limits of resistance', in E. Akçalı (ed.) *Neoliberal governmentality and the future of the state in the Middle East and North Africa*. London: Palgrave Macmillan, pp. 123–42.

Abdalla, N. (2020) 'From the dream of change to the nightmare of structural weakness: The trajectory of Egypt's independent trade union movement After 2011', in I. Weipert-Fenner and J. Wolff (eds) *Socioeconomic protests in MENA and Latin America: Egypt and Tunisia in interregional comparison.* Cham: Palgrave Macmillan, pp. 145–68.

Achcar, G. (2021) 'Hegemony, domination, corruption and fraud in the Arab region', *Middle East Critique*, 30(1), pp. 57–66.

Achy, L. (2011) 'Tunisia's economic challenges', *Carnegie Middle East Center*.

Agamben, G. (1998) *Homo sacer: Sovereign power and bare life.* Palo Alto: Stanford University Press.

Agamben, G. (2005) *State of Exception.* Chicago: University of Chicago Press.

Ahmed, Q. A. (2017) 'Designate the Muslim Brotherhood a foreign terrorist organization', *National Review*. Available at: https://www.nationalreview.com/2017/03/muslim-brotherhood-foreign-terrorist-organization-designation-violent-islamism-jihad/ (accessed 10 July 2019).

Ajala, I. (2019) 'Tunisian terrorist fighters a grassroots perspective', *Behavioral Sciences of Terrorism and Political Aggression*, 11(2), pp. 178–90.

Akçalı, E. (2016) *Neoliberal governmentality and the future of the state in the Middle East and North Africa.* London: Palgrave Macmillan.

Alexander, C. (2010) *Tunisia: Stability and reform in the modern Maghreb.* New York: Routledge.

Aliriza, F. (2015) 'Tunisia at risk: Will counterterrorism undermine the revolution?' *Legatum Institute*. Available at: https://lif.blob.core.windows.net/lif/docs/default-source/publications/tunisia_at_risk_final_-pdf.pdf?sfvrsn=2 (accessed 2 July 2016).

Aliriza, F. (2022) 'Tunisia's Kais Saied becomes an ordinary politician'. *Middle East Institute*. Available at: https://www.mei.edu/publications/tunisias-kais-saied-becomes-ordinary-politician?fbclid=IwAR0LAIXEXC7d-r1StYrZUWqKcRXTDciRlBf8PzrmYWPTzLJtrDJEr-r7jI8 (accessed 20 January 2022).

Allal, A. (2013) 'Becoming revolutionary in Tunisia, 2007–2011', in J. Beinin and F. Vairel (eds) *Social movements, mobilization, and contestation in the Middle East and North Africa.* Palo Alto: Stanford University Press, pp. 185–204.

Amara, T. and Mcdowall, A. (2021) 'Reuter, Tunisian democracy in turmoil after president sacks government', Reuters, 27 July. Available at: https://www.reuters.com/world/middle-east/tunisian-democracy-crisis-after-president-ousts-government-2021-07-26/ (accessed 29 July 2021).

Amnesty International (2003) 'New draft "anti-terrorism" law will further undermine human rights'. Available at: https://www.amnesty.org/en/documents/mde30/021/2003/en/ (accessed 22 July 2017).

Amnesty International (2008) 'In the name of security: Routine Abuses in Tunisia'. Available at: https://www.amnesty.org/en/documents/mde30/007/2008/en/ (accessed 6 June 2016).

Antonakis-Nashif, A. (2016) 'Contested transformation: Mobilized publics in Tunisia between compliance and protest', *Mediterranean Politics*, 21(1), pp. 128–49.

Asseburg, M. and Wimmen, H. (2016) 'Dynamics of transformation, elite change and new social mobilization in the Arab World', *Mediterranean Politics*, 21(1), pp. 1–22.

Aradau, C. and van Munster, R. (2007) 'Governing terrorism through risk: Taking precautions, (un)knowing the future', *European Journal of International Relations*, 13(1), pp. 89–115.

Arditi, B. (2007) 'Post-hegemony: Politics outside the usual post-Marxist paradigm', *Contemporary Politics*, 13(3), pp. 205–26.

Arendt, H. (1972) *Crises of the Republic*. New York: Harcourt Brace Jovanovich.

Ayadi, M. and Mattoussi, W. (2016) 'Scoping of the Tunisian Economy', Brookings Institution. Available at: https://www.brookings.edu/wp-content/uploads/2016/07/L2C_WP17_Ayadi-and-Mattoussi-1.pdf (accessed 27 June 2022).

Ayeb, H. and Bush, R. (2019) *Food Insecurity and Revolution in the Middle East and North Africa: Agrarian questions in Egypt and Tunisia*. London: Anthem Press.

Ayers, Alison J. and Saad-filho, A. (2015) 'Democracy against neoliberalism: Paradoxes, limitations, transcendence', *Critical Sociology*, 41(4–5), pp. 597–618.

Badimon, M. E. (2019) 'From contestation to conciliation: social networks and engagement in the unemployed graduates movement in Morocco', *Social Movement Studies*, 18(1), pp. 113–29.

Baglioni, S. et al. (2008) 'Transcending marginalization: The mobilization of the unemployed in France, Germany, and Italy in a comparative perspective,' *Mobilization: The International Quarterly*, 13(3), pp. 323–35.

Baumann, H. (2017) 'A failure of governmentality: Why Transparency International underestimated corruption in Ben Ali s Tunisia', *Third World Quarterly*, 38(2), pp. 467–82.

Bayat, A. (1997) 'Workless revolutionaries: The unemployed movement in revolutionary Iran', *International Review of Social History*, 42, pp. 159–85.

Bayat, A. (2000) 'Social movements, activism and social development in the Middle East', United Nations Research Institute for Social Development, 3(3). Available at: https://www.unrisd.org/80256b3c005bccf9/(httpauxpages)/9c2b efd0ee1c73b380256b5e004ce4c3/$file/bayat.pdf (accessed 23 January 2022).

Bayat, A. (2017) *Revolution without revolutionaries: Making sense of the Arab Spring*. Palo Alto: Stanford University Press.

Beckett, A. E., Bagguley, P. and Campbell, T. (2017) 'Foucault, social movements and heterotopic horizons: Rupturing the order of things', *Social Movement Studies*, 16(2), pp. 169–81.

Beinin, J. and Vairel, F. (2013) *Social movements, mobilization, and contestation in the Middle East and North Africa*. Palo Alto: Stanford University Press.

Bibliography

Beinin, J. (2016) *Workers and thieves: Labor movements and popular uprisings in Tunisia and Egypt*. Palo Alto: Stanford University Press.

Ben Rejeb, L. (2013) 'United States policy towards Tunisia: What new engagement after an expendable "friendship"?' in N. Gana (ed.) *The making of the Tunisian revolution: Contexts, architects, prospects*. Edinburgh: Edinburgh University Press.

Ben Salem, M. (2016) 'The national dialogue collusive transactions and government legitimacy in Tunisia', *The International Spectator*, 51(1), pp. 99–112.

Berman, S. (2003) 'The roots and rationale of social democracy', *Social Philosophy and Policy*, 20(1), pp. 113–44.

Berman, S. (2006) *The Primacy of Politics*. Cambridge: Cambridge University Press.

Best, J. (2017) 'Security, economy, population: The political economic logic of liberal exceptionalism', *Security Dialogue*, 48(5), pp. 375–92.

Bigo, D. (2008) 'Globalized (in)security: The field and ban-opticon', in D. Bigo and A. Tsoukala (eds) *Terror, insecurity and liberty. Illiberal practices of liberal regimes after 9/11*. Abingdon: Routledge, pp. 10–48.

Binkley, S. (2011) 'Happiness, positive psychology and the program of neoliberal governmentality', *Subjectivity*, 4(4), pp. 371–94.

Bishara, D. (2020) 'Legacy trade unions as brokers of democratization? Lessons from Tunisia', *Comparative Politics*, 52(2), pp. 173–95.

Black, D. (2004) 'The Geometry of Terrorism', *Sociological Theory*, 22(1), pp. 14–25.

Bleiker, R. (2002) 'Rawls and the limits of nonviolent civil disobedience', *Social Alternatives*, 21(2), pp. 37–40.

Boubekeur, A. (2015) 'The politics of protest in Tunisia: Instrument in parties' competition vs. tool for participation'. *SWP Comments*, 13.

Boukalas, C. (2015) 'Class war-on-terror: Counterterrorism, accumulation, crisis', *Critical Studies on Terrorism* 8(1), pp. 55–71.

Boukhars, A. (2017) 'The geographic trajectory of conflict and militancy in Tunisia'. Washington, DC: Carnegie Endowment for International Peace.

Boukhars, A. (2017) 'The fragility of elite settlements in Tunisia', *African Security Review*, 26(3), pp. 257–70.

Bourdieu, P. (1998) *Practical reason: On the theory of action*. Cambridge: Polity.

Brake, S. (2021) 'Muslim and democratic? From Tunisia to Afghanistan, there's no such thing', *Harretz*, 18 August. Available at: https://www.haaretz.com/opinion/.premium-muslim-and-democratic-from-tunisia-to-afghanistan-there-s-no-such-thing-1.10133651 (accessed 8 September 2021).

Breuer, A. and Groshek, J. (2014) 'Online media and offline empowerment in post-rebellion Tunisia: An analysis of internet use during democratic transition', *Journal of Information Technology and Politics*, 11(1), pp. 25–44.

Brody-barre, A. G. (2013) 'The impact of political parties and coalition building on Tunisia's democratic future', *The Journal of North African Studies*, 18(2), pp. 211–30.

Bulley, D. (2016) 'Occupy differently: space, community and urban counter-conduct', *Global Society*, 30(2), pp. 238–57.

Butler, J. and Athanasiou, A. (2013) *Dispossession: The performative in the political*. Cambridge: Polity Press.

Buzan, B. G., Wæver, O. and de Wilde, J. H. (1998) *Security: A new framework for analysis*. London/Boulder: Lynne Rienner.

Cadman, L. (2010) 'How (not) to be governed: Foucault, critique, and the political', *Environment and Planning D: Society and Space*, 28(3), pp. 539–56.

Carothers, T. (2002) 'The end of the transition paradigm', *Journal of Democracy*, 13(1), pp. 5–21.

Cavatorta, F. (2015) 'No democratic change ... and yet no authoritarian continuity: The interparadigm debate and north Africa after the uprisings', *British Journal of Middle Eastern Studies* 42(1), pp. 135–45.

Chabanet, D. and Faniel, J. (2012) *The mobilization of the unemployed in Europe*. New York: Palgrave Macmillan.

Chatterjee, P. (2004) *The politics of the governed: Reflection on popular politics in most of the world*. New York: Columbia University Press.

Chiapello, E. and Fairclough, N. (2002) 'Understanding the new management ideology: A transdisciplinary contribution from critical discourse analysis and new sociology of capitalism', *Discourse and Society*, 13(2), pp. 185–208.

Chomiak, L. (2016) 'The revolution in Tunisia continues'. *Middle East Institute*. Available at: https://www.mei.edu/publications/revolution-tunisia-continues (accessed 25 September 2016).

Chopra, R. (2003) 'Neoliberalism as doxa: Bourdieu's theory of the state and the contemporary Indian discourse on globalization and liberalization', *Cultural Studies*, 17(3–4), pp. 419–44.

Cimini, G. (2017) 'The economic agendas of Islamic parties in Tunisia and Morocco: Between discourses and practices', *Asian Journal of Middle Eastern and Islamic Studies*, 11(3), pp. 48–64.

Cimini, G. and Santini, R. (2021) 'Applying principal-agent theory to security force assistance: The atypical case of Post-2015 Tunisia', *Journal of Intervention and Statebuilding*, 15(5), pp. 665–81.

Collective, C. A. S. (2006) 'Critical approaches to security in Europe: A networked manifesto', *Security Dialogue*, 37(4), pp. 443–87.

Crenshaw, M. (1981) 'The Causes of Terrorism', *Comparative Politics*, 13(4), pp. 379–99.

Dahl, R. A. (1971) *Polyarchy: Participation and opposition*. New Haven/London: Yale University Press.

Dalmasso, E. and Cavatorta, F. (2010) 'Reforming the family code in Tunisia and Morocco: The struggle between religion, globalisation and democracy', *Totalitarian Movements and Political Religions*, 11(2), pp. 213–28.

Dandashly, A. (2018) 'EU democracy promotion and the dominance of the security–stability nexus', *Mediterranean Politics*, 23(1), pp. 62–82.

Darouiche, R. (2020) 'From the Asiatic mode of production to counter-revolution: Re-reading the Egyptian uprisings', in K. Knopf and D. Quintern (eds) *From Marx to global marxism: Eurocentrism, resistance, postcolonial criticism.* Trier: Wissenschaftlicher Verlag Trier, pp. 161–76.

Davidson, A. I. (2011) 'In praise of counter-conduct', *History of the Human Sciences*, 24(4), pp. 25–41.

De Smet, B. (2015) *Gramsci on Tahrir: Revolution and counter-revolution in Egypt.* London: Pluto.

Dean, M. (1999) *Governmentality: Power and rule in modern society.* London: Sage.

Dean, M. (2002) 'Liberal government and authoritarianism', *Economy and Society*, 31(1), pp. 37–61.

Dean, M. (2010) 'Power at the heart of the present: Exception, risk and sovereignty', *European Journal of Cultural Studies*, 13(4), pp. 459–75.

Death, C. (2010) 'Counter-conducts: A Foucauldian analytics of protest', *Social movement studies*, 9(3), pp. 235–51.

Death, C. (2013) 'Governmentality at the limits of the international: African politics and Foucauldian theory', *Review of International Studies*, 39(3), pp. 763–787.

Death, C. (2016) 'Counter-conducts as a mode of resistance: Ways of "not being like that" in South Africa', *Global Society*, 30(2), pp. 201–17.

Debuysere, L. (2018) 'Between feminism and unionism: The struggle for socio-economic dignity of working-class women in pre- and post-uprising Tunisia', *Review of African Political Economy*, 45(155), pp. 25–43.

Deleuze, G. (1992) 'What is a dispositif?' in A. Timothy (ed.) *Michel Foucault philosopher.* New York: Routledge, pp. 159–68.

della Porta, D. (2016) *Social movements in times of austerity: Bringing capitalism back into protest analysis.* Cambridge: Polity Press.

della Porta, D. (2017). 'Political economy and social movement studies: The class basis of anti austerity protests', *Anthropological Theory*, 17(4), pp. 453–73.

Diamond, L. et al. (1989) *Democracy in developing countries: Latin America.* Boulder: Lynne Rienner.

Diamond, L. J. (2002) 'Thinking about hybrid regimes', *Journal of Democracy*, 13(2), pp. 21–35.

Diamond, L. J. et al. (2014) 'Reconsidering the transition paradigm', *Journal of Democracy*, 25(1), pp. 86–100.

Diskaya, A. (2016) '"Don't ask, don't tell": The Israeli nuclear taboo and the limits of global governmentality', in E. Akçalı (ed.) *Neoliberal governmentality and the future of the state in the Middle East and North Africa.* London: Palgrave Macmillan, pp. 105–22.

Drake, C. J. M (1998) 'The role of ideology in terrorists' target selection', *Terrorism and Political Violence*, 10(2), pp. 52–85.

Dreyfus, H. L. and Rabinow, P. (1982) *Michel Foucault: Beyond structuralism and hermeneutics.* Chicago: University of Chicago Press.

Durac, V. and Cavatorta, F. (2009) 'Strengthening authoritarian rule through democracy promotion? Examining the paradox of the US and EU security strategies: The case of Bin Ali's Tunisia', *British Journal of Middle Eastern Studies*, 36(1), pp. 3–19.

Durac, V. (2015) 'Social movements, protest movements and cross-ideological coalitions: The Arab uprisings re-appraised', *Democratization*, 22(2), pp. 239–58.

El-Khawas, M. A. (2018) 'Tunisia's jasmine revolution: Causes and impact', *Mediterranean Quarterly*, 23(4), pp. 1–23.

Fahmi, G. and Meddeb, H. (2015) 'Market for Jihad: Radicalization in Tunisia'. *Carnegie Middle East Center*. Available at: https://carnegie-mec. org/2015/10/15/market-for-jihad-radicalization-in-tunisia-pub-61629 (accessed 23 January 2022).

Feltrin, L. (2018) 'The struggles of precarious youth in Tunisia: The case of the Kerkennah movement', *Review of African Political Economy*, 45(155), pp. 44–63.

Filali-Ansary, A. (2016) 'Tunisia: Ennahda's new course', *Journal of Democracy*, 27(4), pp. 99–109.

Financial Times (2017) 'Tunisian parliament passes controversial economic reconciliation law'. Available at: https://www.ft.com/content/9c09d53b-992f-3a53-8963-918c6b5768d0 (accessed 23 May 2019).

Foucault, M. (1979) *The history of sexuality, vol. 1: An introduction*. New York: Pantheon Books.

Foucault, M. (1996) *Foucault Live*, ed. S. Lotringer. New York: Semiotext(e).

Foucault, M. (1980) *Power/Knowledge: Selected interviews and other writings, 1972–1977*, ed. C. Gordon. New York: Pantheon Books.

Foucault, M. (1982) 'The subject and power', *Critical Inquiry*, 8(4), pp. 777–95.

Foucault, M. (1986) 'Of other spaces', *Diacritics*, 16(1), pp. 22–27.

Foucault, M. (1988) 'The ethic of care for the self as a practice of freedom', in J. Bernauer and D. Rasmussen (eds) *The final Foucault*. Boston: MIT Press, pp. 281–301.

Foucault, M. (1991) 'Governmentality', in G. Burchell, C. Gordon and P. Miller (eds) *The Foucault effect: Studies in governmentality*. Chicago: University of Chicago Press, pp. 87–104.

Foucault, M. (1997) *The Essential works, 1954–1984, vol.1: Ethics, subjectivity and truth*, ed. P. Rabinow. New York: The New Press.

Foucault, M. (2002) *The Archaeology of knowledge*, trans. A. M. Sheridan Smith. London: Routledge.

Foucault, M. (2007a) *Security, territory, population: Lectures at the Collège de France, 1977–78*, ed. M. Senellart. Basingstoke: Palgrave Macmillan.

Foucault, M. (2007b) *The politics of truth*, ed. S. Lotringer and L. Hochroth. Los Angeles: Semiotext(e).

Foucault, M. (2011) *The birth of biopolitics: Lectures at the Collège de France, 1978–1979*, ed. M. Senellart. New York: Palgrave Macmillan.

Bibliography

Fournier, P. (2014) 'The neoliberal/neurotic citizen and security as discourse', *Critical Studies on Security*, 2(3), pp. 309–22.

Gervasio, G. and Manduchi, P. (2021) 'Introduction: Reading the revolutionary process in North Africa with Gramsci', *The Journal of North African Studies*, 26(6), pp. 1051–56.

Gibbs, J. P. (1989) 'Conceptualization of terrorism', *American Sociological Review*, 54(3), pp. 329–40.

Gobe, E. (2010) 'The Gafsa mining basin between riots and a social movement: Meaning and significance of a protest movement in Ben Ali's Tunisia', HAL-SHA, https://shs.hal.science/halshs-00557826.

Grubman, N. (2021) 'Do Tunisians still want democracy?' *The Washington Post*, 1 September. Available at: https://www.washingtonpost.com/politics/2021/09/01/do-tunisians-still-want-democracy/ (accessed 21 October 2021).

Hamdi, M. E. (1998) *The politicisation of Islam: A case study of Tunisia*. Boulder: Westview Press.

Hamdi, S. and Weipert-Fenner, I. (2020) 'Unemployed protests in Tunisia: Between grassroots activism and formal organization', in I. Weipert-Fenner and J. Wolff (eds) *Socioeconomic protests in MENA and Latin America: Egypt and Tunisia in interregional comparison*. Cham: Palgrave Macmillan, pp. 195–220.

Hammami, M.-D. (2021) 'Past as prologue: Kaïs Saïed's prior statements point to upcoming political moves'. *Project on Middle East Democracy*. Available at: https://pomed.org/past-as-prologue-kais-saied-prior-statements-political-moves/ (accessed 1 September 2021).

Han, S. (2020) 'Precarious public sector "site" workers denounce new union agreement', *Nawaat*. Available at: https://nawaat.org/2020/12/08/precarious-public-sector-site-workers-denounce-new-union-agreement/ (accessed 8 December 2020).

Han, S. (2021) 'Securitization of the unemployed and counter-conductive resistance in Tunisia', *Security Dialogue*, 52(2), pp. 156–73.

Han, S. (2021) 'Transitional justice for whom? Contention over human rights and justice in Tunisia', *Social Movement Studies*, 21(6), pp. 1–17.

Hanafi, S. (2010) 'Framing Arab socio-political space: State governmentality, governance and non-institutional protestation', *Contemporary Arab Affairs*, 3(2), pp. 148–62.

Hanieh, A. (2015) 'Shifting priorities or business as usual? Continuity and change in the post-2011 IMF and world bank engagement with Tunisia, Morocco and Egypt', *British Journal of Middle Eastern Studies*, 42(1), pp. 119–34.

Haouas, I., Sayre, E. and Yagoubi, M. (2012) 'Youth unemployment in Tunisia: Characteristics and policy responses', *Topics in Middle Eastern and African Economies*, 14(3), pp. 395–415.

Haugbølle, R. H. and Cavatorta, F. (2011) 'Will the real Tunisian opposition please stand up? Opposition coordination failures under authoritarian constraints', *British Journal of Middle Eastern Studies*, 38(3), pp. 323–41.

Hayes, G. and Fominaya, C. F. (2018) *Resisting austerity: Collective action in Europe in the wake of the global financial crisis*. Abingdon/New York: Routledge.

Heller, K. J. (1996) 'Power, subjectification and resistance in Foucault', *SubStance*, 25(1), pp. 78–110.

Hetherington, K. (1996) 'Identity formation, space and social centrality', *Theory, Culture and Society*, 13(4), pp. 33–52.

Hetland, G. and Goodwin, J. (2013) 'The strange disappearance of capitalism from social movement studies', in C. Barker, L. Cox, J. Krinsky and A. G. Nilsen (eds) *Marxism and social movements*. Leiden: Brill, pp. 83–102.

Hibou, B. (2006) 'Domination and control in Tunisia: Economic levers for the exercise of authoritarian power', *Review of African Political Economy*, 33(108), pp. 185–206.

Hibou, B. (2011) *The force of obedience: The political economy of repression in Tunisia*. Cambridge: Polity Press.

Hibou, B., Meddeb, H. and Hamdi, M. (2011) 'Tunisia after 14 January and its social and political economy'. *Euro-Mediterranean Human Rights Network*. Available at: https://euromedrights.org/wpcontent/uploads/2015/04/exe_Ra_tunisie_En_150Dpi_847268817.pdf (accessed 8 August 2017).

Hindess, B. (1997) 'Politics and governmentality', *International Journal of Human Resource Management*, 26(2), pp. 257–72.

Hindess, B. (2005) 'Politics as government: Michel Foucault's analysis of political reason', *Alternatives*, 30(4), pp. 389–413.

Hobson, C. (2005) 'A forward strategy of freedom in the Middle East: US democracy promotion and the "war on terror"', *Australian Journal of International Affairs*, 59(1), pp. 39–53.

Hobson, C. (2009) 'Beyond the end of history: The need for a radical historicisation of democracy in international relations', *Millennium: Journal of International Studies*, 37(3), pp. 631–57.

Hobson, C. (2009) 'Liberal democracy and beyond: Extending the sequencing debate', *International Political Science Review*, 33(4), pp. 441–54.

Hobson, C. (2015) *The rise of democracy: Revolution, war and transformations in international politics since 1776*. Edinburgh: Edinburgh University press.

Hoffman, B. (1997) 'The confluence of international and domestic trends in terrorism', *Terrorism and Political Violence*, 9(2), pp. 1–15.

Hoffman, B. (2017) *Inside terrorism*. New York: Columbia University Press.

Howarth, D. and Stavrakakis, Y. (2000) 'Introducing discourse theory and political analysis', in D. Howarth, A. J. Norval and Y. Stavrakakis (eds) *Discourse theory and political analysis: Identities, hegemonies and social change*. Manchester/New York: Manchester University Press, pp. 1–37.

Howarth, D. (2006) 'Space, subjectivity, and politics', *Alternatives*, 31(2), pp. 105–34.

Howarth, D. (2010) 'Power, discourse, and policy: Articulating a hegemony approach to critical policy studies', *Critical Policy Studies*, 3(3–4), pp. 309–35.

Bibliography

Huber, D. and Kamel, L. (2015) 'Arab Spring: The Role of the Peripheries', *Mediterranean Politics*, 20(2), pp. 127–41.

Hülsse, R. and Spencer, A. (2008) 'The metaphor of terror: Terrorism studies and the constructivist turn', *Security Dialogue*, 39(6), pp. 571–92.

Human Rights Watch (2015) 'Tunisia: Drop or amend security bill'. Available at: https://www.hrw.org/news/2015/05/13/tunisia-drop-or-amend-security-bill (accessed 1 March 2019).

Human Rights Watch (2017) 'Draft law could return Tunisia to a police state'. Available at: https://www.hrw.org/news/2017/07/24/draft-law-could-return-tunisia-police-state (accessed 1 March 2019).

IMF (2008) 'Tunisia: Concluding statement of the article IV consultation mission'. Available at: https://www.imf.org/en/News/Articles/2015/09/28/04/52/mcs07 0908 (accessed 14 February 2019).

İşleyen, B. (2014) 'The European Union and neoliberal governmentality: Twinning in Tunisia and Egypt', *European Journal of International Relations*, 21(3), pp. 1–19.

IWATCH (2022) 'Negotiations with the International Monetary Fund and the "secret" government program'. Available at: https://www.iwatch.tn/ar/article/ 905 (accessed 19 January 2022).

Jackson, R. (2007) 'Constructing enemies: "Islamic terrorism" in political and academic discourse', *Government and Opposition*, 42(3), pp. 394–426.

Jackson, R. (2008) 'An argument for terrorism', *Perspectives on Terrorism*, 2(2), pp. 25–32.

Joffe, G. (2008) 'The European Union, democracy and counter-terrorism in the Maghreb', *Journal of Common Market Studies*, 46(1), pp. 147–71.

Joffe, G. (2014) 'Government-media relations in Tunisia: A paradigm shift in the culture of governance?', *The Journal of North African Studies*, 19(5), pp. 615–38.

Kaboub, F. (2013) 'The end of neoliberalism? An institutional analysis of the Arab Uprisings', *Journal of Economic Issues*, 47(2), pp. 533–44.

Karl, T. L. (1990) 'Dilemmas of democratization in Latin America', *Comparative Politics*, 23(1), pp. 1–21.

Karray, B. (2020) 'Proposals, intermediation, and pressure: The three roles of the UGTT in Tunisia's post-revolutionary', in I. Weipert-Fenner and J. Wolff (eds) *Socioeconomic protests in MENA and Latin America: Egypt and Tunisia in interregional comparison*. Cham: Palgrave Macmillan, pp. 123–44.

Kienscherf, M. (2016) 'Producing "responsible" self-governance: Counterinsurgency and the violence of neoliberal rule', *Critical Military Studies*, 2(3), pp. 173–92.

Kiersey, N. (2009) 'Neoliberal political economy and the subjectivity of crisis: Why governmentality is not hollow', *Global Society*, 23(4), pp. 363–86.

Kurki, M. (2011) 'Governmentality and EU democracy promotion: The European instrument for democracy and human rights and the construction of democratic civil societies', *International Political Sociology*, 5, pp. 349–66.

Laclau, E. and Mouffe, C. (1985) *Hegemony and socialist strategy: Towards a radical democratic politics*. London: Verso.

Lafer, G. (2004) 'Neoliberalism by other means: The "war on terror" at home and abroad', *New Political Science*, 26(3), pp. 323–46.

Lahusen, C. (2013) 'The protests of the unemployed in France, Germany and Sweden (1994–2004): Protest dynamics and political contexts,' *Social Movement Studies*, 12(1), pp. 1–22.

Laqueur, W. (2001) *The new terrorism: Fanaticism and the arms of mass destruction*. London: Phoenix.

Leitner, H., Peck, J. and Sheppard, E. (2007) *Contesting neoliberalism: Urban frontiers*. New York: Guilford Press.

Lemke, T. (2001) 'The Birth of bio-politics: Michel Foucault's lecture at the Collège de France on neo-liberal governmentality', *Economy and Society*, 30(2), pp. 190–207.

Lemke, T. (2002) 'Foucault, governmentality, and critique', paper presented at *Rethinking Marxism Conference*, pp. 1–17.

Letsch, L. (2018) 'Countering violent extremism in Tunisia: Between dependency and self-reliance, *Journal for Democratization*, 17, pp. 163–95.

Lorence, J. (1996) *Organizing the unemployed: Community and union activists in the industrial heartland*. Albany: State University of New York Press.

Lorenzini, D. (2016) 'From counter-conduct to critical attitude: Michel Foucault and the art of not being governed quite so much', *Foucault Studies*, 21, pp. 7–21.

Lutterbeck, D. (2015) 'Tool of rule: The Tunisian police under Ben Ali', *The Journal of North African Studies*, 20(5), pp. 813–31.

McDonald, C. and Marston, G. (2005) 'Workfare as welfare: Governing unemployment in the advanced liberal state', *Critical Social Policy*, 25(3), pp. 374–401.

McDonald, M. (2008) 'Securitization and the construction of security', *European Journal of International Relations*, 14(4), pp. 563–87.

McMahon S. F. (2016) *Crisis and class war in Egypt*. London: Zed Books.

Malmvig, H. (2012) 'Governing Arab reform: Governmentality and counter-conduct in European democracy promotion in the Arab world'. *DIIS Working Paper*.

Malmvig, H. (2016) 'Eyes wide shut: Power and creative visual counter-conducts in the battle for Syria, 2011-2014', *Global Society*, 30(2), pp. 258–78.

Martin, A. P. (2015) 'Do Tunisian secular civil society organisations demonstrate a process of democratic learning?' *The Journal of North African Studies*, 20(5), pp. 797–812.

Martin, G. (2017) *Understanding terrorism: Challenges, perspectives, and issues*. 6th ed. Thousand Oaks: Sage.

Marzo, P. (2020) 'Solving the security-democracy dilemma: The US foreign policy in Tunisia post-9/11', *Third World Quarterly*, 41(7), pp. 1181–99.

Meade, R. R. (2014) 'Foucault's concept of counter-conduct and the politics of anti-austerity protest in Ireland', *Concept*, 5(3), pp. 1–13.

Merone, F. (2015) 'Enduring class struggle in Tunisia: The fight for identity beyond political Islam, *British Journal of Middle Eastern Studies*, 42(1), pp. 74–87.

Ministry of Development Investment and International Cooperation (2015) 'Mukhatit al-Tanmiyah 2016–2020: al-Majlid al-Awal al-Muhtawa al-Jumli', Tunis, pp. 1–185, https://andp.unescwa.org/sites/default/files/2020-10/Development%20Plan%202016-2020%20First%20volume%20Wholesale%20content.pdf

Mouhib, L. (2014) 'EU democracy promotion in Tunisia and Morocco: Between contextual changes and structural continuity', *Mediterranean Politics*, 19(3), pp. 351–72.

Munif, Y. (2013) 'The Arab revolts: The old is dying and the new cannot be born', *Rethinking Marxism*, 25(2), pp. 202–17.

Murphy, E. (1999) *Economic and Political Change in Tunisia: From Bourguiba to Ben Ali*. London: Macmillan Press.

Murphy, E. (2013) 'Under the emperor's neoliberal clothes! Why the international financial institutions got it wrong in Tunisia', in N. Gana (ed.) *The making of the Tunisian revolution: Contexts, architects, prospects*. Edinburgh: Edinburgh University Press, pp. 35–57.

Murphy, E. (2013) 'The Tunisian elections of October 2011: A democratic consensus', *The Journal of North African Studies*, 18(2), pp. 231–47.

Netterstrøm, K. L. (2016) 'The Tunisian general labor union and the advent of democracy', *The Middle East Journal*, 70(3), pp. 383–98.

Nişancıoğlu, K. and Pal, M. (2016) 'Counter-conduct in the university factory: Locating the Occupy Sussex Campaign', *Global Society*, 30(2), pp. 279–300.

Hill, J. N. C. (2016) *Democratisation in the Maghreb*. Edinburgh: Edinburgh University Press.

O'Donnell, G. and Schmitter, P. C. (1986) *Transitions from authoritarian rule: Tentative conclusions about uncertain democracies*. Baltimore: Johns Hopkins University Press.

Odysseos, L. (2010) 'Human rights, liberal ontogenesis and freedom: Producing a subject for neoliberalism?', *Millennium: Journal of International Studies*, 38(3), pp. 747–72.

Odysseos, L. (2011) 'Governing dissent in the central Kalahari game reserve: "Development", governmentality, and subjectification amongst Botswana's bushmen', *Globalizations*, 8(4), pp. 439–55.

Odysseos, L. (2016) 'Human rights, self-formation and resistance in struggles against disposability: Grounding Foucault's "theorizing practice" of counter-conduct in Bhopal', *Global Society*, 30(2), pp. 178–200.

Oksala, J. (2011) 'Violence and neoliberal governmentality', *Constellations*, 18(3), pp. 474–86.

Owais, R. (2011) 'Arab media during the Arab Spring in Egypt and Tunisia: Time for change', *Middle East Media Educator*, 1(1), pp. 9–13.

Pace, M. and Cavatorta, F. (2012) 'The Arab Uprisings in theoretical perspective – an introduction' *Mediterranean Politics*, 17(2), pp. 125–138.

Paciello, M. C. (2013) 'Delivering the revolution? Post-uprising socio-economics in Tunisia and Egypt', *International Spectator*, 48(4), pp. 7–29.

Paret, M. (2015) 'Violence and democracy in South Africa's community protests', *Review of African Political Economy*, 42(143), pp. 107–23.

Perkins, K. (2013) 'Playing the Islamic card: The use and abuse of religion in Tunisian politics', in N. Gana (ed.) *The making of the Tunisian revolution: Contexts, architects, prospects*. Edinburgh: Edinburgh University Press, pp. 58–80.

Perry, M. (2007) *Prisoners of want: The experience and protest of the unemployed in France, 1921–45*. Aldershot: Ashgate.

Pfeifer, K. (1999) 'Parameters of economic reform in North Africa', *Review of African Political Economy*, 26(82), pp. 441–54.

Pepicelli, R. (2021) 'People want a clean environment: Historical roots of the environmental crisis and the emergence of eco-resistances in Tunisia', *Studi Magrebini: North African Studies*, 19(1), pp. 37–62.

Pilati, K., et al. (2019) 'Between organization and spontaneity of protests: The 2010–2011 Tunisian and Egyptian uprisings', *Social Movement Studies*, 18(4), pp. 463–81.

Pottage, A. (1998) 'Power as an art of contingency: Luhmann, Deleuze, Foucault', *Economy and Society*, 27(1), pp. 1–27.

Powel, B. T. (2009) 'The stability syndrome US and EU democracy promotion in Tunisia', *The Journal of North African Studies*, 14(1), pp. 57–73.

Powers, C. (2019) 'Cartelization, neoliberalism, and the foreclosure of the Jasmine Revolution: Democracy's troubles in Tunisia', *Middle East Law and Governance*, 11(1), pp. 1–37.

Pressman, J. (2017) 'Throwing stones in social science: Non-violence, unarmed violence, and the first Intifada', *Cooperation and Conflict*, 52(4), pp. 519–36.

Przeworski, A. (1986) 'Some problems in the study of the transition to democracy', in G. O'Donnell, P. C. Schmitter and L. Whitehead (eds) *Transitions from authoritarian rule: Comparative Perspectives (Vol. 3)*. Baltimore: Johns Hopkins University Press, pp. 47–63.

Quamar, M. (2015) 'Tunisia: Presidential and parliamentary elections, 2014', *Elections in the Middle East*, 2(3), pp. 269–88.

Radwan, T. (2020) 'The impact and influence of international financial institutions on the Middle East and North Africa'. *Friedrich-Ebert-Stiftung*. Available at https://library.fes.de/pdf-files/bueros/tunesien/16107.pdf

Rapanos, G. (2018) 'The role of human development in the transition to democracy after the Arab Spring', *Mediterranean Politics*, 23(3), pp. 1–23.

Rapoport, D. C. (1984) 'Fear and trembling: Terrorism in three religious traditions', *The American Political Science Review*, 78(3), pp. 658–77.

Rawls, J. (1999) *A theory of justice*, revised ed. Cambridge, MA: Harvard University Press.

Rear, D. and Jones, A. (2013) 'Discursive struggle and contested signifiers in the arenas of education policy and work skills in Japan', *Critical Policy Studies*, 7(4), pp. 375–94.

Rijkers, B., Freund, C. and Nucifora, A. (2014) 'All in the family state capture in Tunisia'. *World Bank*. Available at: https://openknowledge.worldbank.org/handle/10986/20542 (accessed 23 July 2016).

Rose, N. and Miller, P. (1992) 'Political power beyond the state: Problematics of government', *The British Journal of Sociology*, 43(2), pp. 173–205.

Rossdale, C. et al. (2016) 'Everything is dangerous: Conduct and counter-conduct in the Occupy Movement', *Global Society*, 30(2), pp. 157–78.

Rossi, F. M. (2017) *The poor's struggle for political incorporation: The piquetero movement in Argentina*. Cambridge: Cambridge University Press.

Rustow, D. A. (1970) 'Transitions to democracy: Toward a dynamic model', *Comparative Politics*, 2(3), pp. 337–63.

Sadiki, L. (2002) 'Bin Ali's Tunisia: Democracy by non-democratic means', *British Journal of Middle Eastern Studies*, 29(1), pp. 57–78.

Sadiki, L. (2015) 'Towards a "democratic knowledge" turn? Knowledge production in the age of the Arab Spring', *The Journal of North African Studies*, 20(5), pp. 702–21.

Sadiki, L. (2019) 'Regional development in Tunisia: The consequences of multiple marginalization'. *Brookings Doha Center*. Available at: https://www.brookings.edu/research/regional-development-in-tunisia-the-consequences-of-multiple-marginalization/ (accessed 3 January 2022).

Scheinin, M. (2012) 'Report of the special rapporteur on the promotion and protection of human rights and fundamental freedoms while counter terrorism'. *United Nations Human Rights Council*. Available at: http://www.ohchr.org/Documents/HRBodies/HRCouncil/RegularSession/Session20/A- HRC-20-14-Add.1_en.pdf (accessed 14 November 2017).

Schmitt, C. (1988) *The crisis of parliamentary democracy*. Cambridge, MA: MIT Press.

Simoncini, G. (2021) 'Beyond the "Epopee of Ben Guerdane": Exploring the Plurality of Resistance at the South-Eastern Tunisian Border', *Studi Magrebeni*, 19(1), pp. 88–109.

Singer, M. (2018) 'Development loans as a threat to young democracies: the IMF in Tunisia'. *The St Andrew Africa Summit Review*.

Smith, J. G. and Johnston, H. (2002) *Globalization and resistance: Transnational dimensions of social movements*. Lanham: Rowman and Littlefield.

Sokhi-bulley, B. (2016) 'Re-reading the riots: Counter-conduct in London 2011', *Global Society*, 30(2), pp. 320–39.

Stepan, A. (2012) 'Tunisia's transition and the twin tolerations', *Journal of Democracy*, 23(2), pp. 89–103.

Stepan, A. and Linz, J. (2013) 'Democratization theory and the "Arab Spring"', *Journal of Democracy*, 24(2), pp. 15–30.

Szakal, V. (2014) 'One hundred days of lentitude: Jomâa on his work in office',

Nawaat. Available at: http://nawaat.org/portail/2014/05/18/one-hundred-days-of-lentitude-jomaa-on-his-work-in-office/ (accessed 16 Nov 2017).

Tagma, H. M., Kalaycioglu, E. and Akcali, E. (2013) '"Taming" Arab social movements: Exporting neoliberal governmentality', *Security Dialogue*, 44(5–6), pp. 375–92.

Tamburini, F. (2018) 'Anti-terrorism laws in the Maghreb countries: The mirror of a democratic transition that never was', *Journal of Asian and African Studies*, 53(8), pp. 1235–50.

Teti, A. (2012) 'Beyond lies the wub: The challenges of (post)democratization', *Middle East Critique*, 21(1), pp. 5–24.

Teti, A., Abbott, P. and Cavatorta, F. (2019) 'Beyond elections: Perceptions of democracy in four Arab countries', *Democratization*, 26(4), pp. 645–65.

Teti, A., Abbott, P. and Han, S. [n. d.] 'Dancing around democracy'. *Working Paper*.

Thomassen, L. (2005) 'Antagonism, hegemony and ideology after heterogeneity', *Journal of Political Ideologies*, 10(3), pp. 289–309.

Torelli, S. M., Merone, F. and Cavatorta, F. (2012) 'Salafism in Tunisia: Challenges and opportunities for democratization', *Middle East Policy*, 19(4), pp. 140–54.

Tosa, H. (2009) 'Anarchical governance: Neoliberal governmentality in resonance with the state of exception', *International Political Sociology*, 3(4), pp. 414–34.

Truth and Dignity Commission (2018) 'Tunisia: The price of economic reconciliation in the transitional justice process'. Available at: http://www.ivd.tn/tunisia-price-economic-reconciliation-transitional-justice-process/?lang=en (accessed 17 February 2019).

Tsourapas, G. (2013) 'The other side of a neoliberal miracle: Economic reform and political de-liberalization in Ben Ali's Tunisia', *Mediterranean Politics*, 18(1), pp. 23–41.

Young, R. (2015) 'Exploring "Non-Western Democracy"', *Journal of Democracy*, 26(4), pp. 140–54.

Mariana V. (1996) '"Despotism" and ethical liberal governance', *International Journal of Human Resource Management*, 25(3), pp. 357–72.

Valbjørn, M. (2012) 'Upgrading post-democratization studies: Examining a re-politicized Arab world in a transition to somewhere', *Middle East Critique*, 21(1), pp. 25–35.

Valbjørn, M. (2014) 'Three ways of revisiting the (post-) democratization debate after the Arab Uprisings, *Mediterranean Politics*, 19(1), pp. 157–60.

Vatthauer, J. P. and Weipert-Fenner, I. (2017) 'The quest for social justice in Tunisia: socioeconomic protest and political democratization post 2011', PRIF Reports 143 (Frankfurt am Main).

Völkel, J. C. (2015) 'Complex politics in single numbers? The problem of defining and measuring democracy, *Middle East Critique*, 24(1), pp. 67–81.

Jasper, J. M. and Volpi, F. (2018) 'Introduction: Rethinking mobilization after the Arab uprisings', in F. Volpi and J. M. Jasper (eds) *Microfoundations of the Arab uprisings: Mapping interactions between regimes and protesters.* Amsterdam: Amsterdam University Press, pp. 11–40.

U.S. Department of State (2003) 'Press Availability in Tunisia'. Available at: https://2001-2009.state.gov/secretary/former/powell/remarks/2003/26808.htm (accessed 13 November 2017).

Volpi, F. and Clark, J. A. (2019) 'Activism in the Middle East and North Africa in times of upheaval: Social networks' actions and interactions', *Social Movement Studies*, 18(1), pp. 1–16.

Watanabe, L. and Merz, F. (2017) 'Tunisia's jihadi problem and how to deal with it', *Middle East Policy*, 24(4), pp. 136–47.

Weipert-Fenner, I. (2020) 'Unemployed mobilisation in times of democratisation: The Union of Unemployed Graduates in post-Ben Ali Tunisia', *The Journal of North African Studies*, 25(1), pp. 53–75.

Weipert-Fenner, I. and Wolff, J. (2020) *Socioeconomic protests in MENA and Latin America: Egypt and Tunisia in interregional comparison.* Cham: Palgrave Macmillan.

Wiktorowicz, Q. (2006) 'Anatomy of the Salafi movement', *Studies in Conflict and Terrorism*, 29(3), pp. 207–39.

Widder, N. (2004) 'Foucault and power revisited', *European Journal of Political Theory*, 3(4), pp. 411–32.

Wolf, A. (2013) 'An Islamist "renaissance"? Religion and politics in post-revolutionary Tunisia', *The Journal of Nourth African Studies*, 18(4), pp. 560–73.

Wolff, J. (2020) 'Contention by marginalized groups and political change in Latin America: An overview', in I. Weipert-Fenner and J. Wolff (eds) *Socioeconomic protests in MENA and Latin America: Egypt and Tunisia in interregional comparison.* Cham: Palgrave Macmillan, pp.171–94.

Yee, V. (2021) 'Tunisia's democracy verges on collapse as president moves to take control', *The New York Times*, 26 July. Available at: https://www.nytimes.com/2021/07/26/world/middleeast/tunisia-government-dismissed-protests.html (accessed 24 October 2021).

Yehia, K. (2017) 'Tahqiq: al-Maknassy al-Ghadbah al-Maghniyah ... 'Alam Ahly wa Nasi'. *Nawaat*. Available at: http://nawaat.org/portail/2017/02/07/-تحقيق المكناسي-الغاضبة-المغنية/ (accessed 5 November 2018).

Yousef, T. M. (2004) 'Employment, development and the social contract in the Middle East and North Africa', *World Bank*, https://www.semanticscholar.org/paper/Employment%2C-Development-and-the-Social-Contract-in-Yousef/bd516f06dfa61269a68edd2f2fe67c3dbc5b7abf

Zakaria, F. (1997) 'The rise of illiberal democracy', *Foreign Affairs*, 76(6), pp. 22–43.

Zelin, A. Y. (2015) 'Tunisia's fragile democratic transition'. *The Washington Institute for Near East Policy*. Available at: https://www.washingtoninstitute.org/uploads/Documents/testimony/ZelinTestimony20150714.pdf (accessed 13 July 2018).

Zemni, S. (2015) 'The extraordinary politics of the Tunisian revolution: The process of constitution making', *Mediterranean Politics*, 20(1), pp. 1–17.

Index

EU representative:
Easy Access System Europe
Mustamäe tee 50, 10621 Tallinn, Estonia
Gpsr.requests@easproject.com

www.ingramcontent.com/pod-product-compliance
Lightning Source LLC
Chambersburg PA
CBHW050650270326
41927CB00012B/2959